Ministry on the Edge

Ministry on the Edge

*Reflections of an Interfaith Pioneer,
Civil Rights Advocate,
and the First Bioethicist*

KENNETH L. VAUX

WIPF & STOCK · Eugene, Oregon

MINISTRY ON THE EDGE
Reflections of an Interfaith Pioneer, Civil Rights Advocate, and the First Bioethicist

All scripture citations are adapted from the Authorized King James Version.

Wipf & Stock
An Imprint of Wipf and Stock Publishers
199 W. 8th Ave., Suite 3
Eugene, OR 97401

www.wipfandstock.com

ISBN 13: 978-1-60899-506-6

Manufactured in the U.S.A.

Thanks to Sara and the children for their love and support,
to Martin Marty for a most special foreword,
and to Melanie Baffes for being an excellent editor and colleague.

Contents

Foreword

IN THIS BOOK, AS in his others, Kenneth Vaux writes clearly and engagingly, so he does not need a foreword with explanatory comment. What most warrants introduction instead is the genre, because if a reader grasps and welcomes the author's intentions in packaging his stories and thoughts this way, all that follows will turn out to be, yes, "clear" and "engaging."

The genre gets defined several times on these pages as a memoir, and it is that, just as a cart is a cart. What makes carts interesting to all but cart-makers or repairers is what is in them. Their contents can be a giant log or hay or bearings or lunch-boxes, or a combination of these. This memoir, which two lines ago was metaphorically a cart, has a mix of contents, and Vaux rummages around among them with an ease that comes from experience, and through which he can offer samples from the array of contents in ways that will be inviting to readers.

Be warned, however, for this memoir is not an "and then . . . and then . . . and then" chronicle, though many chapters within it have chronologically arranged plots. The pages do move the themes along, not with the neatness one would get from a formal theological ethics treatment—though there is much "formal theological ethics" here—but with an interest in using chronological stopping-off points as places to unload mini-treatises, letters and articles by others, and editorials. Vaux trusts that, taken together, they will form a coherent plot. They do.

An author who chooses such a format also invites speculation as to his pose or stance. His title gives the concept away: his is life "on the edge." One thinks of other books with spatial metaphors for location, such as Paul Tillich's *On the Boundary*. As I read this book and correlated my reading with recall of (many) other works by ethicist Vaux, a different image came to mind. I've elaborated on it before, no doubt because I know a few other people who share Vaux's outlook, intentions, and achievements. It comes from a poem by W. H. Auden and is a noun I had to have defined by a dictionary:

> Arête: *a sharp-crested ridge in rugged mountains.*

The dictionary notes that "etymologically," it is literally a fishbone.

Here are the lines from the Auden poem, "New Year Letter" (1940), which suggest Vaux's situation and circumstance:

> . . . perched upon the sharp arête,
> Where if we do not move we fall,
> Yet movement is heretical,
> Since over its ironic rocks
> No route is truly orthodox . . .

Why think of Vauxism as being preached on a "sharp-crested ridge?" His memoir shows that much of his ancestry reflects Calvinist-Reformed-Presbyterian roots and grounding. That hyphenated religious description not only suggests, it *thunders* foot-on-flat-ground commitment and circumstance. In triadic folkloric imagery, its covenanted communion of members seek each other out, confirm each other's pilgrimages, appraise each other's orthodoxy, and punish the wayward experimenters among them. Author Vaux knows all about that, and the price paid by those who deviate from it. Yet his calling in his times, his places, his vocation perches him on that sharp-crested ridge.

I wrote "times" and "places" in the plural, but left "vocation" in the singular, because it *is* singular, in more senses than one. He has lived "all over the map" and interacted with contemporaries in several generations but, more than that, he knows—and he does know much about it—his vocation has been and is to be "theological ethicist." Like so many others, he has gone to work because he had a job that is part of a career in which he can exercise his profession—because he has a vocation, a calling, to be a theological ethicist. I have known him as professor, colleague, home-repairman, father-and-husband, neighbor, consultant, staffer, preacher, theologian, and ethicist, but he's always at base a theological ethicist. From that firm vocational ground, he takes off to the sharp arête of life.

Always, tensions or contraries are posed here as the "ironic rocks" on which he walks and works. Some of his employers, and many of his colleagues, are able to be described as "simply secular," yet his witness and work and vision among them is frankly religious and theological. He wins respect of the non-religious by showing his respect for them and articulating positions they can recognize as being well thought out, even if they do not share his premises. Similarly, on one side, he is at home in pluralism, inter-faith relations, and ecumenism, but rather than being secure there, he risks staying at home with his Reformed Christian vision. He is deep-down American to the point that even Texans did not distrust him, but he also is a cosmopolitan: just try to keep track of all the locales in which he has worked and in which he and Sara have lived. His natural company can be described as generally liberal, and yet, he can say—as these pages suggest—"Some of my best friends are neo-conservative." He can be critical of religious institutions, but the reader can sense at once, or not be surprised, when he asserts that he is very much at home on a theological school faculty. Those are only beginnings of a list of paradoxical or stressful arrangements and commitments in his life.

Auden wrote that "no route is truly orthodox," and Vaux is orthodox, but not *truly* orthodox. I write not to invite a heresy trial on his head—none is in the offing—but to show that, for all his wanderings *in partibus infidelibus* where the "infidels" roam, his natural company is with Helmut Thielicke and Karl Barth, profound shapers of Christian thought in the 20th century and critical reformers of theology.

The temptation for someone thus poised and posed would be to come down from that figurative mountain ridge, desert the exciting moves on the sharp arête, and turn compromising or wishy-washy. Yet he stays "perched" on the precarious ridge, where he must walk and run.

The reader who follows him will pick up much of an implicit theological ethical system along the way, but it comes here interrupted by serendipities—contingencies and accidents and surprises—which Vaux then accepts as bids and interprets. Let him write systematic books, as he has done; here, instead, he is reminiscent, often arbitrary, taking distractions in stride and effecting balance in every case. Sir Isaiah Berlin wrote a famous essay on "The Hedgehog and the Fox," the hedgehog being the slogging-along beast who cautiously acquires knowledge and finds achievements as he goes his staid and stolid way. A hedgehog Vaux is not. He is instead the fox, who is, first of all, "foxy," making rapid moves from source to source and chore to chore. The reader has to be ready for quick starts, dartings, not lingerings. Life is short, Vaux knows and, with a remarkable family and a diverse batch of colleagues, he wants to make the most of it and its abundant stimuli. One hopes that readers will find and stare up at, or even join, the figurative spiritual journey of "the sharp arête" on which Vaux's book thrives.

Martin E. Marty is the Fairfax M. Cone Distinguished Service Professor Emeritus at The University of Chicago and a collaborator with Kenneth Vaux in a series of books that he mentions on occasion in this book.

Introduction

Why is society relying so heavily on bioethics—a profession that barely existed three decades ago?[1]

A seminal conference in 1968 (convened by Ken Vaux) to gather those engaged in ethical reflection on medicine is regarded by many as the birthplace of the discipline of bioethics.[2]

THE FIRST BIOETHICIST

THUS WROTE SHERYL GAY Stolberg in *The New York Times* in the wake of the stem-cell debate. Al Jonsen echoed this claim in *The Birth of Bioethics*.[3]

"The first bioethicist"—it is not true! The assertion, even the charge, that I was the first ethicist to labor in the vineyards of mid-to-late twentieth-century medicine, fails to gain credence at many points. But we'll take it for what it's worth.

I see the founders of the field of American bioethics as a handful of theologians and philosophers who, were they still with us, would now be in their 80s or 90s. Among these are Paul Ramsey, Joseph Fletcher, Hans Jonas, and Richard McCormick.

I number myself with a wide circle of their immediate successors, now in their 60s and 70s: Leon Kass, Jim Gustafson, Tris Engelhardt, LeRoy Walters, Dan Callahan, Al Jonsen, Mark Siegler, John Fletcher, Art

1. See Stolberg, "Ought We Do What We Can Do?"; Rae and Cox, *Bioethics: A Christian Approach in a Pluralistic Age*, 1.

2. The proceedings of the 1968 Houston Conference on Ethics in Medicine and Technology were published as Vaux, *Who Shall Live: Medicine, Technology, Ethics*.

3. See Jonsen, *The Birth of Bioethics*.

Caplan, Will Gaylin, Ed Pellegrino, and many others. Now a third generation is rising—numbering in the hundreds, if not thousands—of very promising clinicians, philosophers, lawyers, and theologians.

This early emphasis of my career in the mid-1960s was marked by *The New York Times*, when Health and Religion editors Jane Brody and Ted Fiske collaborated in March, 1971 to write a front-page piece on the budding enterprise featuring my story and picture. Today, when Leon Kass retires as chair of the President's Bioethics Commission, and politicians measure their views on stem-cell research, the field has obviously enlivened moral discourse throughout our society. It has exerted a profound influence on my ministry.

MINISTRY ON THE EDGE

Ministry always occurs at what Bonhoeffer called the boundaries (*Grenze*): boundaries of good and evil, truth and "falsehood, hope and despair." This journal is about those membranes of experience, which for me, have become temptations and transitions of opportunity. A minister reluctantly assumes the roles of prophet and priest. Calvin and the older *Munus Triplex* tradition added King as well, but I could make no sense of that unless it would mean the responsibility of governor and administrator—not my forte. I took on the mantle of priest or minister as a Presbyter in 1963 at my home church in New York. The priest (Cohen) bends down and lifts up, offering down the Lord's condescension in prophecy and benediction and lifting up a people before God in supplication for forgiveness and grace. This up-and-down best defines the work of a priest—upholding the broken-down and humbling the haughty. My ministry also has mingled religion and public policy, which I comprehend as a prophetic endeavor. I've seldom been in the sanctuary, more in the streets and the academy, but it's the same oscillating offering.

PART ONE

The Search for a Standpoint

Early Experiences

MEMORIES BEGIN

MY EARLIEST MINISTRY-SHAPING MEMORIES begin on the day Japan attacked Pearl Harbor. I remember stumbling around our small apartment in Mount Lebanon, Pittsburgh. I was nearly 3 years old. Seven decades later, such events frame my consciousness and conscience. I remember an early Christmas at the home of my Pap and Grammy Shoup in the hills of western Pennsylvania. It may have been 1941 or 1942. The snow was clinging to the majestic pines on the steep hills along the Scrub Grass creek. My gift that magical Christmas morning was a wonderful set of wooden boats with spring-fired wooden rockets—a patriotic gesture soon regretted by mom and dad. After several bruises on the folks' legs, the boats disappeared, and my warrior ambitions were nipped in the bud.

My grandparents, and even great-grandparents, on the Shoup side were very special people. The old folks had been born toward the end of the Civil War. They celebrated their 73rd wedding anniversary on IVs and urinary catheters before they were put out of their misery by a loving nurse-daughter. They rooted my life in a long history and remote European cultural background that I would soon get to know and in a rural simplicity, which, for a city priest, was a constant reality check.

Sara has written four volumes on our family history, and I here offer eulogies and a memoir to tell you of two of them. First, I offer my tribute to "Grammy" Shoup, who died of congestive heart failure at home along the Scrub Grass Creek at age 80.

TRIBUTE TO GRANDMA VEDA MAE ARMSTRONG SHOUP

July 13, 1974

We now bring to a close our hours of mourning. We close the casket (a provocation to the folks of Clintonville) and enter some minutes of reminiscence and self-examination and witness to the enduring promise of our God. Then we drive over the hills to the place she was born and lay her to rest with so many of her forebears. Our mood will pass from sorrow to comfort, then to sadness, but sadness chastened by joy and hope.

Veda Mae Armstrong Shoup: born in the verdant northwestern Pennsylvania. She never journeyed far from this place. Abandoned as an infant by her father; her mother taken early by death; reared by relatives in those harsh years at century's turn; meeting the dear companion of her life. The loss of a child, then the birth of twins so small that survival would be a miracle, even today, with advanced neo-natal care.

Then another daughter comes, and she has always been near. School days, sports days, coming and going, she cherished the beauty of nature, teaching all by example to revel at the sight of wildflowers and birds and old hound dogs. Tears came to her eyes, and anger, as she watched the slow destruction of hills and forests and streams.

Persons were her greatest joy. By dim light at night, she finely penned letters to her family and friends. Her home and hearth welcomed both friend and stranger. Travelers who one day stopped by became life-long friends and rise today with her sons and daughters to call her blessed.

Four score years, not so much by reason of health, as by sheer German willpower and by the grace of an abiding sense of humor. A saint and sinner, like us all. She knew it—knew her need of savior in life and death, as the old German Reformed catechism, by which she was raised, had it. She knew her destiny to be to care and she did.

A wife and mother, great to two generations. Keeper of the citadel of a constant home, observer, and commentator on the foibles and aspirations of generations—of wars and depressions—of new starts and inventions. Strange new machines took the roads and the skies in her lifetime; she watched quietly. She watched the profound revolution that fashioned a thousand separate towns and nations into a global village, where brotherhood became the precondition to survival, as well as the gracious thing to do, something she had known instinctively.

Her last evening, she lay beside the window looking up that winding hill that had brought so many travelers to her home in the valley. If her eyes were not already dimmed, she could have seen a black bear ambling across the road. The Indians who once made village along that creek behind her house would surely have sensed an ominous sign of the mysterious fates that cross our path.

As dawn made ready to pierce the eastern sky, she startled as her spirit made its last tortuous cleavage from the shell that was her body, her family at her side, her work completed.

Second, I present a tribute I offered to Grandpa Shoup at a 1995 family reunion. I also conducted his funeral in a more conventional way, given the irascible character of "Pap."

TRIBUTE TO GRANDPA LESTER SHOUP

Family Reunion, July 29, 1995

Thanks Pap, for making it fun to be a kid. Wherever you are in heaven or hell, you old character . . . thanks Pap, for making it fun to be a kid.

For the lime on the garden, the lettuce and cukes . . . and the side porch and the swing and the hummingbirds in the trumpet vine . . .

For the drive one night to pick up Pedro—or was it Tech?—and place him in his mansion. What a fine line of homes, like Levittown, while old Edie, with her fine brunette mane, lay cozy by the gas fire . . .

For the simple, still joy of Christmas '43—snow on the hemlocks and ice on the scrub grass . . . thanks Pap, for making it fun to be a kid.

For the long evenings on the summer porch with Don, swatting flies, for about the same average that we did on the baseball diamond, until Ray came along . . .

For the weenie roasts back at the old stone fireplace up on the creek-bank behind the outhouse, where Grammy's careful script of Edgar Guest hung above the farm journals and Sears catalogs.

This recalls the Fourth of July, rocking on the porch as the cars processed down the hill from near and far . . . like Petersburg.

Then the old outhouse was really put to use . . . and Uncle Bill lost his teeth 'til along came my Dad, ever the fixer of potties and fixtures . . .

Meanwhile, the picnic . . . and the pink angel food cakes . . . and Grammy . . . thanks Pap, for making it fun to be a kid.

And for the old green Hornet left by Uncle Buss that we all learned to drive back and forth around the pump station . . . and down to the swimmin' hole with Pearlie storming down the mountainside, and a flying dive . . .

And the rushing creek behind the house, and memories of the old pioneer village along those banks as we settled after good days to peaceful sleep and sweet dreams.

And the morning pancakes, mixed from scratch from the old Hoosier cabinet, shaped into turtles.

And the berries on the hill by Ross Phipps' farm and the call from Grammy that came so clear to this bored and weary kid, "Come home now boys."

And the tale of my mom's first biscuits, tossed out like cue balls that winter's night, still undisturbed come spring.

And the big dinner table and the game—rabbit, squirrel, venison, and pheasant—and the hand-made pot pie . . . thanks Pap (and Grammy), for making it fun to be a kid.

For the quiet evening reminiscing around the parlor, 'til you headed up the hill at about eight and Grammy remained at the writing table.

And the early morning . . . and the groundhog standing poised across the road, down by the bridge beneath the great long-needle white pines that rose toward heaven before the blight took the hemlocks, and strip mine run-off silenced the spring-fed stream . . . and the bear that ambled across by the Phipps road the night Grammy died.

For the anticipating delight of winding down the hill, then glimpsing the house in the distance; the thrill started for us when we exited the turn-pike—then Harrisburg, Barkeyville, and Nectarine . . . Nectarine—like the peach too sweet and fuzzless . . .

Two churches in a town of 23: the Church of God and the Church of God of Prophesy—fine tuning indeed!

Then Clintonville and the big hill . . . thanks Pap, for making it fun to be a kid.

For the long summer . . . Dick and I wore abners; he busied himself making fishing plugs, carved and colored, a budding craftsman.

Meanwhile up in the bathroom, a fire breaks out . . . who is this kid? P-45 they called him (a bed wetter, a budding theolog), maybe a preacher—you know, fire escape—strange sort!

Then there was fishing . . . Scrubgrass Creek and waders in the pump-house closet and the minnows where the water tank run-off ran down to the creek.

And the big river—fishing from the boat and the evening the moose swam across, long ago.

And Lake Erie one early morning—it died and was born again—as you were about to . . . you'd be glad . . .

And the tromping walks along the pipelines—one just out the road from our cabin lane. And the knowledge and respect for each creature, plant, and animal . . . and the stories—oh, the stories . . . always the roaring side of everyone's foibles . . . and your own . . .

For genes and other memories, for hearty laughs and gentle chuckles . . . and Thanksgiving . . . this kid says, thanks Pap, for making it fun to be a kid.

Though it was a happy childhood, there was nothing auspicious or portentous of future notoriety. I remember one day, when an exasperated Sunday school teacher lamented, "Kenny, you'll either be a good gangster or a minister." A lot of blood and tears poured out in that remark.

Faith moved from the formal to the personal in two decisive experiences: in the fourth grade and in high school. God had begun a lifelong process to "righteous" me through faith.[1] I was being called to service of the gospel of God (Rom 1) . . . the ministry of truth and justice. Ethics would, therefore, be a natural vocation.

The ministry won out over the Mafia. Growing up was liberating and humiliating. A *laissez-faire* home released enormous creativity. Yet, surrounded by so much talent in high school as with Neville Chamberlain, I found much to be humble about. A modestly good athlete in high school would excel in college. When I graduated high school at 6 feet, 4 inches with a 3.95 gpa, I found I was about number 50 in line on both values of height and grades in a class of 1,080. My high-school career was remarkable for its diversity, coming from a very large and excellent school, where most of the teachers held advanced degrees from Columbia University. I had a course in aeronautics (we had an airplane with a hangar), a chef's class (often ended by throwing butcher knives with Rocky Gustino), and a sublime choir (two former members went on to the Robert Shaw

1. Sanders, *Paul: A Very Short Introduction*, 55.

Chorale). I became a music and opera lover in high school when our director, Kathleen O'Donoghue, took us to a dress rehearsal of *Rigoletto* at the Metropolitan Opera in New York City. We had been well schooled, having played and sung through each aria and chorus. Although we didn't know it then, it was a great honor to hear (and meet) Leonard Warren (Rigoletto), Richard Tucker (the Duke), and Rise Stevens (Gilda). The student body at Sewanhaka High School mingled gangsters, white-buck ivy leaguers, scholars, and jocks.

I played baseball in the spring. Jimmy Brown from Port Washington High (and later the Cleveland Browns) once fell on and fractured my arm as he slid back into first base. He later would shine with Syracuse, the Cleveland Browns, and tough-guy films, which was why I cracked and he didn't. I also occasionally tossed back the discus to my friend Charlie Weingarten. He was the number-two discus at Sewanhaka (175 ft.) and went on to set a new ivy-league record at Brown. Our top man, Al Oerter, broke the national high-school record (184 ft.) and then went on to Kansas and to win four Olympic gold medals. It was a thrill to watch the opening parade of the 1996 summer Olympics in Atlanta and see Al leading the athletes.

That spectacle of Oerter started healing the wounds of the 1972 Olympics in Munich, where we lived for a sabbatical year. When members of the Israeli team were killed, my convictions of the signature evils of anti-Semitism, Holocaust, and medical experimentation were sharply defined, as well as my commitment to the need for interfaith awareness.

UPBRINGING

What early experiences prepared me to one day enter this bizarre ministry—civil rights, the highly specialized field of bioethics, and Abrahamic/interfaith Scriptural Reasoning?

Many of my high-school friends went on to ivy-league colleges. I went to Muskingum in New Concord, Ohio—a splendid choice, as it turned out. Here, the reserve of missed achievement and accomplishment was realized. I was Big Man on Campus in several parameters, although always many superior colleagues among the faculty and students challenged me to keep reaching. Four varsity letters: basketball, baseball, and swimming. Student council, YMCA. Fourth in the nation in college oratory. The preacher was budding.

I became keenly interested in science and history, religion, philosophy, and literature. Summers were spent working either on the garbage truck at home on Long Island (lunch on the job) or at YMCA camps in the Poconos for poor kids from Brooklyn. From high school on, I knew I would be a minister, but one with a different twist. Not just your ordinary village pastor; this city priest would make a difference. I was disdainful and disenchanted with the church. Only now, after 40 years in the secular university and medical world, have I gained some appreciation for the mundane parish and the country parson.

When I founded Project X, which became the Park Ridge Center in Chicago, I began to see how vital were spiritual and ethical formation in churches, synagogues, and mosques. I began to see that this was the best source available for moral formation and commitment. Faith commitments became paramount in my judgment. A good part of the delight in finally finding my way into the seminary (a career that started at Garrett-Evangelical Theological Seminary in 1993) was to have some small part in the formation of parish clergy. The *curé de campagne*, city rabbi, and suburban minister are now my superheroes.

How did I come to be in such a place in the mid-1980s? Growing up on Long Island, in a small house where I could climb a maple tree in the back yard and see the Empire State Building, I never dreamed that such events in the latter decades of the 20th century would involve this child born at the beginning of World War II.

A CAST OF MIND

My college oration was entitled "Modern Science: Man's Salvation or His Doom?" Although it won fourth in the nation, it was deemed first by the Michigan State professor who was president of the American Speech Association. Its homiletical tenor turned off the other judges.

The title spoke volumes about that 20-year-old mind. Patterns and circuits were being imprinted that would surface often across the years. In addition to the fascination with secular events in history (and in the natural world), as providential phenomenon or as moments pregnant with spiritual meaning, there was a definite apocalyptic cast to that mind. I don't think I had what Norman Mailer would later call "a middle-class lust for destruction" or some Napoléon-esque *Après moi, le déluge,* but there was a certain tendency to hang on, even thrill at, impending crises, to hover near the fire. To this day, I cling fanatically to the tube, watching Dan Rather's landing on Mogadishu, the bombing of Iraq, and the collapse of the I-35 bridge in Minneapolis. "Why?" some would ask. "Maybe we can do something," I would respond.

In college, I was conscripted to play Mr. Antrobus in Thornton Wilder's play, *The Skin of Our Teeth*. In this, his saga of humanity (quite congenial to this genetic Calvinist, whose brother Amos taught at Harvard Divinity), Sabina, the daughter of Antrobus, who represents the pleasure principle, cries out as the flood sweeps the Atlantic City Boardwalk in one of history's periodic conflagrations: "You know, Mr. Antrobus, I hate to see the war end; people are at their best in war time."

Vaux was typecast. As my tale unfolds, the reader will see a *fascinans tremendum*—a hovering around crisis—be it in the civil-rights struggle and imprisonment in Mississippi in the terrible summer of 1964, the career in bioethics punctuated by dramatic cases in which I was personally involved (like Karen Quinlan and Baby David, heart transplants or cloning human beings), or the general lure of parish, hospital or political work. The more provocative, the more incendiary—for this fire-starter—the better.

I attribute this cast of mind not only to a character trait but to the impact of the Bible on my mind. I started reading it intensely in high school. Whatever you may say about the Bible, it is an apocalyptic tale. In the words of *West Side Story*, something's happening. Regrettably, the trauma of God's appearance has been twice-told by many fools, this one among them. The Hebrew Testament erupts from that perpetually ruptured land of Palestine and has to do with interruption of routine world history by Yahweh, the Lord of space and time. Not only the prophets, but the mythic Genesis sagas, the historical narratives, the psalms, and writings are all convulsive literature—they depict an intruding, disrupting force we call Yahweh. The New Testament is an apocalyptic breaking of Jesus into world history in first-century Palestine. Even today, that same Galilean *Hasid*, made Lord and Christ by God, will soon interrupt any life that will pause there and ask "What's it all about?"

Now at 71 years of age, the apocalyptic tenor of that mind has been tempered. The summer of the year I began to compose this memoir gave Sara and me the opportunity to traverse those same biblical lands. I will conclude this diary with those reflections and what they might mean for contemporary societies and faiths. I believe that one should take the chance to reset one's biblical faith again against its geographical and historical environs: Israel (Palestine), Asia Minor (Turkey), and Greece. Even a little touch with the other three Bible lands—Egypt, Italy, and Syria—would help, but not this trip. In 1996, each of these places was in turmoil.

You can't help be scared as you travel in Ephesus, Pergamon, Smyrna (Izmir), or Istanbul; stop overnight on Cyprus or try to leave from Tel Aviv airport.

In 2007, during the war with Iraq, the crisis had reached ominous proportions. The contemporary turmoil brings to life the tumultuous landscape of the sacred book(s).

CHILD OF APOCALYPTIC

I think if I were to live again, I would seek to be Edward R. Murrow—on the battle front on that early morn at Dunkirk, in the trenches. My neighbor Larry Lichty, the leading scholar of media coverage in Vietnam, is for me today's *karux*, the newsman, the preacher. If theology is about *kerygma* (message), I want to be there and here. I can live with the inevitable schizophrenia. Lord Olsson writes on Mediterranean apocalypticism:

> The Near East and Mediterranean types of apocalypticism (are strikingly like those) of the Americas, Africa, and Oceania . . . The revitalization of mythic material and its reinterpretation with references to a contemporaneous situation is a constant feature in these movements . . . [2]

To me, this is evidence that apocalyptic is a natural part of natural and historic reality and of normative human perception and intelligence. In a recent book, *Being Well*,[3] I argue not only for the perennial recurrence of apocalyptic, but for its validity as a window of insight into reality. It is a kind of urgent schizophrenia, a Dali-esque space-time warp that insists that reality must always be a concourse between two actualities, one sacred, the other secular.

To illustrate: "A Graceful Dialogue: That Day—Wondrous Love" was the title of a sermon presented in chapel at Garrett in early 1996 (scripture texts were Isaiah 58 and Matthew 5). It reflects this dialectical way in which I have always viewed reality.

2. Hellholm, *Apocalypticism in the Mediterranean World and the Near East* , 18.

3. See Vaux, *Being Well*.

A GRACEFUL DIALOGUE: THAT DAY—WONDROUS LOVE

Garrett Evangelical Theological Seminary Chapel, 1996

Isaiah 58 and Matthew 5

After the radiance of Christmastide and the winter light of Epiphany, we have settled into the ever-after glow of ordinary time. While to winter's coldness are added the conundrums of fires and floods pressing our cabin-fever toward agitation, we patiently wait it out as Word proceeds to work in the world. Our only repose, it seems to this bleak mid-winter, was another unbearable Superbowl.

Maybe our 1996–97 Bulls have charged up your batteries, especially the three superheroes—Superman, Batman, and Rodman. Closer meditation to the time at hand discloses a season far from boring, one liturgically and theologically vibrant. The Word God sent has gone out into all the world. Now like growing seed or latent roots, it is gathering strength, never to return empty (but accomplishing its mission). This active and living Word—the veritable music of the spheres—sings a stirring duet. The two voices: "That day" and "wondrous love." Like Richard Tucker and Robert Merrill's "Temps Simple" from Bizet's *The Pearl Fishers* or Kathleen Battle and Jessye Norman's "Lachme," a poignant and expectant song has gone out into all the world. That day . . . wondrous love.

> Like dueling trumpets on old Shechem's mountain of covenant
>   renewal.
> Like the dual thrones of Psalm 89:
> two energies pulsate through the cosmos,
> the entropy of "that day,"
> the negentropy of "wondrous love."
> The weighty matter and drag of sin and law converted by the vul-
>   nerable, yet highly charged, matter of grace.
> That day . . . wondrous love.

Let us reflect for a moment on this graceful dialogue. It is now two years since I joined this august company and offered my first sermon. If I've learned anything from the giants who walk these hallowed halls, it would be this.

The essence of Torah and gospel, of prophecy and parenesis, of wisdom and writings is the complementary tension of judgment and mercy, *sedek* and *hesed,* that day and wondrous love. Two pictures appear on the horizon of world history. They depict these two voices: ominous El Greco skies over Toledo verge back toward Christ's Calvary and a glorious sun rises yet over Lake Michigan, piercing the dark winter sky refracted through Tiffany's resplendent ascension window at Second Presbyterian on South Michigan Avenue. The Bible sings this duet against this panorama as scripture speaks incessantly of "that day" and "wondrous love."

Our service today enacts the oscillation of this alpha and omega wave.

- It is there on Music of the Baroque baritone Doug Anderson's introit from George Herbert and Ralph Vaughan Williams:

  > Such a way, as gives us breath,
  >
  > such a truth as ends all strife:
  >
  > such a life, as killeth death . . .[4]

  That day . . . wondrous love.

- It is there in our processional hymn, recalling fire and 2 Timothy:

  > I know not why God's wondrous grace to me he hath made known,
  >
  > Nor why, unworthy, Christ in love redeemed me for his own.
  >
  > But I know whom I have believed, and am persuaded
  >
  > that he is able to keep that which I've committed unto him against that day.[5]

- It is there in Doug's song with the choir from Fauré's "Requiem":

  > *Dies Irae* (day of wrath)—"that day"
  >
  > *Libera Me* (deliver me)—"wondrous love."

And by the way, Aretha Franklin's "deliver me" is not Domino's Pizza. You should have listened to your preacher dad or your friend Lou Rawls before you did that ad. Unlike Domino's, on that day, we don't get a freebie if the deliverer tarries beyond a half-hour.

---

4. Ralph Vaughan Williams (music), George Herbert (lyrics), "The Call" (1911).

5. James McGranahan (music), D.W. Whittle (lyrics), "I Know Not Why God's Wondrous Grace" (1883).

"That day"—ever so faithful to the Apostle, Luther called it the *Stundenlein*, the *occasio*, the hour, that day. The decisive moment—it's there in our sacrament—the hour cometh and now is.

- It is there in our recessional, the southern folk hymn:

  > What wondrous love is this, oh! my soul! oh! my soul!
  > What wondrous love is this, oh! my soul!
  > What wondrous love is this!
  > That caused the Lord of bliss,
  > To bear the dreadful curse for my soul, for my soul,
  > To bear the dreadful curse for my soul.[6]

- It is there in Kathy Heetland's lovely rendition of Vaughn Williams's plaintive "Rosamunde" prelude and "The Wondrous Love" postlude. In this sacred season of light and darkness, of warmth and cold, of hope and fear, we ponder the eschatological break-in of God's judgment and mercy. The Trinity sings the song. *Deus absconditus* and *Deus adventus* explain the enigma of history full of hope and impending doom. He who has come and is coming illumines the strange paradox of our human condition, glorious and tragic. The restless spirit of God, consoling yet uncanny, makes us aware of the at once infinite distance, yet sublime nearness, of time and eternity. God, Son, and Spirit exude that day . . . wondrous love.

In biblical purview, "that day" is expressed with many terms: the Day of the Lord, Day of Judgment, Day of the Messiah, Day of Christ, Day of God, Day of Visitation, and Coming Day. In the history of theology, liturgy, and music, it becomes *Dies Irae*, day of wrath. "Wondrous love" has an equally rich derivation and tradition, often a counterpoint or transformer pointing to "that day." The wondrous works of the psalms become the wondrous feat of deliverance and covenant. The wondrous loving-kindness of the shepherd of Israel becomes the wondrous love of Jesus. That day can be understood in at least four ways:

- It can be Yahweh's justice in the crises of nations and history.

- It can be Christ's sublime *Parousia*–the second coming.

- It can be the day of our own reckoning or dying.

- It can be today—now.

6. William Walker (music), Alexander Means (lyrics), "What Wondrous Love Is This" (1835).

Yahweh's Justice. Trace these four senses of "that day." In a primal sense, "that day" is when Yahweh joins human events in battle. Gerhard von Rad and Robert Jewett have shown that the zeal of the Lord performs in history the justice that alone grounds peaceable kingdom. In some mysterious—that is, holy—way, historic crisis is always "that day of the Lord." The last rocket launch in Bosnia or a fateful meeting of Israel and Syria can be "that day." We recall the powerful *Dies Irae* tapestry in Coventry Cathedral, England, built onto the bombed skeleton of that church destroyed on those nights of November 14–15, 1940. "That day" cries from the ruins of Kaiser Wilhelm Memorial Church in Berlin. And from the rubble of mosques in Kandahar, the slaughter warehouse in Srebrenica, and the bloodstained floor of the Cathedral in Rwanda.

"That day" is Cyrus the Persian or Nebuchadnezzar the Babylonian. It is the Syro-Ephraimite Alliance, the German-Japanese concordat, the Sino-Soviet Pact. It is the day when nations conspire against the Lord. History and supervening *Heilsgeschichte* are "that day."

Christ's Parousia. "That day" is also the day of Christ—the hour of Christ's awaited appearance. Christ's consummation of history and nature, we confess, will happen in time and space as he returns to judge the living and the dead. The kingdom for which we keep watch is also a coming that transcends those orders. As Ray Brown has shown in the *Birth of the Messiah*, there is a haunting historical quality to advent and second advent. Standing at the close of two millennia of delayed *Parousia*, we can only sigh with W.B. Yeats at 2000 years "vexed to nightmare by a rocking cradle . . ." Yet how silently, how silently, the wondrous gift is given—*Maranatha*, come Lord Jesus . . . my kingdom is within you.

Day of Reckoning. Again, "that day" may be our day of reckoning, of awakening, of epiphany. It may be that ordinary bush—burning, yet not consumed. It may be some call . . . "man, woman, where are you?" It may be the vocation of some still small voice. Some calls may reverberate against our frail, finite, mortal existence. Dying day comes to each of us and to all whom we love. "That day" came three weeks ago to the home across from ours when Claire and Bernie burned to death in a motel fire in Kentucky, leaving three young boys. Even if we are spared some premature death by violence, even if we are granted Dr. King's dream of long years, that day inevitably comes. When hearts fail, or we cannot breathe, or malignancy or senility still our body or mind, we die. When infectious heat overwhelms us and the "fever of life is over, our work is then done."

"The day of dread," said Luther, "is God's gift to us, awakening within us the need for forgiveness." That day brings all into perspective and priority. I have built my house and filled my barns, said one, "take your ease." "Fool, this night, that day your soul is required of you." Therefore, in the ultimate sense, that day is always this day. "Today . . . if you will hear my voice." (Luke 12:18ff).

Today. Today is the implosion of yesterday and tomorrow in God's time. Today is that day. Today is the juncture of heretofore and ever after. The philosophers of time say present doesn't exist—only past rushing into future. Wondrous love is therefore the imperishable bread amid the blaze and substance of "that day." Love is the radiant, high-energy dot at the center of that collapsing black hole, that "dark energy" amid the expanding 40 billion galaxies.

Justice is mercy; mercy is justice. Without mercy, justice is petulance; without justice, mercy is cheap debilitating indulgence. At the axis point of history, at the crux of it all, justice has been transfigured into grace. It happened on a wondrous cross on which a prince of glory ignominiously died. Wrath has been transformed into wondrous love.

In his enigmatic (though rhapsodic) *Ethics,* Dietrich Bonhoeffer wrote of this reconciliation:

> In this figure (of the reconciler) is disclosed the mystery of the world, just as the mystery of God is revealed in it. No abyss of evil can remain hidden from him through whom the world is reconciled to God. But the abyss of the love of God embraces even the most abysmal godlessness of the world. In an incomprehensible reversal of all righteous and pious thought, God declares himself as guilty toward the world and thereby extinguishes the guilt of the world.[7]

It is as if, in *kenotic* emptying, God's wrath diminishes back on the Omega point of sheer love.

So we are left with that wondrous day of love. One of the most moving scenes of this assimilation is in Giordano's opera, "Andrea Chénier." The aria "La Mamma Morta" becomes the epiphany scene in the film *Philadelphia.* Maddalena returns home during the French Revolution to find her house incinerated and her dead mother at the door. She wails:

> They killed my mother at the door of my room;

7. Bonhoeffer, Green, Krauss, West, and Stott, *Ethics: Dietrich Bonhoeffer Works, Vol. 6,* 83.

She died—she saved me. I looked; the place that cradled me was
   burning.

It was during that sorrow that love came to me:

A voice filled with harmony and said, "live still—I am life."

You are not alone; I gather your tears, I walk along your path and
   sustain you.

Is everything around you blood and mud?

I am divine, I am oblivion,

I am the God that descends from heaven to Earth making Earth a
   heaven

I am love.[8]

In the words of Georges Bernanos, "the prisoner of his agony" becomes
the possessor of Christ's wondrous love. In the film *Philadelphia*, the young
attorney played by Tom Hanks is fired from the firm even as he is dying from
AIDS. Like Maddalena, though all around him is destruction, he finds sustenance for that impending day in such wondrous love.

"Do you pray?" he asks his lawyer, played by Denzel Washington. And
as he is transported by Maddalena's song in that hour, that night, that day,
both discover—amid oblivion, amid abyss in the grim face of death—love.
The bread comes down from heaven, the bread of immeasurable, wondrous, unqualified love. In Bernanos' *The Diary of a Country Priest*, as the
young priest receives last rites and a dying benediction is uttered, he faintly
whispers, "*Tout est grace*" (everything is grace).

From the verge of oblivion, the abyss, within Dali's descending arc of
the universe, we sit at cosmic supper—an eternal feast.

One of the windows of this chapel celebrates the appearance here in
1954 at the World Council of Churches' Assembly of the missionary states-
man D.T. Niles. He once defined evangelism as "one beggar telling another
beggar where to find bread."

Our scriptures, Isaiah 58 and Matthew 5 and 25, tell the same story.
Rightful fast before God is the feast of human sustenance, just as salt is the
salience and leaven of life. The leaven of justice is the bread of mercy. The
antidote to sin is the tincture of compassion. Worship and prayer without
justice is noise, however solemn. Our proper response to the day of wrath is
to do justice and love mercy. Beggar to beggar, we are to lead one another to
the hearth of wrath, become the hearth of mercy. There we find sustaining
bread and the refreshing cup. To reenact the Isaianic and messianic voca-

---

8. From the opera "Andrea Chénier," Umberto Giordano, "La Mamma Morta"
(1896).

tion is to feed the hungry as we are being fed, heal the sick as we are being made whole, and bring good news to the poor as we, though impoverished, are being made rich.

The sacrament before us now is the mystery of that day become wondrous love. We realize with the General in *Babette's Feast* that mercy is infinite. Here at altar, mercy and truth are met together as righteousness and bliss kiss. The love feast before us is the conjunction of God's justice and mercy. The commensal meal is both Christ's searching *exposé* and his saving rendezvous. "That day" and "wondrous love" here co-mingle. They cohere in our sure redeemer whom we now greet. Amen!

The sermon with its oscillating dialectic of "that day" and "wondrous love" reveals a pattern of mind. My grandmother, Ethel Stuart Vaux, had such a mind, bordering, like mine, on the depressive, dissociative, psychotic. She was once heard at the table saying "Kenny's deep—like me." She was a devout Baptist Sunday-school woman, who studied her Bible and read the signs of the times with John-of-Patmos-colored glasses. Her biblical view on race, for example was "birds of a feather flock together." It was in the scripture somewhere! I've always admired her ability to shift ground and alter those ingrained neural circuits. When I was thrown in a Mississippi jail for demonstrating for the rights of blacks to vote in 1964, she cross-fired remarkably. When her grandson's face was plastered all over the Pittsburgh newspapers and her shocked neighbors accosted her—"Mrs. Vaux, isn't that your grandson, the preacher?"—she replied with fervent scriptural intensity grounded more in blood than text—"You listen to me, he's a preacher of the gospel, white or black."

FASCINANS CALAMITAS

This bearer of good tidings often relished bringing bad tidings, perhaps the foretaste of those depressive propensities that would surface later in life. I was always thrilled by the thunderstorm, the fire, the siren of the fire truck or ambulance. As a child, I was often caught lighting fires in the bathroom or under the porch. Were I a peasant in first-century Galilee, I probably would have drawn near John the Baptizer or Jesus—at the outer fringe of the crowd. Demons and angels hovered near them. Jesus' ministry consisted simply of healing the sick, exorcising demons, and forgiving sin. Indeed, these were the three dimensions of one healing presence and act. My theology always respected Jesus' diagnosis of the human condition: malady of sickness, insanity, and sin and remedy of healing, soul-cure, and forgiveness.

When this ancient worldview of both Greek healer and Jewish charismatic is accepted, one invariably becomes apocalyptic, schizophrenic, eschatic and, yes, ecstatic. I often stare out into space for long periods of time. Is it ecstasy, dysphasia, autism, or a heart and mind drawn to mystery and wonder?

MOUNT LEBANON

An ethical sensitivity and perhaps a dialectic of acuity/apathy would arise from this character trait and worldview. When I emerged from seminary and was called to the "mother church" of my old denomination—the evangelical, United Presbyterian Church—I was uncomfortable with the disjunction of piety ("love and witness to Christ)" and worldly action ("do justice)." As a brash "know-it-all" young pastor, I felt compelled to "comfort the afflicted and afflict the comfortable." Too often, I visited the wrong cure to each respective group.

The telling event of our early ministry was the assassination of John F. Kennedy in Dallas in November of our first year. Although I had supported Nixon while I was still at Princeton in my first vote in 1960 (out of fear of Roman Catholic power and money), I had come to admire and support the Kennedy brothers, their administration, their cosmopolitan vision, and their programs to address our severe social crises.

I was playing golf with two Catholic priests when the word of JFK's death came from Dallas. We knelt in prayer on the green, then quickly returned home. When the word was announced to Sara's seventh-grade class in Baldwin Township, the children cheered. Although there must have been much innocent grief in this spontaneous cry, their autonomic cheer reflected the not-so-repressed racism and interfaith hatred in Pittsburgh we would later experience in its full fury. I still remember the evening of the assassination. A memorial service was held at the other Presbyterian Church in Mount Lebanon (where I'd been baptized 24 years earlier). John Calvin Reid, the pastor, with deep-south roots, offered a memorable reflection:

Today our president died in Parkland Hospital, Dallas. An old man died in Aberdeen, Scotland, and a hungry child died in Bombay. In the eyes of God, they were all the same.

PART TWO

The Search for Social Justice

Civil Rights

IN THE SPRING OF our first year of ministry at Mount Lebanon (South Pittsburgh), I formed a small study group of pastors to read a book of one who would become my *Doktorvater* in later studies: Helmut Thielicke of Hamburg, Germany. His *A Little Exercise For Young Theologians* was a clarion call for the four of us to get involved. We started to challenge the racial discrimination in South Hills, assisted Donn Clendenon, then first baseman of the Pittsburgh Pirates, as he sought to move to Mount Lebanon. Then in a decisive, life-changing experience, we four—Keith Brown, Bert Fromm, John Mehl, and Ken Vaux—volunteered when the Pittsburgh Presbytery sought workers to send south to the Delta ministry in Mississippi.

Here follows a detailed diary of that experience. It was recorded on scraps of toilet paper and brown paper bags, as I sat and slept in an over-crowded cell next to Vernon Damler, a courageous black farmer whose home was later fire-bombed and he and his family killed. Only in 2000, 37 years later, was the bomber convicted. The language, now 40 years old, is dated but heart-felt.

MISSISSIPPI SUMMER: A PRISON DIARY

Thursday, April 2, 1964. We left Pittsburgh during a slow drizzle. The rain continued through Ohio. We stopped in New Concord, Ohio. Dr. and Mrs. McCleery, my college physician and his wife, were in good spirits, al-though Mrs. McCleery is quite sick. They have discovered a cancer in the uterus. We had dinner, and then they requested we pray with them before we left. It was inspiring to be with them again. They wished us Godspeed and we journeyed on. The sky cleared near Cincinnati and Kentucky. We stopped for dinner at a charcoal pit north of Louisville, Kentucky.

We drove on and stopped about 2:30 p.m. in the afternoon somewhere north of the Alabama border. Here the landscape changed abruptly: flat pine trees and red soil.

Friday morning, April 3, 1964. We had our first encounter with the southern white elder citizens in Sulligent, Alabama. We were sitting on the loafing bench out in front of the general store on the dusty street swept by red dust. We discussed the local school situation. There is a consolidated white school and a state-supported Negro school. "Trouble with them in government is they want to throw them 'damned niggers' in with our kids," one red-necked local said. For this reason, they oppose further school aid and consolidation. We talked about the presidential primaries. They endorsed Gov. Wallace for the nomination. They were very suspicious of Lyndon B. Johnson, because of his foggy stand on civil rights. They despised Robert F. Kennedy and Barry Goldwater, because they wield too much power. One said, "pretty soon I'll be walking down the street and be nabbed and arrested for not doing anything." A big "nigger" then came walking out of the general store door. He had a 100-pound bag of peanuts, which he was planning to sell. He struggled to get through the door. I opened the door for him and our now-suspicious friends' necks glistened in the sun. They conversed about the hypocrisy of the church leaders and churches that preach peace and invite fights and riots: "damned hypocrites," they muttered.

"Billy Graham," they said, "came to Birmingham for a crusade just to be paid off by the NAACP." (Graham demanded integrated meetings.) We took our leave before tempers flared, should they discover they were talking to those very hypocrites.

Friday afternoon, April 3, 1964. It is spring in Mississippi. The last leg of the trip has been refreshing. We passed several dilapidated shacks with dozens of Negro kids running around. In Northern Mississippi, we noticed several teams of whites and Negroes working together on garbage trucks, gas stations, and on farm and construction gangs. The old apartheid south had started to break.

Friday evening, April 3, 1964. We arrived in Hattiesburg, Mississippi, cruised town for one hour then reported to Rev. John Cameron, who is in charge of the project. He is a dynamic, winsome young man who made a very strong impression on us all.

We stopped at the First Presbyterian Church to see the reverend Mr. Stanway. He wasn't there, but we had a very nice discussion with his secretary. All was very cordial, until I mentioned that we were here to work in voter registration. Her mouth dropped, and her eyes became inflamed. We left quickly. We returned to our headquarters, dressed, and joined the picket line at the courthouse.

Later that evening, April 3, 1964. Our amazing experience has been the reaction of the Hattiesburg police. They cruise by in cars and shout obscenities to folks in the line "m. f.," "s.o.b.," "n.l.," etc. If one of the picketers returns any comment (which hasn't happened), he can be arrested. Strange, the perversion of justice. You have to watch your step crossing the street! Bert Fromm and I were nearly knocked down by a Volkswagen truck. He turned the corner sharply and began swearing. With people like these, I agree with Dr. Cliff Smith, my clergy colleague in Pittsburgh, they are driven to deeper feelings of hostility. A great wall that blocks civil rights in Mississippi is the wall of intimidation. I have talked to two people today who lost their jobs for associating with SNCC (Student Non-Violent Coordinating Committee). The fact that we are clergy doesn't make any difference, apparently. Indeed, it heightens the suspicion.

Friday night, April 3, 1964. We traveled by car to the mass meeting with some of the SNCC kids (modern-day saints). They are 18 to 25 years old, wear dungaree overalls, sing, strategize, canvass neighborhoods, and march. The meeting began with clapping, then very inspiring singing, "Go tell it on the mountain," followed by some testimonies. One woman told how she had lost her job when she registered. We (the five ministers) each gave a little message and closed with singing and swaying, "We shall overcome." I realized I was becoming a radically different person. I have never been so taken by the maturity and sense of purpose of these young people. If we had five percent of this dedication in the church, Christ's work would really flourish.

Saturday morning, April 4, 1964. The picket began quietly in 80-degree heat. We marched for one hour. Reverend John Cameron, who is running for Congress, picked up Bob Shaffer and me. When the court officers saw John C. and his friends, we were refused admission to the hearing. The court officer said that he is running the "D" court, and that no "niggers" could be admitted. The scene was televised and reported by NBC and CBS television at the door of the courthouse—to be on TV tonight on the 6:00 p.m. report.

Later in the morning leaving the courtroom, I was greeted by a "white citizen" thinking I was one of his boys. He told me to come out on the porch and see a good group of communists. We looked at the picket line from the balcony. There they are, he said. "If these are communists, our world needs many more of them," I replied. His face turned white, and he huffed into the courtroom. I must record two reflections: the freedom of the Negro and the slavery of the white. The Mississippi white is shackled in a fearful compartmentalized mentality that is eating away at their insides. The Negro, on the other hand, is free in spirit, although his outer life seems to be in bondage. Carlyle Marney's *Structures of Prejudice* has been very helpful in my understanding. God help us! Blacks eligible to vote—425,000, registered—22,000.

Saturday afternoon, April 4, 1964. We went to a rally in Biloxi, Mississippi, down on the Gulf Coast. There were 50 to 60 there. Speakers were good. One of SNCC's kids talked on voter registration. An opinion survey is being prepared to canvass all of Mississippi Negroes and convince Attorney General Robert F. Kennedy that Mississippi Negroes want to vote.

"We have here a wide open proud, unashamed police state"—this statement was made by CORE leader from New Orleans. Certainly this claim is partially validated in the experiences of the day. Noble young warriors for justice are now confirmed defenders of an unjust status quo. To turn a quote of Winston Churchill, "never had so few done so much for so many." In the words of John Cameron, "Every church that refuses to open its doors to every person regardless of color, race, or national origin—Christ is not there."

Saturday night, April 4, 1964. Slim Jones is a laborer who has worked with his hands for many years. We met him in a bar. He spotted us as "the ministers" that were here agitating this week. He expressed more of the southern attitude to us: "the nigger is inferior!" "Show me one who has gone anywhere, who is not three-quarters white! He is thick in the head and in the lip." This man's brutal and sad resentment and prejudice must be fueled by a deep hurt and insecurity. I find in myself mingled rage and pity.

Sunday morning, April 5, 1964. We worshipped in two churches. I was at First Presbyterian with Dr. Stanway, a quiet, intelligent man. He led us in a fine communion service. His sermon was theological, with no ax to grind. I talked with Stanway after the service. He expressed concern for the problem, bewilderment as regards to solution, and a concern to improve the spiritual life of the Negro, not only the "social and political status" (with this I agree 100 percent, how we need spiritual foundations). This depth must be added to all of the social concerns that are surely Christ's work. If we let these works assume a secular character because of our indifference, we have betrayed our calling of being God's people— transforming the world rather than being conformed to it.

Sunday afternoon, April 5, 1964. We learned of General MacArthur's death at 2:00 p.m. as we were listening to Ravel's music. The rainy, bleak afternoon reflected the spirit of the populace.

At 3:00 p.m., we were on the platform with Reverend John Cameron and other Negro ministers this afternoon for the first anniversary of his church. I read the scripture, Bert prayed, John spoke. The singing was emotional and exciting. The sermon turned into an ecstatic chant in the middle of the sermon. Amen!

Monday morning 9 a.m., April 6, 1964. We met with Dr. Barnes, pastor of the largest Baptist church in Hattiesburg. He was very cordial and warm. Then came his statements, "The last ten years have set back the common cause that we have achieved (the brotherhood) . . . We believe that seg-regation is the best context to carry out our common purpose . . . We are called to preach the gospel, not walk in picket lines . . . In the North, you love the race and hate the individual . . . in the South, we hate the race and love the individual." He continually expressed his love for the Negro and his concern for their well-being. He related his experiences preaching in Negro churches, "Jesus never walked a picket line or concerned himself with social related issues." We had prayer together and then I left for the picket line.

Monday afternoon, April 6, 1964. We visited the East Jerusalem section, a Negro slum. We talked with an old Negro lady living near the dump. We asked her why she doesn't register. She said she gets a small check from social security and welfare, and she is afraid that it will be cut off if she registers. Her social security check is $36 a month, and for all her working life she never saw "daylight." She worked at Forrest Hotel for ten hours a day, six days a week, for $12 a week for many years.

This canvassing was very revealing. It showed us the feelings of fear, and yet courage, in the midst of this fear. Folk were resolved to become equal citizens.

Monday evening, April 6, 1964. The rally was well attended. We each spoke a word of encouragement. I spoke on the necessity of identification with the movement on the part of the Negro. Mrs. Gray spoke of the importance of paying the price that freedom requires. Keith Brown said one sentence, "I read that he who says he loves God and hates his brother is a liar. I am here because I am not a liar." (In a few weeks, our first son was born and we called him Keith.) Mrs. Gray, who is running for U.S. Senator from Mississippi, presented her appeal, "Pray like everything depends on God and work like everything depends on you." She closed with a quote from Jeremiah, "Here I am, send me."

Tuesday morning, April 7, 1964. We are now ready to move. Bob Stone, Assistant Executive of CORAR (Commission on Religion and Race), Keith Brown, and Don Mead have arrived and we are looking forward to a few good days with more support. I had an interview with Mr. Lynn (registrar). He answered several questions I had concerning voter registration. No discrimination is made in application processing, except "morality," the clauses that Negroes claim discriminate against them. There is no indication on the registration ballot of race, and Mr. Lynn claimed that no checking is done, although it would be obvious by name and address which applicants were Negroes.

Keith and I discussed the disappointing movement of the local and national civil-rights leadership toward secularism or, at best, into a vague humanism. Many of the leaders are reading Socialistic and Communistic literature. I'm afraid that we in the church must take responsibility here because of our apathy and disinterest. This drive for freedom has substituted secular and humanistic roots for its rightful spiritual basis. How did we dissociate salvation and social justice?

Tuesday afternoon, April 7, 1964. We went canvassing among the black leaders. The level of education and alertness was very low among these people, despite the fact that they are leaders. This is such a tragic commentary on our long suppression of educational opportunity. God forgive us. At one old dilapidated home, a grandmother in her seventies or eighties was at the door. Her son and grandson were with her. Tears came to her weary old eyes as we talked about the life of the Negro.

There is a very amazing psychology at work deeply in the soul of the Negro community. They seem to be so accustomed to motivation by fear only, that they are responding to the voter registration work out of fear. This was illustrated this afternoon, when we discovered that some Negroes had signed affidavits of registration for SNCC kids when they never really had registered. We talked with Mr. Cox, a northerner, pastor of the Westminster Church. He expressed almost shockingly liberal views. He cannot speak out, but I'm sure he will be a significant figure when the Negroes make the final break here. We are starting to have a flood now. The river is quite high and families up north are getting in boats and floating to higher ground.

Tuesday evening, April 7, 1964. Poor meeting. The topic was the Bible and the ballot; it didn't get off the ground. One of the young Negroes, Dick, who asked me to marry him and his fiancée, spoke of the irrelevance of the church to this freedom movement. His words were a stringent indictment on the church: "We don't want politics in the church, but we take greenbacks with a politician on front and signature—we love the Africans in our mission giving, but hate the Negro at our back door."

Wednesday afternoon, April 8, 1964. We interviewed Dr. Stanway this afternoon. He was hot and bothered and expressed at the outset his weariness at much interviewing with Presbyterian ministers in recent weeks (probably around 150). The talk was informative and, I believe, unusually gracious compared to others (Keith Brown is a master at diplomacy). Stanway claims that The Ministers Project has hurt the cause. It has alienated both red-neck and moderate white opinion (this can be questioned). It is not central to the gospel, particularly the picket line. It is arrogant when our own hands are so dirty (good point). Here is a man undergoing deep concern and pain concerning the plight of the Negro and the frustration of not knowing what to do. He is a faithful student of the scriptures and a conservative, theologically (Westminster Seminary). He is somewhat uncertain about the social dimension of the gospel. As a move in this direction, he is beginning to study and preach on 1 John, he says. We assured him of our prayerful support in the trying days to come and then took our leave.

Wednesday evening, April 8, 1964. We had a long discussion after we presented a news release to the press. We talked for three hours with Eric Java, the local white TV commentator. We discussed all the ramifications of the issue. He predicts that the KKK is organizing and that there will be violence this summer (the film *Mississippi Burning* dramatizes the events of 1964). He gave us a very objective evaluation of the impact of the ministerial presence here this spring. He expressed a very strong appreciation for The Ministers Project on the part of the white community. Firstly, it gave substance to the fact that ministers are involved in real-life issues of people and are not entangled and bound to their present social and political web. Ministers have given courage to many whites to discuss the issue of race openly, whereas they kept silent before.

He said that our presence represents the final spoils of the Civil War. This state has never really acknowledged the loss of the Civil War. We are the ultimate symbol of defeat for that old order. Our presence has given dignity to the striving of the Negro for freedom.

Thursday morning, April 9, 1964. "These niggers look all bleached out," commented a local businessman as he came by the picket line this morning. "SHEEEEEIIIT!" said another when I said, "Good morning."

We have forced the Negro spirit to a futuristic eschatology. They never experience the full joy of salvation in this life. They have seen a brutal dichotomy between belief and practice. They will have to wait for heaven to put on their shoes, *i.e.*, to become full and free sons of God (Luke 16). For this withholding of the full love power of the gospel, the horizontal dimension of the cross, we shall be held accountable, I am sure.

A favorite jibe of the police recently has been, "I'll go down and get you a bulldozer," referring to the tragic death of young Presbyterian minister James Reeb in Cleveland, Mississippi.

Thursday afternoon, April 9, 1964. I had a short conference with the chief of police and his assistant down at the station. As I waited outside, I noticed a SNCC worker in a small cell. He was jailed for rape and robbery, which he claimed he never committed. The chief and his assistant were friendly, but extremely anxious and defensive. He told me to tell the college students coming south that their blood is going to be shed this summer along with Negro blood. He believes that there will be blood shed this summer. He said, "The best thing you whites can do is go home, get down on your knees, and pray; pray for forgiveness for the trouble you've stirred up down here."

He talked of having more Negro friends than the Negroes have white friends. His deputy then started talking about his religion. He reads in his Bible that the Negro was created black and is the cursed of God. "They are now like a snowball that is growing larger and larger." He implied that the movement is only among the poor Negroes and does not represent the entire community. The chief asked me why I didn't stay home and feed the poor Negroes there (another good question). He showed how the white community was kind to the Negroes in flood relief and general relief. Eighty percent of relief checks go to the Negro community. The two men were rabid Southern Baptists who believed in "separate and subordinate." They are typical policemen that could be found in any community. They do not want bloodshed, and they constantly use the phrase, "let us both get down on our knees and pray" (there's hope).

I returned to the line at 4:00 p.m. Radio and TV cars were gathered, and the pickets were torn down, as I expected. The governor had just signed a bill that prohibits illegal picketing. Our picketing became illegal when the sheriff and his men took down the barricade. We withdrew with the sheriff's five-minute notice and began to consult with New York and Reverend John Cameron to make our decision. I have been in charge of the ministers. We will consult about our decision tonight.

Friday morning, April 10, 1964. Have you ever spent a night, waiting for morning with the near certainty that you are going to be arrested?

It is 6:30 a.m., and we have presented the challenge of taking off or remaining. Bert and John are making their decision now.

I called Mount Lebanon church and talked with Cliff Smith and Myles McDonald, my senior pastor. They encouraged me to reconsider, in the light of my responsibility in the church and Romans 13 (obey the rightful authorities). They assured me of their prayers and blessings. I tendered my vocal resignation to the session. We were led in our morning devotion by the Reverend Rod Estrada. He read from Romans 8, a very inspiring passage. We each prayed for love and wisdom at this time. The irony and pathos of the time was reflected in the restaurant for breakfast. Some local Negroes turned on the jukebox. It played in a light-hearted way against the backdrop of our uncertainty and fear. We are ready now to move to the line. God help us!

We were arrested that morning for breaking the hastily crafted "demonstration" statute that had the purpose of blocking Negro registration and putting an end to the "trouble making."

Saturday morning, April 11, 1964. We were jailed at 10:00 a.m. Friday morning. We were registered in an orderly fashion and sent upstairs to the city jail. After an hour, we were led into a bus and taken to the county farm. On the way out, I asked the sheriff where we were going. He said harshly, "Never mind and get in." We were held incommunicado for seven hours without food. Then they brought in two sandwiches apiece and bug juice. The police at the door were customarily gross and discourteous: "Their mothers must have been niggers—damn nigger fuckers," etc. We sang the *Gloria Patri* and ate. We retired on the flimsy sleeping bags on the floor at 7:00 p.m. We awoke easily this morning and had breakfast at 7:00 a.m. Still no contact from a lawyer. We read a copy of the *Hattiesburg American* and were impressed by the full objective coverage. When I called her at 8 a.m., Sara implied that national coverage had occurred. We received a first telegram of support from Thatcher and Betsy Schwartz, friends from Pittsburgh. The guys are playing football (a toilet paper roll wrapped in a sock) now on the mattresses—a good time.

It is hard to convey the fear and uncertainty that filled our hearts as we approached the courthouse—jeers and taunts from "white citizens" and red-necks, the full coverage of the press, full police force, and sheriff's department. There was, underneath this fear, a deep resolve and contentment in the rightness of our protest. Should we receive the maximum sentence, we know that the cause of justice, truth, and "Negro courage-to-be" has been strengthened.

Sunday morning, April 12, 1964. Rose early—last night was very hard and sleepless. Several colleagues were sick: Tillman with asthmatic attacks and

John Cameron with stomach pains. We called to the guard for medicine for Tillman that had been ordered. The sheriff came back later, but no one brought the medicine. He panted and cried until morning. We have not yet been contacted by our lawyer—we get to be arraigned tomorrow. The newspaper indicates that bond will be set at $1,000 and that a stiff sentence is in store for us. These seem to be desperation measures that are understandable because of the threat that Negro citizenship presents. We are preparing to have services this morning, hopefully together, but probably separate.

The days in jail have been a profound experience—heights of fun and inspiration and depths of despair and fear. I realize now how it is that much of the world's great literature has been written in prison: Paul, Bunyan, King, Bonhoeffer, Niemöller, etc.

We have each had to weigh the ultimate consequences of our actions: loss of job, cut off from the main stream of church life (the conformity stream), six months hard and miserable imprisonment. We consider these insignificant trials in the light of the magnitude of the truth and justice that focuses on these events.

Let me give you a taste of the way the Negroes are treated here. I would like to introduce all the men in here. There are 17 of us—eight ministers, nine laymen, 10 Negroes, four white men—this jail is the only integrated hotel in Hattiesburg. Our worship together has been especially moving; we have been molded into *koinonia* such as I have never known. Brother Lawrence, an elderly gentleman, is retired, about 70 years old. He worked in a local manufacturing plant, started on a work team making 25 cents an hour doing the same job as whites making 75 cents an hour. I have been greatly strengthened by this old saint's courage: sleeping on the hard floor, the little ration of terrible food, never saying a word. There is Vernon Damler, a farmer, a fine gentleman who lives in the country. (His home was later fire-bombed and he was killed. The clansmen responsible were not convicted until 30 years later.)

Sunday afternoon, April 12, 1964. Ben Smith, our attorney from New Orleans, visited us this afternoon. The primary strategy is to take the case to the Federal court. He is recommending a remand on Monday. We will either be arraigned quickly in the county court, bond will be set at $1,000 and trial set, or we will be here another three or four days while the appeal is pursued.

They just covered up with a burlap sack the sign allowing visitors from 2:00 to 4:00 p.m. Officials here are really beginning to panic, as the pressure seems to be building in community. They have driven the garbage trucks out to barricade the front entrance of the prison. Fifty or more Negroes have attempted to see us. They have been harassed and threatened with arrest.

At 3:30 p.m., Ben Smith came back with a big care package of food, cigarettes, and candy. We were the happiest folks you ever saw.

These days in prison have been a very moving experience. We have Bennie Jackson, Jr., who is 22 years old, vice president of the Mississippi Student Union. He is one of the delightful young men in the movement. He talks so rapidly that understanding is difficult. We have been playing several games, but he always misses the point. He joined the movement back in January.

His most tragic memory was when Rev. Lee, a Negro minister from Berzona, Mississippi was shot one night in his car while driving home. He was a local leader of the NAACP.

The Mississippi Student Union is an organization of students throughout Mississippi, affiliated with COFO (the Council of Federated Organizations), one of the most promising parts of the movement.

John Hall is 19 years of age, a recent high-school graduate with a strong desire to be a doctor. His mom is one of the real saints of the Civil Rights movement. She has cooked and provided for us plenteously. I invited him to come to Pittsburgh to seek enrollment in the university. I hope this contact will work out in the future. John dresses nicely and gives maturity and stability to the younger persons in the movement.

Monday morning, April 13, 1964. The morning has passed slowly. We were fingerprinted and questioned. The morning began with a very moving devotion. Some songs: "Let us Break Bread Together" and "We Shall Overcome." Bert, John, and I gave short meditations. John C. led us in prayer, and this has been one of the most moving experiences. We may be arraigned this afternoon, or we may wait some more days until the adjudication.

Monday afternoon, April 13, 1964. We were arraigned at 4:30 p.m. this afternoon. The judge was swayed by the prosecuting attorney, but he gave us several lee-ways. He denied rights to a shotgun trial next week and lowered the bail from $1,000 to $500. I was immediately freed on bond because of my wife's impending delivery. Keith, Bert, and John are still in jail to give moral support to the Negro kids. God bless them, they are real saints. The flight left Hattiesburg for Atlanta to arrive in Pittsburgh at 6:30 a.m. in the morning.

Before moving to some interpretation of this experience, the reader will enjoy my letter back to the church and two of the many letters of response from the church pillars—of salt, in some cases, but pillars nonetheless—back home.

Hattiesburg, Mississippi
Sunday, April 5, 1964

It has been an emotion-packed, eye-opening experience. We are living as Negroes, in Negro ghettos, eating in their restaurants, drinking from their fountains, etc. I am reminded of William Shirer's book, *The Rise and Fall of the Third Reich*. The situation here is much like Germany during the pre-war period—not much better than a police state. Intimidation, fear, and reprisals continue to convince the Negro that he is sub-human. A full diary and slides will give you fuller detail when I arrive home; let a brief sketch suffice for now.

Our work is under the direction of the Rev. John Cameron, a Baptist minister and candidate for Congress. The movement for equality and civil rights is at heart and soul a Christian movement; one can feel the pulse of Christ's love motivating, inspiring, and constraining the leaders of the work.

Our presence here is a source of strength to the Negro community, a source of questioning for the young generation of whites who are examining the whole messed up power structure here. Our presence is an embarrassment and an antagonizer, apparently, to the white senior citizens. We regret this latter fact, because of the negative feelings that arise, but we rejoice that we can minister to these other sections of the population.

We have been called every name in the book, intimidated in many ways, almost run down by a car. But, all in all, the reception has been warmth from the general public with which we work.

The church has been apostate in the deep South. And the North, as we discover, is little better. It has informed, inculcated, and assimilated sub-Christian social values and structures and, as a result, has lost most of the populace with a sensitive moral conscience. There are signs of revival and renewal, and we must pray to this end. Much sacrifice will be required, much word put to deed, much love put into action. People here in the months to come will discover literally the challenge of Paul in Romans: "Present your bodies . . . a living sacrifice." (Rom 12)

Love to all,

Ken Vaux

June 8, 1964

Dear Mr. Vaux:

Although I heartily disapproved your recent trip to Alabama and your activities in the racial demonstrations in that state, I refrained from sending you any written criticism, hoping that on your return to work at our church, you would refrain from doing anything to further embarrass the membership of our church.

However, since reading and re-reading your article in the *Twin Tower Light* of May 29th, I, as a former member of session for about 25 years (and still one who is vitally interested in the spiritual welfare of this congregation) feel that I must tell you that I deeply resent your statement and implications in the sentence, "We cannot be dragged along reluctantly by the higher judicatories." Such a statement by you is untimely, unjustified, and unwarranted. If such an article should have been written, and I think it should not, but if it were warranted, it should have come from the senior pastor of the church and not from one of the assistants.

You are a young man new in this church in a subordinate position and should remember that it is not up to you to set the policies of this congregation. That is the duty of the senior pastor and session. The main function of the church as a whole, and the members thereof, should be the winning of souls for Jesus Christ.

It is not easy for me to write this type of letter to you, but if I had a son in your position or a similar one, who had done the things you have done recently, I would appreciate some older person calling his attention to what appears to me to have been errors in judgment.

Please accept this letter in the kindly spirit in which it has been written. A copy is being sent to the senior pastor for his information.

Sincerely yours,

George R. Lacy

April 15, 1964

Dear Rev. Vaux,

I would like to write a few of my thoughts on the recent events. I admire you very much for what you did. I think you tried to help our country in its struggle for all men to be equal. I heard you on WJAS Wednesday night, and thought you expressed your feelings well. I have a lot of friends who don't agree with me, and think I'm square, but I'm sure God will guide all of us in this time of trouble.

Respectfully yours,
Deborah L. DeLong
(Intermediate Dept.)

May 19, 1964

Dear Mr. Vaux

We wish to acknowledge your message, coupled with Mr. C. Bryson Schreiner's, which came last week.

It is gratifying to note that there are others in our church willing and wanting to help the Civil Rights movement.

We are glad of the opportunity to help financially, though it is small in amount. We plan to give again a little later.

Five dollars of the enclosed amount is from my mother, who lives with us. She is Mrs. William T. Hardester. The other $20.00 is from us.

Yours Sincerely,
Mary and John DeLong

INTERPRETATION

Let me unpack this tumultuous event and offer a finer-grained analysis of the whys and wherefores, the rights and wrongs of going to Mississippi. What led us to willingly break the hastily conceived law and submit ourselves there to incarcerations? I have already mentioned my penchant for the spectacle. Enough said of the worthiness of that motivation. Any desire for applaud and recognition quickly disappears when you realize that nearly everyone there and at home abhors, or at least disagrees, with what you are doing. I took some strength in those days from the hard charge by some that Jesus was an immoral man (he eats with sinners) and a law-breaker. Sinners were receptors of the kingdom. There was, of course, the justice issue; blacks in the South were getting a bad deal. Since the Civil War, they had been lynched, intimidated, denied rights, and discriminated against. Our gesture, albeit provocative, to plead their right to vote, was just and good. Pragmatically, it was one of the innumerable efforts that brought about the Voting Rights Act of 1965. Forty years later, Hurricane Katrina in New Orleans still cries out of the crucible of our immoral racism and classism.

A primary motivation was present for me, mingling the unworthy one of making a spectacle of oneself with one more worthy display of justice. I knew that persecution, even martyrdom, was the meaning of the word "witness." John the Baptist was imprisoned and beheaded for challenging Herod's immorality, and Jesus challenged the idolatry of Jew and Roman by becoming God to the populace. A cardinal notion in my unfolding theology was that goodness and righteousness provoked that wrath of the world.

Face it—forgiving sins, healing the sick, inviting a following (discipleship), and feeding the hungry is a frontal assault on church and state. The offer of "forgiveness of sins" is an indictment of supposed moral rectitude. Jesus, like John, fulfilled a messianic posture and for that affront was imprisoned and executed. James, Peter, and Paul, the same. Each disturbed the peace (Roman or temple or personal) by condemning that false presumption of self-established goodness and ultimacy by directly reinstating the divine judgment of God's righteousness given in grace. Some day, I need to write an essay on "the immorality of the good." (If I ever muster the *chutzpah* to be a theologian). I now (40 years later and much diminished in *chutzpah*) gather what Barth calls "the simultaneity of command and law, grace and gospel" into the overarching reality of *Akedah* (more on this to come).

Take Paul for a moment. He details the antinomian element in gospel justice. In writing to the church in Galatia, a pagan city back in west central Asia Minor, he says, "for freedom Christ has set us free—do not submit again to any yoke of slavery" (Gal 5:1). The issue at stake was the practice of circumcision, which, of course, had been resolved with the council and dispatch of James and the Jerusalem church (Acts 15) and had even been questioned in Proselyte Judaism. At issue was the whole matter of self-justification. For Paul, it would have been a surrender of the whole gospel to submit again to that oppression (slavery relates to commandment 8). In our mission to Mississippi, state and church were imposing a new requirement (law) on the black citizens of the state before they could register to vote. In place of the simple qualification to read and write, the registrars had substituted elaborate texts of history and constitution (selectively, of course, to blacks) and not surprisingly, even the well-educated failed. The sin was presumed superiority and imputed inferiority. A free society (the legacy of Exodus and Easter) could not submit again to this "yoke of slavery."

Gospel witness, imprisonment, even martyrdom was indeed the price required, not for challenging rightful authority (Rom 13), but for challenging oppressive authority—power that has been put to the service of idolatry and immorality, keeping perpetrator and victim in their sin—a breach of the Commandments, of liberty, of reconciliation. The early Christians went to their deaths for this subtle challenging of the law in the name of the law. They broke Judaic and Roman law (custom) by owning Jesus as *Kurios* (Yahweh). Jesus, indeed, was acknowledged as "the new Torah."

Local Jewish leaders often then sought to incite political authorities to move against them; *e.g.*, Paul in Ephesus, Philippi, etc. The Christian martyrs broke Roman law by acknowledging Jesus Christ as Lord and refused to "confess" Caesar *Kurios*. In each case they were affirming no other gods, no idols, not profaning the divine name (commandments 1, 2, and 3), and condemning church and state for that very abrogation. Injustice is also a violation of the human and divine table of Torah and Decalogue.

The Mississippi experience obviously shaped my life in ways I am still discovering. Many of us trained in seminary in the early 1960s, and thrown out into the turbulent days of the Civil Rights movement and the Vietnam War (following the placid serenity of the 1950s), left the ministry and found other walks of service: social work, university teaching, etc. I would like to know, for instance, how many college presidents in the year 2000 were burned-out theologs of the early 1960s. In some ways, I think my eventual departure from the parish ministry to graduate study, then into the field of medical ethics, was the way I dealt with the unbearable tension of the quest for justice. By 1967, I had launched a new career of ministry in science, technology, and medicine—first as a university pastor and then as a scholar-professor. In one way, it all was an escape to easier ground from what I knew would be the turbulent swamp-crossing of being a priest in the city.

Our legal case wound on for a year. By that time I was pastor in Watseka, Illinois. The law under which we were arrested was appealed to the U.S. Supreme Court by our lawyer, the famous André F. Cournand of Rutgers. We were eventually summoned to an evidentiary hearing before the Fifth U.S. Circuit Court in Biloxi, Mississippi. I remember two of the judges: Mize of Alabama, sophisticated and enlightened, and Harold Cox of Mississippi, an appointee of President Kennedy. I was on the stand for one hour. The reader of the Court Annals will find fascinating material where Judge Cox asks me to take out my Bible while he takes out his. He points to the Genesis passage where the cursed son of Noah, Ham, is discussed. "These are the niggers in my Bible," he said. "God help us!" I thought.

By this time I had left Pittsburgh, along with the other staff ministers. The crisis provoked there was as great as the one in Mississippi. Pennsylvania and Illinois are little different from Mississippi. Years later when a police car drove onto our lawn in Riverside, Illinois and shouted at our black friend who was living with us, "Hey nigger, what are you doing here?" I was reminded that racial bigotry was not a regional matter. Mississippi was eventually to become one of our more enlightened and progressive states.

THE MOUNT LEBANON CRISIS

> There will only be a community of peace when it does not rest on lies and injustice.[1]

From the beginning, my struggle had been the need to synthesize an evangelical and an ethical faith. Whenever these were severed—in Nazi Germany, in apartheid South Africa, in the American South (and North) or in modern day Israel—unrest, *intifada*, and crisis inevitably ensued.

How did these impulses become dissociated? Are there seeds in the Jesus movement itself—perhaps in the mystic and charismatic strands of Judaism—indeed in all religion, that make possible the breach between the ethical and the evangelical? If God's will with humanity is salvific, otherworldly, and pietistic—concerned only with the inner soul, the

---

1. Bonhoeffer, *No Rusty Swords: Letters, Lectures, and Notes, 1928–1936*, 168–9.

realm of spirit, and life after death—then we can easily imagine a religion unconcerned with, or yearning to depart from, this world. That James, Jesus' brother, would couple the two impulses so dramatically staggers me, ". . . pure and undefiled religion is this . . ." "to care for the widows and keep oneself unstained by the world (Jas 1:27) . . ." But Luther and many others reject the Book of James.

True faith must surely be Godly and worldly. After all, what is salvation? From what to what? Jesus enters the ministry of John the Baptist—forgiveness of sins— but what sins? Is not the very substance of salvation a matter of ethics? We have gone wrong; we need to be made right. We need to get back on the good way. That surely is the essential meaning of biblical faith.

At Mount Lebanon, we had the evangelical zeal, but came up short in ethical response. The great Twin Towers was the mother ship of my denomination, the 200,000-strong United Presbyterian Church. Dozens of young men had gone out into the ministry and mission field from her portals. She labored assiduously in scripture study, calling persons to faith. The New Wilmington missionary conference and many other gospel works were inspired in her halls. Why was our demonstration so provocative to this congregation? After I was jailed in Mississippi, the Woman's Association shunned Sara. Some elders called me the devil. Granted, many did affirm my witness or at least the right of my conscience to do God's will as I saw it.

I think of the Bryson Schreiner family. Bryson, a Princeton-trained lawyer, and Jean, his gifted wife, lived out a profound Christian calling, were deeply committed to overseas, national, and local mission. When I started mission work at the church among the junior and senior highs (*e.g.*, service projects among the blacks in housing projects on the North side and Hill district), they were all for us. Today, their children Cathy, Sally, and Sammy are outstanding Christian leaders. They integrate the evangelical and ethical. Reflecting back 40 years, later I've come to the view that social action, including a political dimension, must be a normal and natural expression of evangelical faith in Christ as Lord of all. I think part of the problem at Mount Lebanon was political. It tended to be a Republican stronghold. Civil rights and opposition to the Vietnam War, regrettably, were seen as liberal, Democrat causes. The Republican political ethos had focused more on personal ethical matters—family life, sexuality, honesty, etc.—all well, good, and necessary. Matters of societal transformation—like income re-distribution, racial integration, peace activism, and such—were seen as radical—even atheistic or communistic values. They just weren't the business of the church. The crisis that began at Mount Lebanon has pursued me all my life. It was the signature theological crisis of my doctoral teacher—Helmut Thielicke—in Nazi Germany.

I remember the early months of my ministry at Mount Lebanon. I had succeeded Jerry Kirk, who was a distinguished evangelical pastor whose ethical concerns were strong: pornography, transforming homosexuals, etc. Jerry went on to serve in New Wilmington, Pennsylvania and Cincinnati, Ohio. I was on the planning committee for the pan-Pittsburgh "Back-to-College" conference for young people. The annual conference was built on the convictions of Young Life as these intertwined with United Presbyterian concerns. I was responsible for the book table. I worked hard at this. I ordered hundreds of the best spiritual and theological texts: Bonhoeffer, Barth, M.L. King Jr., Simone Weil, etc. Early in the conference, the pastor of First Presbyterian Church downtown, Bob Lamont, a renowned Christian leader, approached me with a gentle warning: "Ken, to read all of these books is well and good, but we must be careful what we place in our minds and the minds of our young persons. Only what leads to Christ and deepens our relationship with him should occupy our thoughts." Troubling counsel! I wondered, how did we lose Jesus the Jew?

The crisis at this threshold of my ministry was not just the stiff-necked resistance of the church. A 25-year old pastor had much to learn about the psychology of resistance in others. Too often, I sought to lash those of little faith with a wet noodle.

The maturing crisis in me had to do with my mania not for remonstrance but for demonstration. Related to my yearning for apocalyptic breakthrough, I too often expected actions to become provocative and prominent. My faith was also tinged with Gnosticism. *Hoi polloi* (common men) needed to be enlightened by the Gnostics—"those in the know"—like me. There was always a compulsion to make a difference. I wanted people to wake up and take notice. I was too impatient with waiting and working quietly—the grain of mustard seed. I needed to see immediate results. Regarding the living faith in others, I needed to learn the true messianic quality of not quenching "the dimly burning wick," of celebrating even the slightest glimmer. I needed, above all, to mute my own messianic fantasies and trust in Messiah Jesus.

One rewarding moment during my brief sojourn in Pittsburgh was when someone called me "John Coventry Smith come back to life." Smith had been a senior pastor at Mount Lebanon in the 1940s. During the war, when Japanese-Americans were incarcerated around the country and in City Jail, Pittsburgh, Coventry Smith announced one Sunday that he was going to jail to be with his Japanese brethren. He would be back when they were released. He had been a missionary in Japan (and later head of mission of the U.P.s) and felt he had to make this witness of solidarity. When the young whippersnapper Vaux showed up in the "can" in Mississippi, he was derisively seen as cut from the same cloth as that other "troublemaker." To me, the snipe was one of the highest compliments of my career.

ILLINOIS

Our first ministry station lasted only 15 months. With the imprisonment in Mississippi and the subsequent polarization of the Mount Lebanon parish, the three assistants all decided within a period of months to leave. The head pastor, Myles McDonald, a graduate of Gordon-Conwell Seminary, stayed on and built a new team. Many indications show that the congregation grew spiritually and ethically through this crisis. I have never had the chance to visit with Myles and learn how he processed the events. He was caught in a terrible bind. Many conservatives in the church were incensed that this young upstart, theologically suspect, junior partner had overstepped his rights. This church could well have bolted from the denomination in protest of its social positions. Fortunately, the old evangelical-ethical tradition of the congregation prevailed. The church that had sent hundreds into the ministry and mission fields, that had pioneered significant international missions in Egypt, Ethiopia and throughout the world, knew that it had to stand for justice and human dignity at home. I trust that the catharsis that occurred in Mount Lebanon was to reject ideologies of right-wing and conservative political and economic thought. So often counseled to "stick to the gospel," I became more an action-evangelist.

It was October of 1964 when we were able to relocate as pastor of the county seat town of Watseka, Illinois. The chance to preach regularly, to baptize, bury, and companion families across the life cycle, was and still remains for me a season of great thanksgiving. The strife, questioning, discontent, and boredom of my soul were still there. But the affirmation, the love, and the good will of the people of that rural town strengthen me to this day.

PART THREE

The Search for Solemnity

Biomedical Ethics

HOUSTON: NEW HORIZONS

BY 1966, MY RESTLESS SPIRIT had again had enough and I requested a leave of absence that summer to accept a fellowship to study at the University of Hamburg, Germany, with Helmut Thielicke. While beginning those studies, I also began the search for another setting of ministry. This door opened in the early winter of that year when I was called to become Presbyterian University pastor at Rice and the Texas Medical Center in Houston, Texas. Those ensuing years, 1966 to 1978, obviously are the formative center of my career.

We arrived in Houston in December of 1966. Shortly after arrival in this vast sprawling cow town, I had another flare-up of my appendix (which had started during the final Sunday sermons in Watseka). With a hot and throbbing lower-right quadrant, I knew that something was acute. I rushed into the most familiar setting, the First Presbyterian Church on South Main Street. I asked the pastor to refer me to a surgeon. Dr. Lancaster, who later became our family pastor, sent me to the Kelsey Clinic down the block in the exploding Texas Medical Center. The surgeon, whose name I understandably cannot remember, was a suave Southern Baptist gentleman. Trying to break the ice with cordiality he asked, "Where are you from?" I responded through pain-gritted teeth, "I did my seminary at Princeton." "Tell me," he continued as I slipped

beneath the anesthetic, "is that place still filled with communists?" Woe
is me!

Our second child, Kerry Bert, was born in August 1965, back in
Illinois. He was big and beautiful, but something was wrong with his heart.
He was cyanotic (a blue baby) and Dr. Roeder and other consultants said
that we must go to Chicago. After two days, I drove up in Segur's ambulance (I had often gone with Ken, the mortician, for funerals) to Cook
County Hospital. I remember approaching this mammoth and infamous
institution on the Eisenhower Expressway that would one day be my base
of operations. The pediatric heart surgeon was away and one of the fellows checked the baby in. Carrying the incubator into the hospital jostled
the baby and he regurgitated. I learned later that the resident (a gentleman from India) had found the child with aspiration pneumonia and decided not to treat, but let him die. As I recall, I was initially outraged, but
later I accommodated and forgave when I learned from Denton Cooley
in Houston in the mid-1960s that treatments for transposition of the major vessels were not yet well developed. All that awaited the child was an
arduous course of surgeries and most likely early death. I tried to call
Bill Kieswetter, a distinguished pediatric heart surgeon (Siamese twins) ·
in Pittsburgh, whose house we had watched while I was serving there as
pastor. He was also away on vacation that August. Though one can never
perfectly retrieve inner influences and motivations, this experience may
have paved the way for my subsequent career in medical ethics.

The grief was long and hard. For months, Sara and I would cry every
morning and every evening. It was especially tough for her, since she had
to stay in the small Iroquois County Hospital while I transported the baby
to Chicago. Kerry was buried in the Watseka cemetery and later moved
to the family plot in Huntington, Indiana, near his grandparents Anson,
who would follow him twenty-five years later. The grief would ultimately
lessen with the exuberance of the move to Houston (December 1966) and
the birth of another Bert in November of 1968.

Houston would offer vast new horizons for this young couple of 28
and 25 years whose ministry had begun with a rocky parish start, a profound and disturbing socio-political experience, and the loss of a child.
In Houston, young Keith (born on my return from Mississippi) would be
joined by Bert, Catherine, and Sarah. Bert was born in St. Luke's hospital
in the medical center where I worked, as were the two girls. We loved our
house, six-hundred yards from my office at the Institute of Religion in

the Medical Center. Our neighbors—the Allgoods, Jirciks, Cunninghams, Watts, Whiteheads, and Meyerowitzes—remain close friends, even though it has been two decades since we left Houston.

Bert was born distressed (in more ways than one). His umbilical cord was wrapped thrice around his neck and only the alert Will Johnson, our obstetrician, pulled him through—and out. Bert was a blessing who finally put to rest the grief from Kerry's death. The strange psychic-emotive rationalization—"if this . . . then not this"—works wonders in the human psyche. We had to find a way to move on. We never thought that this wild-haired waif would begin his working career as a linguistics professor at Harvard.

Catherine was born half a dozen years later. By that time, I had been trained in the Lamaze birth method by Sara. I knew how to encourage the slow, deep breathing—how to have the paper bag ready, etc. All I remember of Catherine's birth was this: well into labor, Sara sent me home (a 300-yard run) to get Erik Erikson's *Young Man Luther*. Probably she wanted to better understand the compulsive, ill-potty-trained husband that stood at the foot of the bed assisting in this birth. When Catherine was surfacing, her curly head first protruded and it looked like Keith—I shouted, "It's a boy!" "Just a moment," counseled Sara. I next shouted as her glistening body with shiny red hair emerged, "I did it!" Sara simply sighed. "Sure you did!" (Today, Aislinn with her curly auburn hair bears a striking resemblance to Catherine.)

Petite Sarah was born just months before we moved to Chicago. Her delicate torso with fair, thin white hair made her a wispy *Blanche Neige* over that fierce and frosty first winter of 1978 in Chicago. For me, the Houston days were marked by completion of my doctoral studies, the launching of a career in bioethics, and numerous salient experiences—including Sara's completion of her Ph.D. at Rice, the children's growth as excellent scholar-athletes, and my own continuing search for an ethically responsible evangelical faith.

ETHICS IN MEDICINE AND TECHNOLOGY

Helmut Thielicke had set this perplexing agenda forever foremost in my mind. In the small biography I wrote on him for the Word Press Series called *Makers of the Modern Theological Mind* (never published), I explored the paradoxical excellence of this great man who emerged from the *Nazizeit* compelled, with Karl Barth, that faith must be searching, biblical, evangelical, and sociopolitical. Faith must sever itself from the 19th- and early 20th-century liberalism and inculturalism that had so vitiated its substance. Thielicke resonated with Barth, who in the commentary on Romans (*Römerbrief*), spoke candidly about the crisis in history, the church, and the existential soul that set in raw relief the radical grace of Christ, the sin of man, and the gospel of forgiveness and new obedient life—all portrayed in the strange world and Word of scripture.

Thielicke himself was perhaps the last theologian to compose a massive systematic theology and theological ethics. As *Doktorvater*, he taught each of his Doktorans the necessity of doing both, together. Apart from an evangelical faith there is no *Ethik*. Without an ethical system, there is no theology. His ethics spanned a wide range of classical and novel topics: politics, war and peace, and family life, as well as sports, the nuclear age, and homosexuality. He was pleased when I announced my dissertation topic: Cybernetics and Ethics. Working on the *Gottes Mitarbeiter* theology of the Lutheran and Calvinist heritage, I explored the way in which the electronic age—the age when computers augment the human brain, communication media, and the senses, and prostheses replicate the organs and outer body parts—was an age that needed a renewed doctrine of divine-human cooperation. I was searching for a moral vision that would ground a responsible, humane, and just ethic for the use of these new technologies.

In March of 1968, when we convened one of the first major conferences on Ethics in Medicine and Technology,[1] Thielicke spoke on "The Ambivalence of Progress." This paper summed up my own emerging ethic concerning science, technology, and medicine. He argued that biomedicine was a worthy service in favor of human needs and goods, but that it should not be made a god. Science and technology, like medicine, are two-edged swords. They help people, but with the considerable risk of harming at the same time. Thielicke was continuing the utopia critique and human-sin-reminder of neo-orthodox theology.

He was also holding forth a hopeful prospect for human culture, especially the prophylactic (preventing harm) and ameliorative (healing) culture of medicine. When we used our technology (Fr. technique) to heal the sick, feed the hungry, exorcise demons, and proclaim good news

---

1. Vaux, *Who Shall Live.*

to the poor, and when this was done in the spirit of justice and peace and not hubris, it was blessed by God—*cooporatio Dei.*

I finished my dissertation with Thielicke in the summer of 1968 (after the Houston conference). It was published by John Knox Press[2] with a foreword by the astronaut Buzz Aldrin. During my early years in Houston, I also became interested in the space program, frequently speaking at the Presbyterian Church near NASA where Buzz and an old college colleague, John Glenn, were members. When Thielicke visited for the 1968 conference (along with Paul Ramsey, Joe Fletcher, Margaret Mead and others), he wanted to visit NASA and had an engaging conversation with John Glenn. Although my own association with John was cordial, we later crossed swords at a Muskingum College Forum on the question of whether the Soviet Union should be seen apocalyptically as an evil empire. While I was influenced more by Andrei Sakharov and the peace (disarmament) efforts, John was passionately animated by his patriotic anti-Communist, soldierly perspective. I still find John and Annie Glenn to be one of the exemplary couples of our generation, expressing Christian conviction in public life.

When the Challenger spaceship exploded in space, I published an essay on Space and Spirit. The themes of my dissertation continued in an unpublished symposium (*Journey into Space and Spirit*), a conference with Wernher von Braun and others. Some of this reflection is in the 1997 Abingdon volume, *Being Well.*[3]

Our concern for the ethics of space utilization, present in the Star-Wars and missile-shield programs, was accented when our young family watched Christie McCullough and the others joyously march to the space ship, then the lift off, then the spray of fire in the sky. The kids asked, "Where are they, Dad?" Typically, this theologian had no answer for the great whys of life. But I listened that night to the memorial remarks and the music. WFMT played Gabriel Fauré's "Requiem," and there was the answer to the question of where: "Heaven and Earth are full of your glory."

2. See Vaux, *Subduing the Cosmos.*
3. See Vaux, *Being Well.*

SPACE: WHY DO WE DO THIS?

Chicago Tribune, February 1, 1986

Crisis forces reflection. There is mean reflection: "I told you this would happen!" There is the easy brush-off: "Just a temporary setback; we'll soon be on the move again." The tragedy of the space shuttle Challenger, poignant because it touches technocrats and schoolchildren, Americans and Soviets, invites us to move beyond blame and blasé enthusiasm to both immediate and profound reflection.

There is the immediate question: Why the great haste? What was the rush? Do we need to have one shuttle a week? Who is pushing us? Is it the old Sputnik legacy of frantically catching up with the Russians? Are they getting the better of us?

Is the Department of Defense moving to take over the space program, forcing the civilian program into a rush for survival?

Perhaps our fascination with Star Wars, satellites, and space shuttles is at root a glance of shame, not to the ground but now to the sky, a glance away from Earth's misery and our complicity. The agonies of Beirut and Botswana, of Addis Ababa and Achille Lauro, pale in insignificance as we gaze into the heavens. But G.B. Shaw reminds us, "Beware of the man whose God is in the sky."

Norman Mailer writes of the irony of this great distraction in *Of a Fire on the Moon*:

> The century would seek to dominate nature as it had never been dominated, would attack the idea of war, poverty, and natural catastrophe as never before. The century would create death, devastation, and pollution as never before. Yet the century was now attached to the idea that man must take his conception of life out to the stars. It was a world half convinced of the future death of our species, yet half aroused by the apocalyptic notion that an exceptional future still lay before us.[4]

The why also goes deeper. Not only why did this accident happen, but why do we probe the universe in the first place? Ethical values, those purposes that justify or condemn our actions, emerge from our basic beliefs about human destiny in the cosmos. One view of this celestial purpose holds that the Earth is too confining to captivate the imagination and ingenuity of

4. See Mailer, *Of a Fire on the Moon*.

man. We must explore and exploit the cosmos to fulfill our manifest destiny. Science fiction writers from H.G. Wells to J.B.S. Haldane have argued that humans must go to the stars or end up on an endless hamster wheel here on Earth.

Others contend that the flight away from Earth's confines is part of a frightful removal from terrestrial responsibility, and evasion of fundamental duties of justice in the face of misery and serenity in the face of mortality. C.S. Lewis describes Professor Weston in *Out of the Silent Planet*:

> He was a man obsessed with the idea . . . that humanity, having now sufficiently corrupted the planet where it arose, must at all costs continue to seed itself over a larger area . . . [those] vast astronomical distances which are God's quarantine regulations. This is for a start. But beyond this lies the sweet poison of the false infinite—the wild dream that planet after planet, system after system, in the end galaxy after galaxy, can be forced to sustain, everywhere and forever, the sort of life which is contained in the loins of our own species—a dream begotten by the hatred of death upon the fear of true immortality . . .[5]

After three astronauts burned up on the pad in the 1967 disaster, John Glenn, with whom I collaborated during my years in Houston, told me: "It is just a matter of time until a fire occurs, an explosion happens on ascent or in orbit, or a ship escapes from controlled orbit and drifts endlessly in remote space. We must know why we are doing this."

Are we the pioneers of a new humanity or, in the words of St. Jude, are we "wandering stars, for whom the deepest darkness has been reserved forever?" (Jude 1.13).

Today, a picture dances ruthlessly on the screens of our minds, a picture of a great rocket and Leviathan ship exploding to smithereens, spraying fire into the heavens. A picture of those special seven people—chosen with what seems to be lovely randomness out of the glory of the human family: scientist and layman, man and woman, black, white and Asian, Christian and Jew—poised in their seats, excited like children in their small cabin atop the craft.

> And while these pictures flood our minds . . .
> Children ask, "Where do we go when we die?"

A disheveled and deranged New York City street preacher cries, "We are all vapor, we are here, we are not here."

---

5. See Lewis, *Out of the Silent Planet*.

A choir sings at a memorial service, the haunting words of the Mass, that great hymn of Earth and heaven, life and death:

Sanctus, Sanctus
Dominus Deus Sabaoth
Pleni sunt coeli et terra gloria tua.

(Holy, Holy, Lord God of Hosts, heaven and Earth are full of Your glory.)

Although space and environment, energy and computers fascinated me by reason of my dissertation research, my main concentration was on the issues of medicine. When we arrived in Houston in December of 1966, there was tense anticipation as to who would transplant the first human heart. About six groups in the world were ready: Cooley and DeBakey in Houston, Shumway in Palo Alto, and yes, Christiaan Barnard in Capetown, South Africa. I remember a highly critical founding session of the Hastings Center in New York City when I was castigated for defending the heart surgeons in Houston against the intellectual establishment "east of the Hudson," which bemoaned that such primitive savagery could only happen in the racist bastions of Houston, Texas or South Africa. The ire subsided only when one of their own—Harvard blue-blood Henry Beecher, the Dorr Professor of Anesthesiology—rose and quietly remarked, "Be still gentlemen, you are only jealous that Houston has better surgeons than Boston!"

Actually, Beecher, whom I came to know quite well in founding Hastings, was intriguing not only because of his rich family heritage (Harriet Beecher Stowe, Henry Ward Beecher), but also because of the ringing indictment he was then writing on American surgery. It was called "Knifing." The last I inquired, the estate was withholding publication permission, for obvious reasons.

First, there were heart transplants, then abortion, then genetics, behavior control, dying well, and euthanasia. This parade of anguishing human experiences would mark the next 25 years of my career. Barnard transplanted the first heart by himself, declaring the donor dead and the recipient ready. Obviously, one of the first ethical guidelines needed was to insist on separate teams to look after and advocate for donor and recipient. Across the years, I would be party to the formulation of guidelines for research and treatment in numerous biomedical fields: transplantation, DNA research, abortion, discontinuing life-support, the Genome project, etc. In 1968, I wrote an essay on the "Ethics of Heart Transplantation" in *The Christian Century*. Across the years, the two widely circulated theological news magazines *The Christian Century* and *Christianity Today* would publish numerous pieces on biomedical ethics, including a good number of my own.

The Heart Transplant: Ethical Dimensions

The Christian Century, March 20, 1968

> We must be on guard, lest science, however noble its professions, violate human dignity.

And I will give them a new heart and put a new spirit within them. I will take the stony heart out of their flesh and give them a heart of flesh . . .

Ezekiel speaks symbolically of spiritual things. But this prophecy of his highlights two phenomena of our time: first, that man's yearning for "a new heart" has been answered in a literal sense, that a new heart of flesh is now a medical possibility and second, that the heart of man is indeed the essence of life, spiritual and physical. Hence, the lively discussion we have been having on the ethical dimensions of heart transplantation.

The Judeo-Christian tradition that informs Western culture views the heart of man as the locus of the emotions that structure his life. Anger and hostility, love and compassion are all thought of as proceeding from the heart. Witness not only our common speech, but also our poetry and art, our religion and philosophy. Thus Erich Fromm, in his recent book *The Heart of Man*, writes of the ambiguity of the impulses that proceed from the "heart," impulses at once creative and destructive. Fromm of course is speaking symbolically. But translated into physiological terms this view seems rather primitive. The fact is, however, that recent medical discoveries support the notion that the heart is the center of life. A human body can survive for years with very low-grade cerebral activity, in a complete coma. But without the presence of the pulsating heart, life is soon extinguished. As *Time* magazine put it, ". . . the heart is essential to life in a more immediate temporal sense than any other organ, even the brain."[6]

---

6. "Surgery: The Ultimate Operation," 71.

This paper is not directly concerned with the techniques of heart transplantation. Our purpose here is to analyze the ethical dimensions of this operation as these emerge in the literature on it. We shall note three ethical problems related to the technique, and then discuss three options of ethics in medicine that give direction to those involved in day-to-day decision-making. The three problems are the time and meaning of death, the question of donor and recipient, and the rejection phenomenon. As our point of departure, we take the surgical feats around the world which, in the past few months, have confirmed that heart transplantation is a viable option in the treatment of radical coronary disease.

The Time and Meaning of Death

Our first problem of ethical significance concerns the time and meaning of death. When Denise Darvall arrived at the Cape Town hospital she was at the threshold of death. Although the electroencephalograph showed lingering impulses in her body, her heart had stopped. Dr. Marius Barnard explained how his brother, Dr. Christiaan N. Barnard, and the surgical team made their decision to remove her heart. "I know," he said, "in some places, they consider the patient dead when the electroencephalograph shows no more brain function. We are on the conservative side, and consider a patient dead when the heart is no longer working, and there are no longer any complexes on the electrocardiogram."[7]

What is the correct index to determine the time of death? Is it heart or brain function? Is there a distinction between existence and life? Is sustained physiological activity without any relational capacity really human life? When a man has lost the capacity to respond to both external and existential environment, is he still a man? Are we justified in hastening natural death? Are we justified in extending life through extraordinary measures? Our culture is now being forced to grapple with these extremely difficult questions.

In heart transplantation, it is urgently necessary that the donated heart be as fresh as possible. This necessity raises the profound ethical problem of who decides—and how—whether and when a person is dead. The case of Clive Haupt, the second of the South African heart donors, points up this question. After his stroke on the beach, he was immediately treated as a potential heart donor rather than as a present stroke victim—a fact that raises the shocking specter of a future day of corpse snatching.

7. Ibid., 64.

Newsweek quotes a public health official in Washington: "I have a horrible vision of ghouls hovering over an accident victim with long knives unsheathed, waiting to take out his organs as soon as he is pronounced dead."[8] Here, perhaps, is the ethical issue on which heart transplantation focuses. As Dr. Michael DeBakey—a pioneer in the field of heart surgery—notes in an article soon to be published: "The controversy has resumed on this point, with proposals for a new criterion of death based, for example, on electroencephalographic findings and other demonstrable evidence of cessation of vital cellular function. The legal, moral, and theologic aspects of this problem are intricate and formidable, but not impenetrable."

The cultural optimism that whispers excitedly through the populace clouds for the moment the ambiguity of our life and makes the Aesculapius legend profoundly contemporary. Aesculapius, you remember, practiced the art of medicine so well that the angry Zeus feared he would make the children of Earth immortal, and so slew him with a thunderbolt. The classic deception of chilianism naively believes in a coming life free from the imperfection of human existence. But man is born to die: this is the only certain universal axiom. Only the man who acknowledges the finality of death can know the meaning of life. And all the discussion of heart transplants may reveal the meaning of life and death to a society that evades the deep questions to run after superficial ones.

THE QUESTION OF DONOR AND RECIPIENT

Our second ethical problem area concerns the question of consent by donor and recipient. In the Cape Town case, to be sure, the problem hardly arose. Louis Washkansky, Dr. Barnard's patient, needed only two minutes to make a decision that he could have taken two hours. He agreed at once to have his heart cut out and replaced with a donor's. Edward Darvall, Denise's father, also made a decision immediately. When the doctors told him, "There is no hope for her. You can do us and humanity a great favor if you let us transplant your daughter's heart," Darvall answered, "If there is no hope for her, then try to save this man's life."

But the problem of consent is frequently much more complex. What, for instance, if neither the donor nor recipient is able to decide for him- or herself—which member of the family has the power of decision? The Clive Haupt case illustrates this problem. His bride of three months collapsed when she was asked to permit removal of his heart. His mother finally consented to the removal.

8. "Transplant Surgery," 87.

More difficult, however, are the psychological and spiritual factors involved in decisions of this nature. John Holden of the Institute of Social Ethics at Chicago's West Side Medical Center has pointed out—in his article "Some Ethical Considerations in the Transplantation of Organs"[9]—how traumatic the decision can be for a person, for example, who is challenged to give one of his kidneys to his own brother. What of the guilt he would feel if he refused? Dr. John R. Elkington, editor of the *Annals of Internal Medicine*, describes the "risk to the medical well-being of donors and potential donors" in the February 1964 issue of his journal. "There was the case," he says, "of a man who refused to donate his kidney to a brother, with resulting severe emotional problems. And a family was torn apart by a mother giving a kidney to a child, against the wishes of her husband."[10]

There is also the identity problem that may arise on the side of both donor and recipient. Thus Philip Blaiberg, Dr. Barnard's second transplant recipient, said he felt like a different person, and he appeared so to his daughter when she flew to his bedside from her studies in Israel. And to Louis Washkansky's death, Mr. Darvall reacted pathetically: "I have nothing to live for. My daughter lived on for a while; now all is gone."

But the most difficult question in this matter is that of which among the many persons who need it is to receive one of the few available hearts. Perhaps some day, there will be organ banks and a multitude of card-carrying donors. Not so at present. Moreover, in a television interview on December 24, 1967, Dr. Barnard revealed a medical attitude that compounds this problem. "My duty as a doctor," he said, "is to treat the patient. The donor I could treat no longer. I had only one way to treat my patient: transplant. To me that's not immoral."[11] Of course, he is absolutely right. The genius of the medical profession is the single-minded devotion of the physician to an individual patient. Yet, when there are hundreds of thousands of desperately ill coronary patients, who decides who shall be given a new heart? What are the criteria of this decision? Will the transplant technique be available only to people who have money or connections? In other words, there is a social-ethical issue here. The physician's devotion to the patient must be augmented by social concern. In the interview cited above, Dr. Barnard commented on ethical decision-making: "If you want to know what is right, you must not ask the people around you—you must ask yourself." The ethi-

9. Holden, "Some Ethical Considerations in the Transplantation of Organs."

10. Elkington, "Moral Problems in the Use of Borrowed Organs, Artificial and Transplanted," 309–313.

11. Barnard, "Face the Nation" interview.

cal imperative of the hour is that concern for an individual and concern for humanity enrich each other.

THE REJECTION PHENOMENON

A third aspect of the heart-transplant problem is the body's built-in ability to reject foreign intrusion. The blood's white corpuscles, for instance, fight disease. But in the case of a heart transplant, this power becomes the enemy.

The few cases of heart transplantation have not yielded any knowledge regarding the rejection phenomenon. Despite the progress medicine has made in the area of immuno-depressant therapy through drugs and radiation, the problem of rejection remains formidable. For while such therapy reduces rejection, it also reduces resistance to infections such as pneumococci. It is true that every medical treatment intervenes in the natural processes of the body in some way. Are we, however, justified in so radical an intervention as that required in heart transplant cases? Should we force the body to contradict its genius?

CONCLUSION:
INQUIRY AS TO HUMAN ESSENCE, ETHICAL OPTIONS

We come again to the basic question: the meaning of human existence. Helmut Thielicke, the German ethicist, speaks to this question in a lecture, "Ethical Problems in Modern Medicine," soon to be delivered at the Texas Medical Center: "The substitution of organs by machines or by organs from other persons confronts us again with the inquiry for the essence of man. Here this inquiry appears with a particular implication: Is man to be understood in analogy to the machine whose parts are exchangeable? We have to observe carefully the tenor of the question: We do not ask—as do certain engineers of a utopian biology—whether "man" is to be exchanged and re-structured, but we rather ask, what "in" man can or should be exchanged."

Let us now look at this whole problem in the light of three ethical options that shape our culture: the Jewish-humanitarian, the situation-ethic, and the Roman Catholic natural-law options.

Rabbi Immanuel Jacobovits, chief rabbi of the British Commonwealth, has said (in the issue of *Newsweek* cited above) that the most profound ethical question regarding heart transplantation is the termination of the life of the donor. He holds that even the minutest fraction of life is precious and that morally speaking, we have no right to terminate life, though only minimal hope exists or none at all.[12] This view seems to agree with popular opinion. As Edmund Leach, provost of King's College, Cambridge, pointed out in a *London Times* article, "The vast majority is still deeply shocked at the idea that the doctor should ever willfully terminate the life of anyone who had already acquired a human personality by the fact of being born."[13]

The Jewish position, of course, is based on a deeply sensitive interpretation of the commandment "Thou shalt not kill"—an inviolable principle that protects the sanctity of human life.

Christian theology also emphasizes the sanctity of life. Opposed to the fatalism of "When your number's up, it's up," Christianity declares that man must struggle for life incessantly. As Dietrich Bonhoeffer put it: "It is only when one loves life and the Earth so much that without them everything seems to be over that one may believe in the reserrection and a new world."[14]

Our second option, that of situation ethics, holds that each particular person, each particular instance, is unique and must be evaluated in its uniqueness. The remarks by Christiaan Barnard cited above emphasize the high humanism of a decision motivated by concern for a specific person in a specific situation. Dr. Barnard's posture shows freedom from legalistic norms, along with compassion springing from deep ethical principles.

Apropos of the many recent heart transplants, Joseph Fletcher, of the Episcopal Theological School in Cambridge, Massachusetts, has declared that "speeding up a donor's death, when death is positively inevitable, may be justified if the transplant provides another human with valuable life."[15] In other words, as he sees it, the basic principle of sustaining and extending life justifies radical technique. Unlike the "natural law" theologians, Fletcher would say that the only intrinsic principle is the love principle, and that this demands different decisions in different instances.

At this point, the situationist could refer to what both Christianity and other world religions consider the highest ethical act man is capable of; namely, the sacrifice of his own life for another's. Christians believe that this principle was personified in Jesus Christ, who said "Greater love hath no man than this, that a man lay down his life for his friend" (John 15:13). Thus the situationist in ethics would say that the decision to transplant a heart, though fraught with dangerous concessions all the way, is one that basically

12. "Transplant Surgery," 87.

13. Leach, "Doctors' Powers 'Unbelievable,'" 2.

14. Bonhoeffer, *Letters and Papers from Prison*, 157.

15. "Transplant Surgery," 87.

affirms the preciousness of human life, and at the same time opens an opportunity for the highest form of self sacrifice.

We turn now to the Roman Catholic option, which, because it is organized around a single principle, offers the most systematic moral theory in regard to our problem. That principle, simply stated, is that any violation or abrogation of the natural process is wrong; for such intervention strikes at the mysterious beauty of that divinely instituted and directed process, the origin and development of life.

Bringing this principle to bear on the question of heart transplants, the Vatican newspaper, *L'Osservatore Romano*, declared that the heart is a physiological organ with a purely mechanical function. This view has been echoed by Dr. Thomas O'Donnell, former lecturer in medical ethics at Georgetown University School of Medicine, a Jesuit institution. O'Donnell (as cited in the issue of *Newsweek* mentioned above) regards the heart as "an efficient pump with no moral significance." In other words, the natural-law position would consider radical techniques justified when they enrich and extend the life of man, provided that there is no moral violation at any other point. Specifically, the requirements are approval from the next of kin and the assurance that the donor is medically dead.

The best recent Roman Catholic scholarship, the work of Pierre Teilhard de Chardin, for example, emphasizes that the humanitarian benefit science can now render is good, a part of a cosmic evolutionary fulfillment—of Christogenesis, or God enriching and humanizing human life. Helmut Thielicke in the lecture above says: "Without doubt man has been commissioned, in the command given with creation to subdue the Earth . . . not to accept her passively, but rather to use her as material in responsible creativity." In other words, this third option considers developments in the biological sciences to be blessings discovered under providence by men who faithfully seek to extend and enrich human life.

We must admit, however, that so far as heart transplantation is concerned, no clear moral directive issues from any one or all of these positions. This is not surprising. Such directives have never been easily arrived at; in our complex society they are almost always ambiguous. The one thing that is clear in our time is this: technology can be used for the benefit of the individual and of society, or it can be used for destructive and dehumanizing ends. We must continually affirm the goodness of science when it works for the welfare of mankind, and we must continually be on guard lest science, however noble its professions, violate human dignity. With Robert Oppenheimer, we must remember that what is technically desirable is not necessarily good.

Apart from this dramatic beginning on the issue of heart transplantation, the first enduring matter I would confront was, of course, abortion. In Texas, the outstanding attorney, Sara Weddington, was already preparing what would become the landmark case, Roe vs. Wade (1967). Early that year I was invited to speak at a forum on abortion in Lubbock, Texas with my new Chicago colleagues, Don and Anne Marie Coleman. (The Colemans were university pastors at the University of Texas campus there.) I set forth my own nuanced view on abortion: that it was sometimes right and sometimes wrong. For 30 years, I have been unable to convince anyone of this view, especially die-hard, pro-life and pro-choice partisans. Here is the distillation of my views from *Birth Ethics*.[16]

ABORTION: A MORAL POLICY

This ethical analysis requires that we differentiate abortion cases along a moral spectrum. It is simplistic to say that abortion is always right or always wrong. Even though philosophy demands consistency, and the law requires uniformity, more subtle decisional criteria should be applied when our choices involve human beings.

Therefore, we need to distinguish among differing situations and admit that there are times when the technique of abortion must be used. In the public policy arena, we need to develop an ethic of reason and prudence. Then, in a nuanced way, we can assign value or disvalue to a given case according to some balance of the principles to beneficence, nonmaleficence, justice, and freedom.

A suggestive grouping of cases might be these: abortion would be strongly advised in incest, child rape, and cases where profound genetic defects (*e.g.*, Tay-Sachs, Lesch-Nyhan syndrome) are present, or the pregnancy or delivery is life threatening. Abortion is permissible but not obligatory in coercive out-of-wedlock pregnancy, situations where pregnancy offers a physical or mental risk to the mother, moderately severe genetic or congenital abnormalities discovered in the fetus (*e.g.*, Siamese twins, Spina bifida, Down Syndrome). Abortion is permissible, but discouraged, in illegitimate pregnancies, mild and treatable genetic or congenital accidents, (*e.g.*, hairlip, cleft palate). Abortion is proscribed

16. Vaux, *Birth Ethics*, 90–91.

for reasons of convenience, population control, and sex selection. Who should be the judge to say whether any of these conditions exist?

The answer is obvious. The final choice should lie with the mother and father, together with medical and pastoral counsel. The law should convey general contours, but abortion should not be seen as a criminal act unless the specific case falls under this last category.

This proposal suggests that neither "right-to-life" nor "freedom-of-choice" doctrines satisfy. Both abandon the subtleties of freedom and conscience. Our society appears to be groping for some nuanced abortion policy that will more appropriately honor our cultural values of "sanctity of life," "freedom," and "justice." We must reject the morally simplistic reduction of this complex of issues into the one hand, and the equally absurd "freedom-of-choice" doctrine on the other. We need some carefully nuanced public policy that avoids the dangers of being restrictive or conducive for the tragic interim, until completely reliable and trustworthy modes of contraception are available and used. In this tragic interlude, our sense of judgment and our schemes of ethics will be severely put to the test.

BEGINNING-OF-LIFE ISSUES

Perinatal ethics joined space and energy technology as early interests. Timely events converged to precipitate these interests, such as the AIDS epidemic and ethical cases regarding children.

HIV/AIDS

"Where is God?" asks Martin Scorsese in *Mean Streets*, as they drive by the old Catholic church. "God is there in the streets." Often streets, hospital, and university came together, as in the following essay I offered in the *Chicago Tribune* in 1987. As the Center's ethicist, I had convened a workshop on AIDS in 1983, when very few medics even had heard about this new disease. My university, the University of Illinois at Chicago Medical School, was trying to assure patients at our hospital and at neighboring Cook County Hospital, where we practiced, that none of our workers were HIV-positive. I share this essay at the outset of this journal to begin to illustrate for you the person offering this story. Pope John Paul II had just made his "Natural Sanctions" speech in San Francisco, where he implied that AIDS victims suffer the natural consequences of the sins of promiscuity and homosexuality.

ETHICS, AIDS, AND COUNTY HOSPITAL

Chicago Tribune, September 18, 1987

The litmus test for the ethics of any society lies in its treatment of the vulnerable: the poor, the old, the children, the sick. Cook County, Chicago's hospital for the sick poor, once again has become the focus of the value crises and conflicts of our community.

At issue now is not the abandonment of the beautiful, but decrepit, structure or the dumping of green-card patients into its pain-throbbing corridors and clinics after "wallet biopsies" have been performed on them at the suburban "for-profit" hospitals.

Now, concern centers around the decision to restrict the activity of a staff physician with AIDS, and what to do about the fact that numerous healthcare employees in inner city institutions are infected with the virus. What shall be our moral response?

Initially, we need to remind ourselves of the ethical excellence of this great old health center serving Chicago's poor. Not only is the burn and trauma unit world renowned, but the gravely ill can expect to receive expert and compassionate care—as our family discovered with a dying child twenty years ago. Anyone who spends any time at County is immediately impressed with the social conscience, the human warmth, and the sacrificial care expressed in the midst of this desperate atmosphere of acute need.

Today, as AIDS changes its epidemiologic portrait from the San Francisco to the New York visage, from a disease afflicting the middle class and well educated homosexual community, now to the impoverished, black, drug-scene culture, we should not be surprised that County becomes the focal point of not only ethical anguish and disputes, but, of our more basic inquiry about what makes for a "good and just" community. How does such a community express itself on institutional ethics, professional ethics, and the more general societal ethics? Our present search for institutional ethics is an encouraging sign. It may signal recognition that we have erred in focusing moral attention too much on individual liberties and rights and too little on commensurate duties and communal goods. As city governments adopt ethics ordinances, or as work places debate substance abuse policies, we witness an exciting ferment and dialogue on those vital questions too long relegated to the sphere of personal will.

But is a public ethic possible in a society so committed to personal rights? Reinhold Niebuhr reflected on the contradictions in *Moral Man and Immoral Society*. We create "value-free" societies based on privacy, because of the terrible residue of human injury that has been inflicted on persons by collectivist ideologies and states, whether they be religious or the more modern secular-humanist forms of tyranny. Religion (*lit. religare*) is the ligature that binds us into a common memory, hope, and value system.

When we entered the post-religious age, when Descartes parted ways with the French Jesuits and Locke with the Puritans, Hobbes with the Anglicans, Spinoza with the Synagogues, Hume with the Presbyterians, and Kant with the Lutherans, a fundamental cleavage between the ethics of individuality and of solidarity was fashioned. The modern mind and our derivative political institutions, formed from the teaching of these great political philosophers, have yet to recover from this estrangement. Now we need rapprochement. We need to recover the essential complementarity of personal and public ethics.

What has this venture into the history of ideas to do with AIDS? As Defoe in *A Journal of the Plague Year* and Camus in *La Peste* made clear, historic crisis or natural calamity drives a people to recall the binding ligatures, the common bonds. The AIDS crisis provides us opportunity to reformulate our covenants of life and the mutuality of our existence. At County Hospital, indeed at all of our public institutions of housing, schooling, and healing, we shall need to draw together the representative boards of governance, the professional servants, and the community of those served to draw up new contracts of obligation and protection.

Professional ethics are also cast into bold relief by the AIDS crisis. In Chicago, we hear not only of two physicians with AIDS, but of two priests and a Benedictine brother similarly afflicted. Showmen like Rock Hudson and Liberace we can understand, but not our honored and pristine professionals. Again, the impulses of shock, condemnation, and fear must be balanced by those of understanding, clemency, and creative help. In health care, we rightly demand an aseptic clinical setting, and we can indeed be confident that there is very little chance that a physician, nurse, or even the phlebotomist will transfer infection even if they have AIDS, ARC, or antibody positivity. We do have the right to ask that those who are sick or impaired withdraw from responsibilities of intimate care. Indeed, we do need to ask if the Hippocratic standards of "holiness and purity" of practice or the Hebraic-Christian strictures of prophylactics and purification should not pertain to professional conduct. In the medical tradition of Luke the physician-evangelist, of Maimonides, Sydenham, and Osler, the healer, though not perfect, must be worthy of trust with one's life and health.

But, at this point, we must also remember that such moral excellence is founded in grace and humility and not in arrogance and achievement. Our moral expectation of physicians is concerned with avarice and apathy, just as much as it is with AIDS.

But the servant is also a wounded healer. Dr. David Hilfaker has pointed dramatically to the frailty and fallibility of the medical profession. We must establish exacting standards, all the while supporting and shielding those who fall. This pertains to the impaired physician as well as to one with AIDS. The spiritual director who refuses to extend mercy to the fallen Benedictine brother may be expressing puritan zeal, literal obedience, and calculated deterrence, but he is not expressing the searching forgiveness of Torah and gospel, our social charter.

The controversy at County and the broader community concern it represents ultimately pushes to a deeper societal ethic. At the root of our disturbing, indeed highly dangerous confusion about AIDS is a defect in our theology, which I define as the Greeks did, as our cultural matrix of beliefs and ultimate values. In the gay literature, one is greeted by the deity of exuberant freedom, in the hyper-straight press, the wrathful vengeful deity belching brimstone. In reality, God is neither a sugar-daddy nor a terrorist. God, as Whitehead spoke, is the righteous energy granting direction, destiny, and discipline into his creation. Even the God known in nature and history is a force of justice. God is also a being of tender mercy.

Finally, since AIDS is a crisis, literally an event with ominous and creative potential, we need to proceed with accommodating and ameliorating measures. We need to act with urgency and intensity to make sterile needles available free (as in England and Holland), not to endorse the drug culture but to blunt its morbid effect. It is unconscionable that one child should die from AIDS because of a contaminated needle carrying the lethal virus to its mother. We need also to unravel the "condom conundra" and educate for "safe sex." Finally, we need widespread voluntary, perhaps even compulsory testing for AIDS antibody status. The estimated 1.5 million infected persons must know for their own sakes and the sake of those whom they contact. Society must know so that it can track the disease and safeguard its people. I suggest we begin with free, completely anonymous, testing in shopping centers, results going only to that person. (San Francisco scientists report an antibody test 95 percent accurate that will cost 25 cents).

At the same time we undertake these proscriptive measures, we need to formulate prescriptive measures: healing, reformative, ameliorative actions. Can we redemptively influence the cultures of advertising, television, film, and education and so retard the ascending style of promiscuity and compulsivity in sex and reaffirm chaste and faithful love and the integrity of family? Cosby is doing his best. Let's halt our long burned-out tirade against chastity and support with renewed vigor family vitality through economic, tax, and business policies. Most crucially, let us rediscover that reverence for persons that leads us to respect and shield them from harm. As Cicero reminds us, we are all the dying, caring for the dying.

HOMOSEXUALITY

My own views on homosexuality and AIDS have been mollified across the years. While, as an ethicist, I affirm sexual fidelity and man-woman love, as will be clear as this autobiography unfolds, I seek to integrate more closely a biblical-Judaic ethic into Christian thought. I cannot envision second-temple Jewish ethics, Qumran teaching, or early Christian morality ever condoning polygamy, divorce, abortion, infanticide, or pederasty. But, I cannot cast blame on our brothers in the gay community for the first horrible wave of the AIDS pandemic. They had no foreknowledge that injection into human flesh would concentrate initially in the gay population. This occurrence, I have come to feel, was more a quirk of natural cause-effect processes than a moral sin. Human actions are always a strange admixture of freedom and determinism. Our responses must be merciful and just. The gays, gypsies, and Jews who went to Hitler's gas chambers suffered for righteousness' sake. Matthew Shepherd was an *Akedic* martyr. Somehow, homosexuals are woven into a theology of persecution. The redemptive mystery of the complex of righteous demand, sinfulness, sacrifice, forgiveness, repentance, and reconciliation is what I call the *Akedic* complex. Somehow AIDS is about this.

I've thought of my newspaper writing as "moral essays" in the tradition of Jonathan Swift (though dramatically less fleet-footed and sure-footed). The editors of the *Chicago Tribune*, for whom I wrote some 30 essays beginning in 1980, spoke of my style as scientific-poetic or mystical-historical. Like my artist-brother in New York, I refer to my work as iconic or sacramental. It is more impressionistic than Flemish. I seek to discover the sacred in the secular.

One year, when I served Second Presbyterian Church in Chicago as pastor, I offered a 20-sermon series on the theme of sacraments, "Intimations of the Sacred." Subjects included faith, love, hope, snow, light, grace, peace, joy, and life.

HOSPITAL ETHICS CAREER BEGINS

Called on by the media to place Baby Fae (recipient of a baboon heart transplant) and William Shroeder (recipient of an artificial heart) in a context of meaning took me back to Karen Quinlan and Louis Washkansky. My career as an instant pontificator and prognosticator began when we moved to Houston in 1966. In a few short weeks, the first heart transplant occurred in South Africa. Drs. DeBakey and Cooley had been upstaged. For me, a new career as "bioethicist" had begun. Yes, Ms. Stolberg, 38 years ago. My approach was always irascibly theological and cross-referential.

"Baby Doe" regulations in 1985 recalled Roe vs. Wade in 1973. Cloning arose on the radar in 1960, 1980, and 2000. Terri Schiavo was Nancy Cruzan who was Karen Quinlan. Issues always come full circle. I've always found the themes of moral response to be constant and perennial. Medicine is now business and business is medicine, food, goods, comforts. Healthcare issues are also intertwined with broader societal concerns. Convictions on abortion seem to be rooted in deeper religious and political values.

Decisions of medical triage (*e.g.*, Can we afford liver transplants? or How ought we to distribute limited quantities of anti-lymphocyte globulin for aplastic anemia cases?) seemed to devolve back on fundamental, economic, and national defense policies. Before debating with the cardiac surgeon in the Baby Fae case, Dr. Bailey, I offered the following reflection on this most exotic transplant. I was with Dr. Cooley when he transplanted a ram's heart into a human patient in 1969. The man's body seemed to boil away in rejection. But here we went again in desperate, albeit caring, heroism. Reneé Fox called it "the courage to fail."[17]

---

17. See Fox and Swazey, *The Courage to Fail.*

Baby Fae: Layers of Meaning

Chicago Tribune, November 8, 1984

As we approach Advent, the season in the Christian calendar when our world's attention is again drawn to a child born to peasant parents—a child, in Menotti's words, "the color of Earth and thorn . . . the color of wheat and dawn"—in Adventist Hospital in Loma Linda, California, a little child has invited our world to gaze into its cradle, now an incubator-oxygen tent, and examine what we believe about good and evil, health and death, and life's meaning.

Baby Fae has caused us to ponder both the immediate ethical issues of medical treatment and the deeper metaphysics of the nature and destiny of our bodily life. Fascinated, we have marveled at this bold act of implanting a nonhuman (baboon's) heart in a human breast, and, puzzled, we have sought to penetrate the layers of meaning that encapsulate the scientific event. Our response begins simply, in surprise, but grows thick and complex as we begin to consider responsibility of the human agent to the things he creates and also to those others with whom he is linked by threads of duty, affection, or reverence.

Responsibility: Human to Animal

At a simple level lies the issue of animal rights. One might expect that some members of that remarkable faith community, the Seventh Day Adventists, with their ovo-lacto vegetarian diets, might object to the sacrifice of a baboon to supply a heart to replace the terribly distorted hypoplastic organ that lay in Baby Fae's chest. Actually, Adventist vegetarianism is based on a prophylactic and eschatologic ethic that seeks to keep the body a fit temple for the Holy Spirit.

Protesters, whether anti-vivisectionists or merely animal lovers, call our attention to the moral issue of sacrificing animals to serve human needs. Although careful guidelines against insignificant research usage and cruelty to animals are now being developed (as indeed they should be), animals have always been the sentinels and servants of man. Birds have been sent into coal mines to see if they die in the shaft; if they come back, the miners enter. Deformed and dead fish and cats give first warning of environmental pollution. From the days of our hunter-gatherer ancestors, animal flesh also has served as a protein source and gustatory delight.

Yet the noblest human service offered by animals is not found in the restaurant or zoo, but in the corridors of medical therapeutics and investigation. And now the generic beastly sacrifice for man has been symbolized in the most profound and focused life-giving sacrifice in human-animal interplay: that of the baboon whose heart beats in Baby Fae.

Responsibility: Human to Human

Hans Jonas, the great German philosopher, has argued that human experimentation may be a contemporary expression of the traditional rituals of animal and human sacrifice to assuage the gods' wrath and assure Earth's fertility. Whatever the deeper cultural significance of the act, human experimentation and its ethical bearings is a theme in this case. While the human/animal interface generates one level of responsibility, the human-human responsibility is greater. The most troubling aspect of the Baby Fae case concerns the moral dimensions of human experimentation.

The Nuremberg code, which guides the medical profession in its investigational activity, says that appropriate animal studies must precede human studies and that fully informed consent must be obtained.

On the first point, many scientist-clinicians feel that the time had not yet come for an interspecies transplant. Such had been performed before: James Hardy of Mississippi performed an ape-to-human transplant in the 1960s. I was in Houston in 1969 when Dr. Denton Cooley placed a ram's heart into a human when a suitable donor was not available and when his patient lay near death. In all these cases, early and fulminant death ensued. For this reason, most major transplant centers in the United States do not feel the time has come to use animal hearts, even given the shortage of human donors and the sullied yet still bright promise of Cyclosporin A and immunosuppression.

Second, did the research intrigue and the interest of this center in xenografts override the obligation to obtain fully informed consent? More important, did the ambitions of the center's staff serve the best interests of the child? Were all alternatives fairly laid out for the parents?

Four courses of action appear to have been open to the family. The first was the action it initially took: to take the baby home and keep her comfortable as she died. The family returned to the hospital when options two and three, a xenograft from a baboon or an allograft from another human, were raised. Was a fourth option—the Norwood procedure—discussed? In this procedure, a conduit is placed to lift the burden of the compromised left heart, an operation now around 50 percent successful. The question of consent remains to be answered, as does the other question raised by the Nuremburg Code, the question of the benefit to be gained.

Do no harm; save life. This is the essence of the medico-moral creed. Whether we look to biblical ethics or to the Greek humanist tradition of Hippocrates, the first obligation of the doctor is not to harm. This means not to cause or amplify pain or suffering (unless, that is, it is momentary pain that will yield to recovery and health), not to unnecessarily mutilate, not to prolong dying. We cannot know, I'm afraid, whether we are helping Baby Fae or compounding her affliction. As one never could justify war on the grounds that increasingly sophisticated technology issues from it, so also would one hesitate to justify suffering inflicted on this child by saying that the benefits to medical science would be immense. Is this not a costly purchase of insight? We watch the rosy daily bulletins from Loma Linda (free breathing, feeding) and wonder about the agony of post-operative pain and/or rejection of the heart.

The wisest physician I know thinks the major moral issue in the Baby Fae case is the imposition on her parents of an uncertainty, even a dread, of what will happen to their daughter for the rest of her life. The concern is well-founded, not only because of the rejection threat, or concern over whether the heart will grow as the infant develops, or concern for the long-range effects of the immunosuppression—but also the more profound human injury that might ensue by virtue of being for all her life an object of scientific and technological manipulation and curiosity.

Nonetheless, some say a societal economic cost-benefit equation must be added to this personal equation of suffering and saving. That we spend a billion dollars a day on health care, though this is an impressive figure, is a specious argument. I understand that the cost of one aircraft carrier would underwrite the entire perinatal budget for five years. We live not on a lifeboat but on a luxury liner. Yes, we are beginning to confront limits on health care; but I would argue that they are the good and provident boundaries calling us from our space-time idolatries to an appropriate bodily destiny and an accession to the ultimate mystery of life and death. These are enduring life-lessons Baby Fae is teaching us.

RESPONSIBILITY: HUMANS TO MYSTERY

What is the horizon of human spare-parts replacement medicine? Should we seek to enhance the acceptability of alien tissues and create animal farms from which we can grow and harvest the organs we need? Or perhaps we should fund genetically-engineered tissue banks or impose societally coerced organ retrieval systems? Should we see the unique fingerprint of our immunological system—that "I" that recognizes "not-I," and combats it—as a messenger of our inviolability, or as a destructive power to be muted, a problem to be solved? And, finally, should we continue on our present course of transforming our concept of the human person from that of an unrepeatable, unique, mysterious, yet finite, being, to that of an infinite collocation of interchangeable parts?

A raging thirst for life, gratitude in life, is perhaps the most profound characteristic of our Hebrew-Christian culture. This spiritual and moral tradition also forms the structure and impulse of the world of modern science. Perhaps this is the reason we ventured against all odds, neglected some conventions, and clung to life for this little child.

Bret Harte wrote of a tiny baby abandoned in a rough and violent mining camp. The dirty and debased miners were transformed into a redeemed community through the "The Luck of Roaring Camp." Baby Fae has been laid on the doorstep of our world in these waning weeks of Orwell's 1984. Like the miners of Roaring Camp, we are challenged to ask ourselves questions, ponder meanings, and reorient our lives.

In the spring of 1968, two philosophers were invited to join a distinguished panel of scientist-physicians testifying before the U.S. Senate Health Committee chaired by Mondale and Kennedy. The question was whether a commission to study the ethics of biomedicine was needed. The ethicists, Jerry Brauer (Dean at University of Chicago School of Divinity) and Ken Vaux said "Yes." The parade of medical experts—Barnard, Kornberg, Lederberg, DeBakey, Shumway, etc.—said "No!" Good fellows (like themselves) needed no snooping or supervision, especially from clergy-types. Vaux and Brauer dissented, as did Harry Beecher. It took 15 more years for the commission to be established. Now, my then-colleague Leon Kass heads it.[18]

Behind the limelight and the accolades, what was unfolding through my patchwork career as pastor, theologian, consulting bioethicist, and public policy *Pontifex Minimus*? The parade of scholarly articles, newspaper essays, and books for popular consumption tell the story. But what was going on inside the mind of this 30-year-old man? Like Michael

---

18. See Vaux, *An Abrahamic Theology for Science.*

Jordan, this youth was thrown into extraordinary notoriety, too soon (in my case because of events; in his, raw talent).

In retrospect, it seems we were entering a new era of human influence, if not control, over the forces of life and death. As in the Faust legend, these developments cast us against theological depth. We now stood within the judgment of heaven and hell. With Oppenheimer, all could say "we scientists have known sin." Even though theology had become publicly irrelevant, events drew us back into a kind of sacramental age of mystery and power. Theology would have to be resurrected as a societal instrumentality of understanding and influence. The new cooperation of the sacred and secular spheres must not be oppressive and retarding as of old, but now visionary, prophetic, and encouraging—another compelling reason to unite the evangelical and the ethical. We had abandoned faith-based ethics just when we could not live (or die) without them.

To sum it all up, I wanted our society to continue its biomedical quest, just as today I want it to continue its business quest, its global-economy quest, its quest for peace, the communication revolution—but all with prophetic and pastoral moral cognizance and guidance. I offered the following overarching perspective in the *New York Times*.

ETHICS OF MEDICINE AND THE SPIRIT OF WESTERN CULTURE

New York Times, January 31, 1975

The spirit of Western culture, which is the spirit of modern scientific medicine, is today an erratic wind that cannot sustain full-blown the sails of our technological voyage.

Distinguished scientists at the World Food Conference in Rome suggested that perhaps famine should take its course among the peoples of India and Africa. Some argue that disease has a natural place in the history of our species and should be allowed to have its play because the side-effects of the conquest might be worse than the disease itself.

Yet today's physician and scientist, indeed any human, faced with a malnourished child or a young adult dying from leukemia cannot accept this verdict of resignation. And so a deep ambivalence of the passions of conquest and submission, of compassion and resignation, war within us as in the breast of Faust.

Discerning the spirit of Western culture is essential to the task of precise analysis of the current ethical questions in medicine. Unless we understand where we are coming from and where we think we are going, we are in danger of being swept along in some "directionless" and "valueless" progress, the end of which we do not know and may not desire. Many clinical dilemmas are clarified by understanding this conflicted spirit of Western man.

Consider the following: the delicate decisions requiring a balancing of needs against limited resources, decisions of triage and priority, decisions to impede, accelerate, or merely attend a patient in the dying process.

In these cases, the ability to understand the conflicting values of hope and resignation is necessary in order to avoid two unfortunate responses. On the one hand, there is empathy that can foster debilitating guilt; the biologist Garrett Hardin has pointed up in recent papers the destructiveness of thoughtless benevolence. On the other hand, there is that systemic repression that slowly renders one an automaton without conscience. Those forced to render without conscience. Those forced to render decisions in medicine must delicately transact the tension between hope and resignation.

In *Young Man Luther*, Erik Erikson locates this same dialectical tension in man's psychological nature. He speaks of the mood of a certain period of time (the early 16th century) as reflecting "mood cycles inherent in man's psychological structure."

> The two most basic alternating moods are those of carnival and atonement: The first gives license and leeway to sensual enjoyment, to relief and release at all cost; the second surrenders to the negative conscience, which constricts, depresses, and enjoins man for what he has left unsolved, uncared for, unatoned.[19]

At this moment of history, both the carnival mood of scientific ingenuity, exploration, and creativity, and the atonement mood of reflective and evaluative concern are intense. We have initiated a war on vascular disease and cancer and we are not sure that we should. What new force in nature will we be making room for to be the messenger of our death?

I would suggest that holding the two moods in tension is essential to the genius of our civilization, and to the sanity of any therapist at work within this ethos. Let us label the moods Nordic and Mediterranean, northern and southern.

The Nordic spirit in our consciousness is symbolized by our unwillingness to accept the necessities of nature, including death. It is characterized

19. Erikson, *Young Man Luther*, 75.

by the abandon with which we intervene at the sacrosanct thresholds of life: birth and death. In Nordic mythology, the gods are man's friends, fellow warriors against the fiends, and monsters let loose in the creation. One day, man becomes godlike in his prehension and power and the gods say good-bye. A *Götterdämmerung* is perceived, whereby he inherits through his knowledge and technology the formerly prohibited abilities. Nordic man attacks the unknown. He challenges the alien forces in nature; he rides in pursuit of the Four Horsemen of the Apocalypse.

The Mediterranean spirit is different. It is born in the same sun of Spain, Italy, and Africa. Unlike the dark, cold winter nights that nurture a Luther and a Dostoevsky, here on warm days, life throbs on the vines, in the marketplace, and in the temples.

Southern man seeks to harmonize with the rhythms and cycles of nature. In the North, the Lord must cover his Earth with the white death in winter, lest man cut and till it year round. In the South, man walks more gently and cries to Earth as his mother. He does not rise about the Earth in mastery.

We are fortunate that life has its Nordic and Mediterranean elements; its North and its South, East and West. In a world such as ours, an intense oscillation of these dialectical impulses is necessary and should be sustained. The great questions of medical ethics can be posited within this structure:

- Should genetic disease be evaluated as communicable disease and be brought under public health quarantine?

- Should deformed children be allowed to die?

- Should health be seen as a right insured by public financing?

- Should elective death and non-election of prolonged suffering be socially accepted and professionally administered?

In the case of these decisions the delicate equipoise between conquest and resignation must be sought. For the sake of our sanity, for the integrity of our spirit, for the moral legacy we bequeath to the future, we have no other option.

To return to abortion for a moment, in light of this theological paradox and dialectic, in the ensuing years after Roe vs. Wade, I would often put forward the preceding abortion views (*e.g.*, in the Presbyterian Commission on Life issues I chaired for the denomination). The polar views were always so strident that, when added to the law's insistence on uniformity and philosophy's requirement of consistency, we were never able to move beyond shouting and polarity.

I am still unnerved by one letter I received on the abortion issue from a young minister serving a 20-year jail sentence. I'm not as certain of the rightness of his action as I was of our civil rights activity. In fact, quite the reverse. I have lost his letter, but it went like this.

Dear Dr. Vaux,

. . . I want you to know that I have followed your views that abortion is wrong and contrary to the will of God, and I have decided to take a stand. I planted a bomb in the_____ abortion clinic in (an eastern state) and have been imprisoned for my action . . .

My conserving and nature-respecting views on biological matters of ethics—fertilization, abortion, homosexuality, etc.—often got me into trouble, but never like this. While I realize the nobility of the Maccabeans standing for the law of God against the sacrilege of Antiochus Epiphanes, or Luther boldly proclaiming "*Hier stehe ich*," this was not an act of the same order (although it yielded the same result). Civility and non-violent ethical protest, I had resolved since working with Dr. King on "Operation Breadbasket," must always be the Christian *modus operandi.*

In 1970, we organized a second major conference under the leadership of Sara's brother, Bert Anson, a scientist who had come to Houston to begin a teaching career. He helped develop a fascinating program on "Science, Technology, and a Human Future." I had been serving on a National Council of Churches (NCC) Task Force on this subject, which had become a major emphasis of NCC and WCC work in the 1960s. The ecumenical movement, then at its zenith, produced outstanding work in this subject. Our conference assembled Jørgen Randers (Norwegian physicist, member of The Club of Rome), Ivan Illich from Cuernevaca, and others. Margaret Mead, who was a member of our NCC Task Force and a deeply committed Christian laywoman, wrote the foreword to that publication: *To Create a Different Future.*[20]

20. See Vaux, *To Create a Different Future.*

The conference pointed up two tendencies in my changing career. I was thoroughly committed to bringing people together from across disciplines and faiths in dialogue on major world problems. Second, I was committed to publishing small study guides for classes, congregations, pastors, etc., to help deal with these issues. There is a great reservoir of talent and insight in the church, synagogue, and mosque that can be marshaled in the ongoing work of theology and ethics in the world. We have made a serious mistake by not calling on our physicists, economists, health professionals, business leaders, etc. and directing their gifts into the work of theology for the world. Could the day come again when the church would sponsor great art, music, architecture and also works of the mind—philosophy, political analysis, public ethics?

I suppose there has always been in me a desire for *Corpus Christianum*. I yearn for an era of vibrant faith that animates all aspects of culture—literature, the arts and, most of all, the decisional spheres of personal and public life.

In this regard, it was the spring of 1968 when I invited my other Hamburg professor Carl Friedrich von Weizsäcker to Houston to lecture. Weizsäcker had been a young physicist at Göttigen in the 1930s with Fermi, Heisenberg, Teller, Oppenheimer, et al. As a university student, he had asked the elder Heisenberg what he should do to study philosophy. Heisenberg replied "first, study physics." He did so, and became world renowned, both for his defense of the Kant-Laplace theory of the origin of the universe and for his work on heavy metals and nuclear principles. When the emigré Albert Einstein, also from this circle, learned of Weizsäcker's work and noted that his father was Hitler's ambassador to Denmark, he put two and two together: the Germans were building a bomb. In recent revelation surrounding Michael Frayn's play *Copenhagen*, he may have been right. This concern prompted the famous Einstein letter to Roosevelt and the resulting Manhattan Project—the beginning of the nuclear-military age.

While at Houston, I invited Weizsäcker to lecture at Rice under the auspices of physics chair Bud Rorschach. The work at this time in my career in physics, astrophysics, and theology is a thread I wish I had been able to continue, had not medicine become so all-consuming. Eventually, I would return to the interpenetration of theology and science. Weizsäcker lectured that day on "Creation in Theology and Physics," and drew on themes of his 1949 study with the University of Chicago Press, *The Unity of Nature (Die Einheit der Natur)*. My ideal of a thrilling seminar would be to have physicists and theologians read together Stephen Hawking's *A Brief History of Time* and Langdon Gilkey's *Maker of Heaven and Earth*.

That evening, we retired to the Rice University's Faculty Club on Fannin Street for a dinner hosted by Ken Pritzger, the university president. At about 9:00 p.m., our dinner was interrupted by word that Dr. Martin Luther King, Jr. had been shot in Memphis. There to support the garbage men's strike, he was resting on his motel veranda when he was shot and killed. The 1960s, such an age of promise, had ended in such devastating tragedy that year with the murders of Dr. King and Robert Kennedy. Weizsäcker, who had deep sympathies with Dr. King (he himself had been nominated for the Nobel Peace Prize), was deeply shocked with the rest of us. After dinner, he asked me to take him out to some of the black ghettos and shanty towns of Houston, where the grief was doubly poignant. With some of my black friends who were students at Texas Southern University, we sat on stoops around town well into the morning, sharing this deep grief and loss. Together we asked, "Where do we go from here?" I'm not sure if our society has ever recovered from that night. While the fires burned in Chicago, the politicians vowed to carry on his vision. But we remained numb and bewildered, and still are. Many social scientists see only regression on the racial front over those succeeding years.

I was on the road a lot during the late 1960s and early 1970s. A new age of ethical sensitivity about science and medicine grew out of the larger social awareness associated with the rapidly deteriorating environment, the civil-rights struggle, the Vietnam war, and the Women's movement. It seems that I was called on a lot by hospitals, colleges, and churches, especially around the South. I was often in Arizona, Arkansas, Georgia, Texas, and Oklahoma. Chicago, the east coast, and California had their own philosophers. I had established a personal association and an association in the public eye with cultural pioneers in Houston: Dr. DeBakey (later consulting on Boris Yeltsin's surgery in Moscow), John Glenn and other astronauts, and leaders of the petrochemical corporations. Their pioneering efforts created new theological and ethical questions and Vaux was often a commentator.

From the 1968 hearing before the Senate Health Committee—when you could count the country's bioethicists on one hand—to 1975, when it was a rapid growth industry, until 1993 when thousands called medical ethics their specialty, my life was defined by those questions. At the same time my own concerns were moving in three directions:

1. More lay involvement at the grassroots level, *e.g.*, nurse bioethicists.

2. Moving to fundamental questions in my own research, *e.g.*, the meaning of death and life.

3. Encouraging faith communities to articulate their beliefs and values in these matters (eventuating in the 20-volume series co-edited with Martin Marty on *Health and Medicine and the Faith Traditions*[21]).

M.D. ANDERSON HOSPITAL

A deeply formative part of the Houston experience was work I was able to do at M.D. Anderson Hospital. One of the world's half-dozen great cancer centers, Anderson pioneered many of the new treatments for tumors in the 1960s. Two scientist-physicians, Frei and Freireich developed multi-drug treatments for childhood leukemia, for example, that changed this once-hopeless and fatal situation into one where regular cures are expected.

I often engaged Jay Freireich in debate. This distinguished graduate of the University of Illinois in Chicago chafed against the atmosphere of law and ethics that developed just as miraculous cures were unfolding. Jay would have preferred completely unregulated research, no informed-consent criteria other than the doctor-patient relation, immediate access from animal lab testing into human beings, etc. I admired Freireich immensely and was able to argue and dialogue with him in mutual respect (Denton Cooley, on the other hand, saw me as a priest meddling with another Galileo—himself.) Freireich was a consistent proponent of a "pro-life" ethic. I remember in a M. L. King, Jr. "Breadbasket" march in 1967, I saw the two doctors, Frei and Freireich. He opposed abortion, and advocated crazy schemes like removing mammary glands from female babies with high genetic (familial) propensity to develop breast cancer. He adamantly insisted on treating malignancy aggressively with any new procedure; the rules and regulations, be damned!

21. See Marty and Vaux, *Health/Medicine and the Faith Traditions.*

JAN VAN EYS

When Jan Van Eys came from Vanderbilt, a new scientific and ethical excellence began at M.D. Anderson. Van Eys was also a distinguished scientist-physician. A neurologist-nutritionist with specialty in brain tumors, he became chair of pediatrics at Anderson, then at the University of Texas Medical School.

A serious theologian, Van Eys worked with me to develop a series of conferences and publications on ethics and pediatric cancer. We collaborated on church task forces and worked together to strengthen the Institute of Religion. Van Eys eventually sponsored a *Festschrift*, which I organized in honor of Paul Ramsey (and whose teaching post I eventually assumed at Garrett-Evangelical Theological Seminary).

Van Eys organized the Pediatrics Department at the University of Texas in Houston with the most participatory process I have ever seen. Patients and parents, nurses and social workers, doctors and pastors all collaborated in intensely involved team-care. The models of care for the dying that had been pioneered at Anderson a decade before by Dr. John Stehlin and Beatrix Cobb (the original source of Elisabeth Kübler-Ross' stages of dying) were now reactivated. There was a profound respect for research, cutting-edge therapy, human protection, and personal involvement—all undergirded by a deep spiritual and ethical sensibility.

Van Eys once involved me in the case of a patient, a teenaged boy from West Texas. The youth contracted Hodgkin's Lymphoma when it was still a usually fatal disease. His family did their grief work and came to terms with his imminent death. His friends and classmates also came to terms with the loss. Then, suddenly a new treatment brought him a remission and cure.

When I was consulted, Dr. van Eys was involved in a court case in a small West Texas town. The lad had returned home, his hair was gone, the kids thought he was infectious, and they had already given him up for dead. How dare he come back like this, uninvited? He was rejected at home, school, and community. In rage against a world that had saved his life, but not accepted his resurrection, he shot the sheriff— the representative of the world that had rejected him.

I remember at the time reading of the Lazarus syndrome in pediatric cancer, where a child unexpectedly comes back from the dead. In an article I wrote, I drew on Eugene O'Neill's troubling play, "Lazarus

Laughed." When Jesus comes up to Bethany on the south ridge of the mountain of Olives across from Jerusalem, he hears that his dear friend Lazarus (the brother of Mary and Martha) had died. The Bible story of the raising of Lazarus from that deep stone tomb (which you can still visit if you accept the early church tradition of place), is retold by O'Neill. But Lazarus is not welcomed back. In fact, he is taunted and hounded until he is finally chased back into the tomb—the Lazarus syndrome. The event may be the crux cause of Jesus' crucifixion.

The following essay illustrates the work done in M.D. Anderson. Laurie was a precious person who in teaching us about death and dying also taught us life and loving.

Laurie's Story:
Ethical and Religious Issues in Childhood Cancer

The opportunity to write this chapter is an outgrowth of my work as a consultant in medical ethics at M.D. Anderson's Hospital's Department of Pediatrics. For several years, Dr. Jan Van Eys, chairman of the department, and I sought different ways of considering moral and spiritual issues in the experience of patients, families, and caregivers. We planned conferences, published essays, convened patient and staff seminars, and agonized personally with one another. This distinguished center of pediatric oncology, where so many of the new treatment protocols were pioneered, has matured to the point that it has overcome the need for secrecy, inhibition, and defensiveness and has found the security to grapple with the profound psychosocial, moral, ethical, even theological, aspects of childhood cancer.

It was at M.D. Anderson Hospital that I met Laurie, a 14-year-old schoolgirl from Missouri who had come to the hospital for experimental treatment of head-neck tumor. Her courageous fight against cancer included several surgeries and multiple courses of radiotherapy and chemotherapy. A final effort to save her life involved the administration of 14 grams of methotrexate, one of the largest doses ever given to a human being. She was a devout Roman Catholic. Her experience with disease enabled her personally to appropriate that noble tradition's vision of the meaning of life and death. Her moral decision-making in the high-risk experimental therapeutics, along with her religious experience during this portion of her life, form the framework of this reflection.

When Laurie got into the car from her last ride from M.D. Anderson Hospital back to Missouri, she shouted, "Has your baby arrived yet? I hope she's a little girl." Our little Sara is now 3 years old. Those transpired years have given all of us time to assess the moral and spiritual lessons Laurie taught us.

"You ask me how people can help a person who has cancer and is dying," she wrote, "Well, lots of people really mean well. They say they are sorry and that's good, but sometimes people can be a real bother, especially if they feel sorry for you. That's just a sign they don't understand death and the real meaning of life."[22]

After presenting some background material. I shall discuss in turn the ethical and spiritual aspects of childhood cancer. In Laurie's experience and that of all of us, these elements intermingle to form the nucleus of what she calls "the meaning of life."

BACKGROUND

Thirty years ago, childhood cancer was considered one of the great, unsolved areas of medical knowledge and therapy. It was considered categorically a lethal disease unless a miracle intervened. Even if the anecdotal accounts of cure are believed, it is clear that miracles seldom occurred. Since the pediatric tumors seemed to have volatility and virulence that accomplished their morbid and mortal effects swiftly, affected persons saw themselves confronting inscrutable fate or divine will and hopelessness in terms of cure. The word cancer has been, and in many cases is, synonymous with death.

The last three decades have changed dramatically the phenomena of pediatric oncology therapeutics. We now talk of cures and of the truly cured child.[23] Perceptions and interpretations of the experience of cancer also have changed for children and their families.

In the first place, the age-old question, "What did I do to cause this?" has taken on new and frightening force. Questions now focus on: Was genetic transmission of an oncogene, or some inherited predisposition to develop cancer, my fault? Could I have done something about it, or was it a chance mutation outside of my control?

Laurie had transitional carcinoma of the head and neck. It began with a small nodule in the neck identical to one that had been successfully excised in her mother. What did the parents think about that occurrence? What did

---

22. Laurie's journal (unpublished), 9; Spinetta, *Living With Childhood Cancer*, 68.

23. See Van Eys, *The Truly Cured Child*.

Laurie think? The emerging cognizance of the heredity element in cancer has lifted the age-old theme of familial guilt into new prominence.

Then there is the question of environmental etiology. This also raises the issue of our own complicity, as it becomes clear that the air we breathe, the substances we eat and drink, and the habits we have developed may have carcinogenic effects. Why did we move near this chemical plant? If I had only fed the kids good and wholesome foods! Maybe we should have kept Johnny on dialysis and not agreed to a transplant, since the immuno-supression is now the cause of this malignancy.

Not only are feelings of guilt and responsibility heightened by our increased knowledge, but the moral quandaries are intensified. What had been called courageous resignation now may be seen as the sin of inaction. Now there is something to do, and that sustenance of a people throughout history, although sometimes tragic, provides a clue to the meaning of the human race. As Matthew Arnold said, "The Hebrews are the people who know the way the world is going." For the Christian, the psalm's meaning also is shown in the journey of Jesus to and through the crucifixion and resurrection.

How are the theological themes in the texts, scriptures, hymns, and prayers of church and synagogues relevant to the experience of children with cancer and to their families? Practically, the first level of meaning in childhood cancer is the level of common ministry: the priest, the prayer, and the thousand tokens of concern and benediction from the faith community.

Dealing with Pain and Suffering

One contribution of religion to childhood cancer is found in the endurance of pain and the interpretation of suffering. Close behind Dostoevsky's question in *The Brothers Karamazov*, "Why do little children have to suffer?" is the question, "Why is this happening to me?"

The following passage from Laurie's journal expresses her conceptual and practical struggle with this issue:

> One thing that helped me with the pain and not to complain was thinking about all the pain the Lord went through. It couldn't be one half the pain He went through all his life. He had so much criticism the same as some of us. He said if you can take this cup away from me do it (I said that too; either end this now or just get rid of it). He always had to fight for people even to understand who He really was. You really have to learn to send different messages to your

brain besides pain. At first that takes lots of effort, but if you put forth that effort early, it becomes easier later.[24]

Most religions attempt both to probe and to interpret the problem of pain. Many Eastern faiths stress the transience, even the unreality, of pain. The Western philosophies—Platonism, Epicureanism, and Stoicism—counseled responses of ecstasy, serenity, and self-control. Laurie, in the tradition of Roman Catholicism, focused reflection on Christ's *Via Dolorosa* as the meaning of her painful journey. To her, the anguish and accomplishment of the pain was found in its excruciating character. It crucified her life. This was her way of becoming pure and fresh and ready to meet her Lord.

The delightful note of distraction is found in the closing words of the passage. How remarkable this 14-year-old girl could so faithfully embrace and express the principal patterns of Catholic devotion. In mortification, one reflects on death in the midst of life. In vivification, one reflects on life in the midst of dying. The practical impact of this kind of diverted concentration is found in another passage:

> It was also important not to draw back and feel sorry for myself. There's always somebody who's worse off than you. That may be kind of hard to imagine, but it's true. I can have cancer and get it over with. Some people suffer for years and years. Some people are born retarded and all their life are shunned and shoved back by society, never being brought forward. Whenever I started to feel sorry for myself, I had a hell of a time coming back and being part of things.[25]

Both the daily transaction of the endurance of pain and the search for meaning in it are facilitated through religious experience. The injections, the nausea, and the pain— postoperative, chronic and acute, existential, social—are all manageable and are all drawn into some pattern of meaning through elements in one's religious experience.

DEATH AND DYING

The most significant religious issue that comes to bear on the experience of childhood cancer concerns death and immortality. Religious thanksgiving and hope foster anger and resistance to death, as well as acquiescence and resignation. People who view life as a gift from the creator cherish and relish life in themselves and in others. One clings to life, styles life in terms of

24. Laurie's journal (unpublished), 18.

25. Ibid., 14.

habits that will allow one to live long and well, and works to counter forces that cause disease and debilitate and destroy life. The mood of anger and resistance is born in the love of life. William Stringfellow speaks of resurrection being verified where resistance to the demonic thrives. The energies that resist death in the name of life range from immunological surveillance and salutary neurochemical impulses to commitment to build hospitals and fund biomedical research.

Religious faith also affects the way one receives death. Does one give oneself to experimental treatment protocols that may not be of personal benefit but may help others in the future? Does one look at the economic and social justice constraints in weighing decisions of life prolongation? Does one register a living will? How does one feel about resuscitation orders? All these dispositions are shaped by beliefs about death and what lies beyond death. Is dying a process of purification and maturation, or is it purposeless suffering? Is death itself a door or a wall? Is it the culmination, where people discover what life is about and have the opportunity to have their story placed in a divine perspective, or is it a dead end? One's religious worldview determines these perceptions and responses.

It is at this point that religion becomes not so much the handmaiden, but the adversary, of biomedical commitments. Theology critiques the position that death is univocal evil and that preservation of vitality is the overriding value. As Karl Barth has affirmed, faith stands against the idolatry of religion: the religion of technology, the religion of medicine, and the religion of religion.[26]

A rabbinic story tells of an old rabbi dying in an upstairs apartment. Inside the physicians struggle to prolong his life. He is ready for the world beyond. Outside, his congregation prays to hold off death. Finally, he pushes the doctors aside and goes to the window, and drops a flower pot on the praying faithful, shattering Goethe's diabolical yearning that this space-time life moment endure. He returns to his bed and dies.

The paradox of loving and relishing life and yearning for death as release is commonly experienced in cancer care. Laurie's reflections might sound morbid and suicidal if her gusto for life were not taken into account.

> Death is a joyous occasion—something beautiful. I am where we'll all be. If He made this world this beautiful, what must it be like to be there? We should all think about that before it happens. The biggest goal in my life right now is to get out of here. Jesus is like a goal to

---

26. See Barth, *Church Dogmatics*.

me, a leader, someone to look up to, someone I want to be like. I'm anxious to meet Him.

Facing death is like facing marriage. You have to be willing to communicate with the doctor or whoever is there. Sometimes you don't have a big choice about who you talk to. But if you don't communicate you'll have a lot of trouble in dealing with life; you'll find yourself in a bind lots of times. If you don't ask questions to find out things, you'll always be wondering and not be able to learn. Doctors and family have no right to keep anything from you. When you are sick or dying, tell people. Because you'll find out how many there are who care, more than you can ever imagine, people who you thought would never concern themselves. They often become your truest friends.[27]

Laurie dealt with the daily chores, the daily challenges. She instructed all of us who knew her in wisdom and faith. She lived tenaciously, hoped incessantly that she would get better, but ultimately was ready to leave this world.

There is a spirit of weariness of this world and yearning for the next in much religion. Our faith traditions also sanctify this time and space and dignify this life. The secret wisdom of all faiths is the serenity that is power, the release that is replenishment, the dying that is life.

He who seeks to save his life, he will lose it. He who loses his life for my sake will find it (Matt 10.39).

As the years went on, there were fewer and fewer dramatic cancer cures, more and more sobriety about the ambivalence of our progress. Van Eys spearheaded the work of the ethics committee at Anderson and U. of Texas, helping to develop an institutional process that has become a model around the country. Upon retirement back to Nashville, Van Eys has made a major commitment to help develop the Ethics Center at Garrett-Evangelical Theological Seminary. Active Methodist laypeople, Jan and Catherine Van Eys, whose son is a Methodist pastor, are trustee-leaders of the center. We have together assembled major conferences and *Festschriften* on two ethicists with whom we often worked in Houston: Paul Ramsey and Joe Fletcher. They also devoted untiring energy to the healthcare ministries of the Methodist Church.

27. Laurie's journal (unpublished), 2, 7.

My three teachers and mentors in ethics were Helmut Thielicke, Paul Ramsey, and Joe Fletcher. Each of these three gentlemen exerted profound influence on my theological ideas, on the ethical themes and problems I was drawn to, and to my personal faith and well-being.

HELMUT THIELICKE

Helmut Thielicke, my *Doktorvater* in Hamburg, was immensely gracious in accepting me as a student in 1966 and in sponsoring a rather *avant garde* piece of work on "Cybernetics and Conscience." He influenced me most in two ways: his person and the scope of his thought. He was a preacher-theologian. All of his life, he sought to combine the pastoral and homiletical dimension of faith with the work of systematic theology and social ethics. He loved people. He always sought to be near the common folk in the crises and challenges of their lives. Although my career has been confined more to the academy, I have always emulated his synthetic ministry and have sought to be involved in the church, in the clinic, in the city. If the reader will take this immodest remark with some reservation, I've always wished I could be a preacher-pastor theologian like Luther or Calvin. The ideal life for me would be to completely integrate those responsibilities, as Calvin did in Strasbourg and Geneva, Barth at Safenwil, Niebuhr at Detroit. The range of Thielicke's interests—in medicine, technology, the arts, literature, politics, sports, etc.—have found a dilettante *chez moi*.

PAUL RAMSEY

Paul Ramsey took me under his wing when I returned from studies with Thielicke. Paul knew that I had no sponsor or academic contacts in this country and, since each of our interests gravitated toward medicine in the late 1960s, we found ourselves involved in many common tasks: the "Who Shall Live" conference in 1968, the founding of The Hastings Institute, involvement in the Karen Quinlan case, etc. The fact that Paul began his teaching career in the classrooms, where I now ply the trade, is great challenge and constant inspiration. It is a great honor to present a *Festschrift* for him, which includes his final writings in bioethics.[28]

28. See Vaux, Vaux, and Stenberg, *Covenants of Life*.

JOE FLETCHER

Joe Fletcher was a particularly dear and kind friend and associate. He also came down to the Houston "Who Shall Live" conference in 1968. As I write this, Dr. DeBakey, who supported our conference and wrote the foreword to the book *Who Shall Live*, is consulting surgeon in Moscow as they perform a multiple bypass operation on Russian President Boris Yeltsin. This feat of the 85-year-old pioneer heart surgeon recalls an incident in 1968. Mike DeBakey was called to the (then) Soviet Union to perform aortic surgery on the Director of the Soviet Academy of Science. When he returned, an irate Texas right-winger chided DeBakey for not killing the high official on the operating table while he had the chance. DeBakey was speechless, but asked me to formulate a response. I traced for him the doctrine (Hippocratic, Hebraic, and Christian) of not using the art for retaliation or political purpose, but rather seeing the medical and operative (surgical) occasion as a kind of sanctuary in which the sick one is protected. When a doctor treats the fleeing John Wilkes Booth after Abraham Lincoln's assassination, or when M.A.S.H. doctors in Vietnam treat the Viet Cong captive, they exhibit this non-discriminative quality of moral medicine.

Joe Fletcher was a renegade from cover to cover. My publication of his personal diary captures this spirit.[29] Joe was the first American (with Gordon Allport) to be hauled before McCarthy's House Committee on Un-American Activities. His life was characterized by controversy and confrontation.

From un-American activities, to pioneering business ethics, to radical and provocative bioethics, to the maddening and liberating "situation ethics," Fletcher always was the calm and gentle eye of a whirling storm. His collegiality, warm support and, above all, constant reminder ("Ken, you're the only theologian trying to remain one while doing secular bioethics—keep it up!") follow me to this day.

One of our many joint appearances was in Geneva in the 1970s for a conference of the World Health Organization on "The Ethics of Vaccines and Biologicals." As the world project of eliminating smallpox was coming to a conclusion, the conference was asked to develop moral guidelines for the use of various prophylactic substances to prevent diseases. We talked about childhood vaccinations around the world. We pondered norms for

29. See Fletcher, *Joseph Fletcher*.

the commonplace and exotic inoculations for a variety of diseases and frontier substances that might prevent viral diseases, such as those which would appear ten years later in the AIDS epidemic. It was the inspiration of this pioneering panel (including the Ministers of Health of most countries in the world) that led me to convene a meeting on HIV at the University of Illinois in 1981, some time before most realized that there was a problem with AIDS.

Fletcher and I proved to be a good team. He was the innovator open to radically new insight. I was the interpreter and, in some ways, champion of the heritage of ethics (Hippocratic, Hebraic, Hellenic, Christic). My system was steeped in normative insistence, his in exuberant situational freedom.

We both commended strong social conscience and concern for the weak and poor, especially children. While my emphasis was on informed consent and human rights, he was a strong advocate of innovation, risk, even (to my surprise) hurting some few to help the many. Fletcher, for example, supported (with his friend Garrett Hardin) the vaccination program of Mao Tse Tung's China, which gave biologicals to all citizens, to two effects: killing 50,000 persons and instantly transforming the public health of the most populous nation on Earth.

I still have on my desk a book on each of these persons. The Thielicke theological biography languishes for lack of a publisher after Word Press (which commissioned it in the *Makers of the Modern Mind* series) went out of business. A 500-page *Festschrift* on Paul Ramsey is available, and the Joe Fletcher volume was published by Westminster John Knox.

CHURCH COMMISSIONS: HOMOSEXUALITY IN THE PRESBYTERIAN CHURCH

The unique experiences I was privileged to learn in the corridors of M.D. Anderson and Baylor, of the Rehabilitation Institute and Ben Taub (Harris County) Hospital were quickly recognized as an asset to the church. I was invited to lecture on theology and medicine at the Institute of Church and University in Frankfurt, Germany. I was invited to dialogue with Hermann Kahn of the Hudson Institute in Florence, Italy. The most challenging service, however, was on the church commissions (NCC and WCC) and on two task forces of my own denomination, the United Presbyterian Church in the U.S.

In 1976, the one and only time I have been a commissioner to the General Assembly of our church, I was appointed to the study commission to advise the General Assembly on the ordination of "avowed, practicing" homosexual persons to the ministry. The Presbytery of New York City was confronted with this challenge and asked the church in General (annual) Assembly for advice.

The Presbyterian Church, which has given the Western nations the model of democratic and representative political assembly, meets each year with an equal number of laypersons and clergy to adjudicate matters of all of the fury, controversy, compromise and lobbying that we have come to dread and enjoy in the parliaments of Western Europe and the Congress of the United States. All these are patterned in one way or another after John Calvin's Geneva (and English Puritans' London) model of deliberation and adjudication of issues.

This commission of 17 persons (scientists, theologians, laity, etc.) worked hard for two years, held hearings across the country, and struggled through to a final report that was one of the finest pieces of theological work by a Christian denomination ever produced. The Blue Book (1978) was distributed in half a million copies and studied assiduously around the country. We examined in detail the data from biology, medicine, and psychiatry. We considered the social, legal, cultural, and ecclesiastical factors and ramifications. Above all, we committed ourselves as Christians to surface the biblical, historical, theological, ethical, and pastoral themes that pertained to this volatile subject.

As with most biomedical issues (if this really is one), it is extremely complex and pretty much impervious to satisfying resolution. Even now, almost 30 years after this task force, our church and others (Methodist, Episcopal, Lutheran, and others) are no closer to resolution of the issue than they were then. It is a classic quandary of an issue that involves facts and values. Homosexuality is a biological condition characterized by certain genetic, biochemical, psychological, and behavioral components that, as of now, are only imperfectly known, described, and understood.

Homosexuality is also shaped by sociological, familial, and cultural forces. Are these able to alter the biological condition? No one knows. The theological underlay of these issues is even more conflicted. On the one hand, religion commends compassion and understanding for all manner of persons. The Christian tradition, in particular, has had a most diverse history with reference to matters of human sexuality. It has extolled the ministries of women even in highly patriarchal settings. Celibacy and marriage have been seen as noble vocations. Homosexuals have exerted important ministries for centuries.

On the other hand, Christianity stands with Judaism and Islam in the Abrahamic-Mosaic tradition with its strong traditions of sexual responsibility, family obligation, discontinence of *porneia* in any form (sexual activity apart from marriage), and emphasis on the procreative and unitive purposes of the love between men and women.

The process of study undertaken by our commission severely amplified my cynicism about the church when it functions as it then had, at its worst. As the 1978 General Assembly in San Diego approached, I was aware that not only was the expected lobbying and pamphleteering going on, there was an even more insidious process underway. Many members of the Presbyterian Church, especially on the right and left wings of the denomination, do not believe in Democratic process. They feel that guerilla tactics and coercive manipulations are required. That year delegate commissioners were chosen for G.A., not in their rotation schedule or on their record of service, but on how they promised to vote on the "homosexuality" issue. Persons whose turn had come to be a commissioner were turned down in Presbytery votes (if they favored "gay" ordination in most of the country and if they were against in the "city" Presbyteries). This violation of due process and mutual respect so "turned me off" that I didn't return to the issue (except an abortive reappearance in 1992) until a couple of years ago.

Moral reflection on homosexuality turns on the basic motif of this diary, of whether the evangelical and the ethical, or the ecclesial and the secular are separate, coterminous and always in tension, or simultaneous realms. Take the Decalogue, for example: Is this a universal or a parochial mandate? Is Israel alone, or is the Christian community as well covenanted to the law? Is there a generic and universal ethic that can be derived from the peculiar and particular dispensation to Israel and the church?

The Polish filmmaker Krzysztof Kieslowski argues "yes." In one interpretation of his work, he moves after the Decalogue to the films *Red*, *White* and *Blue* (*Liberté*, *Egalité*, *Fraternité*) to address secular moral principles that are "closer to the common life" of people. In a similar way, secular (or religiously pluralistic) societies have sought to ground public ethics in these general humanistic principles.

On the matter of homosexuality, for example, the issue is not, it is argued, to be placed within the biblical realm of *porneia*, idolatry, cleanliness, purity, even the relation to God or any such religious context. It is a matter of personal liberty, freedom of expression, perhaps "do no harm" in terms of medical or civil damages, but largely a matter of private choice. At this point early in the 21st century, much of society, especially in Europe and North America, full civil rights and domestic partnerships have gained acceptance.

We still have some tension between the different ways of looking at concrete moral issues. In some sense, the evangelical impulse is not conservative at all. It is exuberant in its freedom. It may be, therefore, in profound tension with the ethical impulse, which tends to be definitive, nomian, and conservative. More generally in this diary, I am searching for a synthesis, a concerted expression of what I am calling the evangelical (the gospel call to faith) and the ethical (living faith out in responsible action in the world). There is no doubt that a lively, evangelical faith community is to be found within the gay community. Edward O. Wilson ventures the thought in several of his writings that homosexual persons traditionally served as priests and Shamans because of the freedom from family obligation entailed in their vocation along with an inherent spirituality, perhaps honed by their peculiar sexuality and their martyrical social existence.

In any case, the reader will note a change of perspective in my recent writings. Several facts have nudged my mind toward acceptance and affirmation of ordination and ecclesial celebration of unions.

- The homosexual community will always be a part of the human community. It will not be converted away. If anything, it will increase in this complicated, congested, city-culture that is our future.

- Homosexual persons are experiencing calls into ministry.

- Chaste, monogamous partnership is necessary for the community's survival in the age of the AIDS pandemic.

BABY DAVID

The saga of David is a memorable part of our Houston sojourn. The issue had gone on for almost 15 years when a correspondence in the *Journal of the American Medical Association* accused me of endorsing unethical human experimentation. It began in the early 1970s, shortly after we came to Houston. David was born in the heyday of biotechnology and abundant cash. From the dawn of time until 1971, all babies born with the disease SCID (Severe Combined Immune Deficiency) looked healthy at birth, but after their mothers' still-circulating immune bodies (white cells, etc.) wore off, the child became infected from the omnipresent bacterial ocean that surrounds us all, inside and out, and soon died. This had happened to an older brother born to David's parents. When David's mom became pregnant again, they asked their doctor if anything could be done. They were told to first have an amniocentesis to check if the baby was a girl, if so everything was okay since this disease appears only in male children. It was a boy. Now they had two choices. They could abort (an option morally unconsidered because of their Roman Catholic faith) or they could pursue the other option. They chose that course.

From here, the saga is well known from the television documentary and the movie with John Travolta as the grown David. He was delivered into a bubble—a germ-free environment—and he stayed there until the very end of his 12½-year life. Now, new genetic knowledge and therapy may cure the disease.

The following essay, written at the time of his death, recounts the experience.

Seeing Hope in a Bubble Boy

Chicago Tribune, March 9, 1984

Child of the pure, unclouded brow
And dreaming eyes of wonder!
Though time be fleet, and I and thou
Are half a life asunder,
Thy loving smile will surely hail
The love-gift of a fairy tale.[30]

---

30. Lewis Carroll, *Through the Looking Glass: What Alice Found There* (New York: Harper & Brothers, 1902), iii.

My friend David died the other night. He was a living experiment. Since his birth 12½ years ago on September 21, 1971, until very recently, he lived in a germ-free bubble.

I remember when he was born. Gnotobiologist Dr. Raphael Wilson had constructed a germ-free capsule in which he was placed at birth. Dr. Wilson is a Holy Cross brother and one of the most distinguished germ-free scientists in the world. He was David's closest friend for the first years of his life. They shared the same faith tradition. Even David's communion wafers had to be sterilized.

David once told me he hoped to be a priest, the influence of Dr. Wilson, no doubt. A good vocation, I thought to myself. A priest is in some sense sealed off as David was from this toxic world. A priest must live in a fish bowl. A priest lives a mortifying existence, preparing for death.

David was a living experiment in his plastic house. He looked out on us. We looked in on ourselves. Yes, David was and is a priest. He was a living showcase.

The saga began because of the interplay of medical power and a faith tradition. David's brother, like all children with SCID, had died some years before. Severe combined immunological deficiency is an X-linked genetic disease transmitted from mother to son. Those who have the disease cannot resist infections with either arm of their immunological system. Both the thymus-mediated resistance (T-cells that provide cellular immunity) and the bone marrow fighters (B-cells that provide humoral antibodies) are impotent. This brother died when he was several months old, when maternal immunity wore off and he became susceptible to infection.

The experience tipped off David's parents. "How can we avoid this happening again?" they asked their doctors. They could avoid becoming pregnant, or they could adopt a child. Their Catholic consciences were troubled by the contraception proposal. "Is there any way we could try to have another baby?" they asked. Doctors could do an amniocentesis during pregnancy to determine if the fetus were a boy; if so, the child has a 50 percent chance of being affected and the parents could choose to abort. But what if the baby is normal? Again, qualms of conscience. There was one other option, but it was risky and expensive.

It was 1971, the age of national affluence, of the National Institute of Health, NASA, and the Texas oil boom. The blush of biomedical intrigue and confidence was high. Why can't we save this life? Let's take a chance; maybe we can get him through.

A living experiment. Some felt that making the baby an involuntary guinea pig was unjustified. The child certainly had no opportunity to consent to the experiment in the first place. These recent months, he could be seen pounding on the walls of his bubble. He wanted to come out. He opted for the marrow transplant.

I assume his caretakers explained the implications of this choice clearly to him. I was recently asked to monitor informed consent with a young girl who required a bone-marrow transplant to save her from death by Fanconi's aplastic anemia. "Do you understand the picture?" I asked. "Yes," replied the girl's street-wise young husband. "It's like we're driving our car down the highway. A semi is barreling towards us. We will either swerve and be safe, or we'll be smashed to smithereens." A pretty good understanding of the risks and benefits of bone-marrow graft and graft-versus-host reaction, I thought. While David did not consent to the experiment's start, as Barney Clark did, he was given the option to discontinue the experiment.

Raphael, the doctor, was David's soul brother. I remember one afternoon he and I went in to see David. This was shortly after another doctor and the psychiatric staff came to the conclusion that personality autism might set in if there weren't more touch and contact for David.

"Ken, take these gloves." David pointed to big rubber gloves attached to the side of the bubble. "Now, hold me," he said, and we wrestled for a few minutes. He never knew skin touch, with all the meaning that entails, until the waning days of his life, when his mother was able to hold and kiss him at last.

As an ethicist thinking about medical situations, I am fascinated with our fascinations. Why did we peer with such intense interest for 12 years into the looking glass with the smiling, bouncing boy inside? Why the *Nova* documentary? The John Travolta movie? Was it hope on our part that he was the first immortal? He was never sick a day in his life, not even with a common cold—that is, until the marrow graft from his sister triggered the uncontrolled B-cell growth in the intestines, the fevers, bleeding, pulmonary and pericardial edema that eventually choked his breathing and sent his heart into terminal arrhythmia. Had he stayed behind glass, he might have lived forever, at least if the thesis is valid that all disease is caused by some eternal, environmental trigger, toxin, virus, or the like.

David caused us to look at our own mortality and fragility. In a sense, we are all fragile bubbles floating on a precarious and tumultuous sea. The auto accident, the divorce, the loss of a job, the lump in the belly or breast can shatter us in a moment.

In another sense, David was a precursor of the dawning age of medical genetics. We are approaching an age when we will be able to know much about a person before he or she is born. We can discover the sex of children on the way to being born; we can uncover diseases that can be treated either by fetal therapy or by eliminating the bearer of the disease. What will we do when we can see whether the baby on the way will develop breast cancer when she is 40 or heart disease when he is 50 or schizophrenia when he is 60?

David was a harbinger of this new age of completely rationalized birth. We now have impressive controls over when, how, and of what kind our offspring will be. It is a new age of eugenics, the craving for good birth, fully understood, planned, programmed. Yet life in its mystery defies us. Who are we to say that this is undesirable and abnormal, that that is beautiful and gracious? How do we know that sickness is not health, that death is not life?

Most poignantly, David's life expressed our hope, hope for a world that will one day be free from war, injury, disease. This is why we gladly spent more than $1 million on David's care.

David, we can no longer look in on you. Do you still look on us dimly through that dark glass? Or do you see all now face to face?

When my friend and then colleague, Ray Lawrence, a chaplain at St. Luke's Texas Children's Hospital raised the issue later of my complicity in this unconsented human experimentation, I was taken aback. There was truth in Ray's point. David came into this world like each of us—without giving his permission. As Heidegger reminded us, we are all cast into a traumatic existence without ever having given consent to life. David's career was even more complicated since his parents (with all of us family, friends, and consultants) made decisions for him. Quite early in his life, as I recall, when he was 5 or 6, he was taken on as a partner in all decisions and the final judgment of whether to try a marrow graft and come out of the bubble was, in many ways, left to him. As the essay contends, I have always seen David's story as a human epic of hope against the constant force of failure and finitude. That babies now born with SCID are treated—and survive—is testimony to this brave pioneer.

A general reflection about health and illness comes to mind as I reflect on David's story. I have always projected a heroism on patients, holding that their experience not only helps us learn things to help future patients (a strong theme in Emil Freireich's and the general M.D. Anderson ethic), but that their ordeals/adventures are purposive in an even deeper sense than the pragmatic.

My theology of pioneering humanity, where resurrection and life are the yield of righteousness, suffering, and sacrifice, is found developed in my book *Jew, Christian, Muslim.*[31] Here *Akedah* becomes the interpretive paradigm for the human project. In one essay that I offered to a National Alzheimer's Conference, I spoke of persons afflicted with that disease as pioneers of a new humanity. In the early 21st century, we have exposed the human family to a new range of diseases if only because of our elimination of older diseases, like infection. Persons who go out on to those horizons go there both for and because of us. In my present thinking, they are Abrahamic or *Akedic* pioneers. Their experience is vicarious. The human vocation of coming into this world, living, suffering, experiencing illness, and dying transpires under the grace and justice of God (Ps 90). God, I believe, gives to each person and to the human family a purposive destiny. Nothing that happens to any one of us is absurd. Quite the contrary: every experience and burden that any one of us receives at the hands of life is fathomed and ennobled by the life giving Savior in whom "all things work together for good" (Rom 8:28) and that "in all things we are more than conquerors through him who loved us so that neither death nor life . . . nor things present or things to come, nor powers, nor height, nor depth, nor anything else in all creation will be able to separate us from the love of God . . ." (Rom 8:35ff.).

Early works (*This Mortal Coil: The Meaning of Health and Disease*), mid-career works (*Health and Medicine in the Reformed Tradition*) and recent works (*Being Well, Dying Well*) are, in addition to *Jew, Christian, Muslim*, works in which I have explored these ideas.

THE INSTITUTE OF RELIGION

The Institute had begun in the early 1950s, as a religious presence in the burgeoning Texas Medical Center. At first, it supplied chaplaincy programs in a few of the hospitals, offered continuing education events for clergy and health professionals, and gave some lectures to the nurses in training. By 1978, this great medical center had two medical schools, five nursing colleges, each with excellent programs in medical ethics and humanities, and 12 hospitals, all of which had formidable programs in pastoral care and training. The Institute, like fluoridated water for dentistry, had worked itself out of a job. In my view, the only future for the Institute

31. See Vaux, *Jew, Christian, Muslim*.

would be to become an excellent, high-level center for work in theology and medicine. This vision had little appeal to the laypersons from religious congregations who were her body of support. Time to move on.

But with great thanksgiving! No human being in the fourth decade of his life and the first of his career ever had such encouragement, such support. Every bold idea and expansive program was enthusiastically received.

Jean and Dominique de Menil are one example. I came to know them when I was offering a course in religion at St. Thomas University as an adjunct professor. The de Menils had built had built an outstanding center of art and art history in Houston, in part centered at St. Thomas. The Philip Johnson architecture (eventually the Rothko Chapel) exemplified their grand vision. When some controversy arose at St. Thomas, the de Menils decided to transfer their artistic interests to Rice and their religious concerns to the Institute of Religion. I was then acting director and Jean and Dominique asked me what was needed. The brash 30-year old said calmly, "five chairs." "How much?" they asked. "Half a million to endow each," I said. "You've got it." As I staggered out of their lovely *Rue San Filipe* home with the accoutrements of the Paris XVI, I was not sure what I had gotten myself into. After trips to the North, Chicago (John McKenzie), Pittsburgh (George Tavard), New York (Raymond Brown), and even Europe (various French, Dutch and German divines), I realized that no one would come to Houston even with a well-funded chair, when we didn't have a library, students, an existing faculty, etc. The enthusiasm of support and the ethos of those imaginative propensities, sometimes verging on the megalomaniacal, was *magnifique*. One lasting regret I have about Houston is that, despite magnificent support, we were not able to build a permanent center of religion commensurate with the medical megalopolis that today stands as the Texas Medical Center. Surgery, yes! Ecumenical theology, no!

CHICAGO

The summer of 1978 seemed an appropriate time (if ever) to leave Houston. The offer to assume the Davis Professorship in Ethics at the University of Illinois College of Medicine in Chicago was inviting, even compelling. Two experiences in the transition deserve sharing. When the invitation to interview in Chicago came, we had all the stock prejudices towards the city. This was the town of Al Capone and the great Mafia intrigues of the 1920s through the 1950s. The film *The Sting* captured the ethos. Therefore, I was surprised one evening to hear President Jimmy Carter extolling the city of "Broad Shoulders" (Carl Sandburg). Even with customary political rhetoric (toward Mayor Richard Daley, Sr.), his words seemed overdrawn: I am happy to be here in the best-run city in the nation (OK, we know the ward spoils system, "vote early and often," etc. . . . but then . . .) and also the most beautiful city in America (now that was too much!).

Until we drove into town that warm autumn evening, came north from Hyde Park along Lake Shore Drive and saw that magnificent panorama of architecture jutting out into Lake Michigan. We then learned what we later realized about a lot of things: Jimmy Carter most often had it right.

The time was right. Keith was ready to start high school and the younger children could make a smooth transition at that point. Sara's parents, Dr. and Mrs. Bert Anson, were still strong in their mid-70s and it would be good to be near their Muncie, Indiana home. I think I had given about all I could to Houston. Trying to stabilize the Institute of Religion was particularly challenging, so with gratitude, we bid *adieu*.

So as fall chill descended in 1978, we found ourselves living in a mammoth Chicago home designed by either distant relation Calvert Vaux (designer with F.L. Olmsted) of Central Park or, more likely, William Le Baron Jenney. The second transition experience has to do with the Jenney mansion at 84 Riverside Road in Riverside, Illinois.

I visited the Medical School of the University of Illinois on a frigid December day in 1977. Dean Bill Overholt, my host, arranged an exciting agenda of meetings with a range of colleagues from the health professions and university humanities who were doing excellent work. Whether it was the cold or dark, I still was not excited. As I set to return to Houston, I decided to divert my way to O'Hare airport through Riverside, since I knew that Vaux and Olmsted had designed this "first planned suburb in the United States." After the Chicago fire in 1871, there was a need for an in-close suburb for business leaders of the city. The New York team was commissioned. Riverside possessed a haunting beauty on that icy winter day, even to this Texas preacher without a warm coat.

Our kids, almost all born in, but all raised in Houston, had for the most part never seen snow. We did have a crocus-like blizzard one

February, which brought Houston to a standstill. I remember the day, because medical students built snowmen around Baylor Med School and Methodist hospital all with Jimmy Durante-shaped "schnozzes" that unmistakably meant Dr. DeBakey. It was the day that Richard Nixon's "wanted" list of political enemies was published in the *New York Times*. There between Carol Channing and Daniel Ellsberg was Michael DeBakey. We were all extremely proud of him finding a place among these *persona non grata* in Washington. We believe it was for his stand supporting the Kennedy-Mills Health Plan, a bit too socialistic for the president with such fragile rectitude.

I stopped by a realtor on Burlington Road and asked about housing in the village. The realtor asked my name and she gasped, "You won't believe this but we have a Calvert Vaux home about to go on the market." She showed me the noble structure, and I fell in love with it. Over the protests of Sara and her justified fears of endless dusting in the *grande maison*, we decided to look favorably on the University of Illinois, Chicago, and Riverside. In August of 1978, we trekked north from Texas as Cornelia Earhart Anson (Sara's mom) and her family had done 50 years earlier.

My work now moved into a clearly structured, highly professionalized mode. I felt none of the medical hostility that I knew in Houston at the dawn of the bioethics era. By now, lots of people were working in the field, and it had developed into a well-developed and well-defined discipline. We now had two major national centers in bioethics—Hastings in New York and Kennedy at Georgetown. I had been privileged to be in on the foundation of both programs. I was officed in the department of surgery and affiliated with the Department of Medicine. The strong recommendation of Tony Gotto M.D., chief of cardiology, then chair of medicine at Baylor (now Dean at Cornell), did much to get my work off to a credible start.

Ruy Lournço, the Chair of Medicine, was most gracious in his support of everything I proposed. He made me a section-chief, asked me to come to morning report, where residents reported cases on the floor, and invited me to occasionally present ethics grand rounds. The remarkable colleagues at University of Illinois—Truman Anderson, Stan Schade, Bill McGuire, Neal Kurzman, Amurat Vidyasagar, Tapas Das Gupta, Lloyd Nyhus, Olga Jonnassen, and others—made the work a delight. I often remember trudging through the snow as dusk settled south into that no-man's land that is Chicago's West Side to my parking place on Roosevelt

Street, feeling so thankful that I had the chance to serve here. I loved the patients, who often represented the poorest of Chicago's poor; the nurses who, with Helen Grace, Myra Levine, Bev McElmurry, Olga Church, and others pioneered a new strength and involvement into American medicine; the students and the residents—so bright, so committed!

DEATHICS

One of my colleagues in Chicago, medical historian Norm Gevitz, suggested the term *Deathics* for the title of my book. Many of the cases and themes that engaged my heart and mind during those good years were matters of terminal care. While still in Houston, I had been called to consult in the Karen Quinlan case in New Jersey. At the University of Illinois, I was always drawn in on the transplantation and termination of care decisions. Long before Kevorkian, I became known as "Dr. Death." I usually counseled the acceptability of "letting go" when this was the will of the patient and family. In the cases of babies, I often counseled stopping treatment. Typically, I sided with the nurses who found "life prolongation" measures with imperiled newborns morally problematic.

This concentration of work is not surprising, since death issues are the major way that medical and theological concerns intertwine. But I was somewhat surprised to find myself engaged so deeply in these issues, since my death-phobias were as strong as those of any physician. This became clear when I needed to attend my own grandmother, as she was dying in her small home in the Pennsylvania hills that had meant so much to me as a youth. She was dying with congestive heart and lung failure and went to bed for the last time some months before her death. She had made it clear that she didn't want to be hauled out in an ambulance or be confined to a hospital or nursing home. Although I never discussed euthanasia with her, she found ethical offense in the supposed "hastening" of death in Pap's parents over in St. Petersburg. On the other hand, she did not believe in prolonging the dying process, and she strongly affirmed her own autonomy and right to stay at home. In this rural area, I don't think she ever had contact with a physician. The local doctors were all osteopaths. This first exposure to osteopathy led me to the profound respect I've always had for this alternative path to medical training.

What came hard for me in her dying was the awkwardness of being a grandson and pastor. Starting in college and during seminary, I was called on to say grace at the table. I was both honored and embarrassed. Now, as a young pastor-teacher, I felt it appropriate to gather the family around her bed whenever we were there, for scripture, song, and prayer. Was this fear of death deep in the subconscious? Was it just my reluctance to own my faith within the family circle? Beneath the pastoral serenity, the forceful scriptures and prayers, the seeming confidence of Christ's resurrection, power over death, was there a disbelief and denial? When I conducted Grammy Shoup's funeral, my mother said that I approached it somewhat impersonally, and I wonder why? I remember that some family and locals wanted to keep the casket open for the service. I insisted on closing it—perhaps too dramatically—before the service began. In any case, a familiarity with death would soon be a major aspect of my career.

To date, I have written or edited 23 books and more than 100 articles and essays. At least half of these publications pertain to death and dying. I, therefore, always appreciate the counsel of Sara and our kids, "Dad, get more with life and living! Get a life!"

At the outset of reflection on the topic, let me share with you a meditation on the subject I offered at a church in Houston. It states in stark terms the rather high Christology of death I have.

THE DEATH OF CHRIST

For the Christian, the death of Christ, or rather the death/resurrection event, is the clue to the meaning of all that is. This crucial and excruciating moment—a young Palestinian hanging on a crude tree outside the wall of Jerusalem during the administration of Pontius Pilate—is an event that speaks to faith about the enigma of life. Why do the planets whirl in space? Why do the azaleas bloom in the spring? What is my destiny? What are my life and death all about? *Crucifixus est pro nobis* (he was crucified for us).

First, a starting point, a presupposition on which the following analysis will be built. With the gospel of John, Paul the Apostle, and Martin Luther, I make two faith assumptions. They concern the relation of God to Jesus and the centrality of the crucifixion to the Christ event. (1) Jesus is God's word, he is *Logos tou Theou*. "The Word was with God, the Word was God, the Word (meaning of the cosmos) became a person and pitched his tent with us" (John 1:14). God made the world through Jesus Christ (Col 1:16 ff). Indeed, God was in Jesus reclaiming the world to Himself (2 Cor 5:19). In the language of the Apocalypse, He is the "Lamb slain from the foundation of the Earth" (Rev 13:8). Luther puts it more bluntly. Jesus is *Gekreuzigte Gott* (God crucified). Paul summarizes this view in the Corinthian correspondence, when he boldly claims *Logos tou Theou* (2 Cor 2:7) is *Logos tou staurou* (1 Cor 1:18). The Word of God is the word of the Cross. God is crucified. Reality is cruciform. The death of Christ is the meaning of all that is and all that happens. His death is the interpretative paradigm of space and time, of nature and history.

Six brief statements draw out the implications of this central notion. They contend in turn that Christ's death is the meaning of (1) creation; (2) nature's evolution; (3) Israel; (4) the rise and fall of nations (that is, of world history); (5) the nature of one's being; (6) one's destiny in time (that is, death).

Creation. This planet and solar system that is our home is billions of years old. Whether formed in a big bang or in slow evolution of life forms from organic and inorganic structures, it is being fashioned within some process of death and renewal. We find in creation a cosmic agony, the meaning of which can only be fathomed in the cross, a paradigm of cosmic death and resurrection. Creation speaks to us of death and resurrection. Conversely, the death of Christ is seen as a cosmic event. The moment of Christ's death shattered Earth and sky as the evangelists saw it. Paul listens to nature's groaning and travail in Romans 8. Like the howl of the wind, the thunder of the oceans, all nature quakes in death throes yielding redemptive birth. The world is brought into being with divine intention. It has meaning because of the Creator who means it. It is becoming something. It is going somewhere. All its *telos*, its purpose, is signified in the death of Christ. The structure and process of the world, wrote Teilhard de Chardin, "resembles nothing so much as the Way of the cross."

Nature's Evolution. Christ's death is the meaning of nature's evolution. The solar system is evolving within the universe. This Earth is a sea of shifting plates, moving to and fro, throwing up land out of the sea, great cleavages, faults, and ridges. The biosphere, the circle of living beings is evolving. Subtle transformations are going on within the web of life. Seasons come and go, seed time and harvest, and nature reconstitutes itself. The hour has come for the Son to be glorified. Unless a grain of wheat falls into the Earth and dies, it remains alone. But if it dies, it bears much fruit (John 12:23–24).

The savior deities of all primitive and ancient near-Eastern cults mimic the vegetative and fertility cycles. Baal and Astarte, Osiris and Isis—birth, growth, death, rebirth. The barge of life sails under the world. Tut's body and soul are reconstituted, then at the far edge of the underside of the Earth disc, the dawn comes, the solar disc rises, life is reborn. But the Hebrew story differs from pagan rituals. All worldviews before the Hebrew speak of ever-recurring cycles of life-death, death, regeneration. With the messianic interpretation of reality, the doctrine of eternal returns becomes the doctrine of eternal life—not endless repetition, but the rebuilding of a kingdom in time. Nothing created in God's image can be obliterated. "We know if this earthly tent is destroyed we have a building from God, a house not made with hands, eternal in the heavens" (2 Cor 5:1).

Darwin's voyage on the Beagle gave him a glimpse of the majestic branches of the tree of life, growing organically from common stock. Species come and go. We must protect the golden eagle and the green turtle, not because they are Aristotle's eternally immutable species, but because they are God's creatures in the history of nature—color and joy, as well as darkness and death. It's all His story.

The death/resurrection of Christ is God's assurance to us that absurd natural apocalypse will not end history. It cautions us to temper our utopian schemes of perfecting nature through genetic, environmental, or any other mode of human engineering. It says that here is a dynamic process of nature's emergence, of which human ingenuity is a part, and we are invited to a cooperative task of building the Earth into its promise.

Israel. Jesus' death is the meaning of Israel. Yahweh chooses a servant. As the tribes are drawn into His will, they must die to their idolatries. He cleanses and consecrates this recalcitrant lot into an obedient people. Van Leeuwen writes concerning Kingship in Israel: "In the paradox of Kingship we see the paradox of Israel's history as the chosen people; and that in its turn bears witness to the paradox of the whole history of man in this Earth which the Lord has made. The history of Israelite Kingship is the history of creation, of sin, of destruction, of creation 'anew.'"[32]

---

32. Van Leeuwen, *Christianity in World History*, 87.

As Judaism is purified, the servant is envisaged as a suffering figure, and the messianic destiny of a people and an anointed individual becomes a destiny of profound pain, bearing identification with the human race in its suffering, plight, and death. Jesus becomes the new Adam, the temple, the Messiah, God's future. The mystery of the Hebrew race and faith in modern history, the establishment of the state of Israel, the visit of a current-day Pharaoh (Sadat)—all of these events transpire mysteriously within this framework of meaning.

Rise and Fall of Nations. Perhaps the greatest historian of the modern world, Arnold J. Toynbee, argues that the cross is the clue to the vicissitudes of history. Cultures that become vitalistic, power-obsessed, and introverted ripen, wither, and die. Only cultures that live in self-sacrifice, justice, and universality will prevail. Peter took Jesus aside and rebuked him (Mark 8:32). "You must not go to Jerusalem." Even Jesus demurred, "If possible, let this cup pass from me." "Do you love me? . . . feed my sheep." "Nevertheless, not my will, but thine, be done."

The great economist Kenneth Boulding was once asked what he thought the phrase meant "the meek shall inherit the Earth." "When all is said and done," he answered, "the civilization and the person that endures after all others fall is the one who knows when to back off." "God is in the world," wrote Bonhoeffer, "where the sufferings of the poor signal the presence of Christ." Now, as always, the clue to what is going on in history is the pedagogy of the oppressed.

Nature of Being. Christ's death and resurrection provides the clue to discovering who I am, my being. Understood most profoundly is an ever-deepening life in the midst of a withering, weakening organism. All growth is a dying—a not-I, an ego negation. All movement is pain. All maturation involves fracturing open, an excruciation. Conversely, clinging to life, building barns, denying death, frantic obsessions with self-gratifications impede, thwart, even kill, the development of my being. In André Malraux's *magnum opus*, he reflects on his life-threatening illness, his impending death. In Lazarus, he writes, the only sacred experience is common human cause against that which "paralyzes" and "rots" man: "Myself, though I do not believe in redemption, I have come to the conclusion that the enigma of cruelty is no more tantalizing than that of the simplest act of heroism or love. But sacrifice alone can look torture in the face, and the God of Christianity would not be God without the crucifixion."[33]

Destiny in Time. Finally, my story is also illuminated by the death of Christ. Not only am I someone, the possessor of being, but I move in time. Heidegger says we are *Sein zum Tod*, "being toward death." Each of us goes to his or her own death. This is destiny. My death is not a problem for biomedical technology to solve. The thought of death is not some discomforting distraction from life to be evaded. Awareness of death is not a neurosis for psychoanalysis to render conscious or pharmacology to render unconscious—usable and, therefore, trivial. It is the secret of what life is all about. My finitude signals me that I am incomplete, needy, and dependent. While the sirens sing the seductive song that I can be "well adjusted," self-sufficient, and autonomous, this deep call of God to my life reminds me to whom I belong. Christ's death and my participation in that death through my death is the secret of my destiny.

Therefore, the first word of life is a word that only two thieves can literally say, but we can figuratively say: "With Christ, I have been co-crucified. Ego lives no more, Christ lives in me" (Gal 2:19–20).

"All I want," writes Paul as his own violent death draws near, "is to know Christ and to experience the power of his resurrection. To share in his sufferings and become like him in his death, in the hope that I, myself, will be raised from death to life" (Phil 3:10–11).

Involvement in the areas of death and dying came in the areas of personal cases, public policy, and conceptual analysis. Cases such as Quinlan and Cruzan, Solovecik and Kevorkian represent for me what seems, as I look back, to be hundreds of involvements.

Involvement in these cases impressed on me the necessity of holding in lively tension the personal, parochial, and public parameters of ethics. In Solevecik, where an Orthodox Jewish family of rabbis struggled over "letting-go" the life of a young son with a brain tumor, we realized that personal and family ethics often run into conflict when exposed to the faith dimension. In this unusual case, we also saw the limitation of what I have frequently called for: religious adjudication of cases through rabbinical courts, canon law, or pastoral process. In public policy (both court decisions and legislation), I have argued for a *laissez-faire* respect for an

33. Domenach, "Malraux and Death," 37–38.

idiosyncratic approach. On the "aid-in-dying" issue, for example, I have argued for an absence of law. In this approach, we should not pass prohibitive legislation as Michigan keeps trying (unsuccessfully) to do in the Kevorkian cases, nor should we pass conducive legislation as in the state of Washington, Holland, and the more recent law in North Australia.

In public policy formation on death and dying issues, I have spent countless hours attempting to embody theological ethics, but also to enhance personal freedom and the sanctity of the physician-patient relationship. I testified in several states on the development of "natural death acts" and "living will" kind of laws. I was involved in the formulation of "definition of death" (brain death) statutes in the 1960s. Many interesting hours were spent in developing the guidelines for the state of Illinois "agency" statutes, where the dying person's nearest relative was empowered with proxy judgment. I participated in the Hastings Center, as we developed guidelines for the "cessation of life-prolonging treatment." During this time, I often consulted hospitals, medical schools, religious orders, and the like as they formed in-house ethics committees and guidelines for terminal care. I worked hard as well, helping professional groups such as the AMA, chest physicians, nursing associations, and religious communities (*e.g.*, the Presbyterians) develop their own policies and guidelines. The following article comments upon the AMA guidelines on "feeding" to which I had made input.

Opening a Doorway to Death

Chicago Tribune, April 8, 1986

"What a strange machine man is! . . . You fill him with bread, wine, fish, and radishes, and out of him come sighs, laughter, and dreams."[34]

A machine, yet a mystery, fearfully and wonderfully made. Both our manipulative zeal to sustain life and our foreboding restraint not to harm the terminally ill were chastened by the American Medical Association's new guidelines, "Witholding or Withdrawing Life-Prolonging Medical Treatment." The text reaffirms ancient creed and responds to novel need:

> For humane reasons, with informed consent, a physician may do
> what is medically necessary to alleviate severe pain, or cease or

34. Kazantzakis, *Zorba the Greek*, 254.

omit treatment to permit a terminally ill patient whose death is imminent to die. . . Even if death is not imminent but a patient's coma
is beyond doubt irreversible . . . it is not unethical to discontinue
all means of life-prolonging medical treatment . . . (This) includes
medication and artificially or technologically supplied respiration,
nutrition or hydration.[35]

This brief, but potent, document acknowledges the historic ethical covenant of medicine requiring that we stand in respectful awe before the mystery of a person's being. This means we sustain one another with the sacraments of life: food, water, warmth, and breath.

What is the metaphysical background of this practical commitment? We believe that these ingredients of divine provision must be safeguarded and mediated one to another. These vitalities of the world are entrusted to our care. They are not our possessions.

To allow a child to starve to death or, through sociopolitical neglect, to deprive an impoverished mother, is like severing a lifeline to an auto-accident victim in an intensive care unit. To spill acid rain and destroy a watershed is like poisoning a well or dehydrating a burn victim. To fill the air with mustard gas or to seize by the throat to choke or suffocate is like clamping an oxygen or respirator line.

It was Easter season in 1983 when Elizabeth Bouvia checked into a Tijuana motel to starve herself to death and gain release from crippling cerebral palsy. Several years later, in 1987, Nancy Ellen Jobes died after seven years in a coma, sustained in a New Jersey hospital by a feeding tube. Her case was pled in light of the AMA guidelines.

In Passover, Lent, Ramadan, and Pentecost, we celebrate (and vow to be trustworthy with) the sacraments of food and fluid, fire and spirit. In the medical covenant, as a facet of this sacrament of life to life, we pledge to sustain well-being via the ministries of Earth and water, fire and air. This is epitomized when, while asleep under the care of an anesthesiologist, our nutrients and electrolytes are monitored and modulated, our airways are cleared and respiration sustained, and our vital temperature balance is maintained.

But exhaustion is the correlate of inspiration, feasting inevitably leads to fasting, and metabolic heat yields to that still chill. Rather than the terror of nonbeing and extinction, we discover here that mystery where loss becomes gain, impotence becomes power, death becomes life. Our obsession

35. The American Medical Association Council of Ethical and Judicial Affairs, "Withholding or Withdrawing Life-prolonging Medical Treatment."

with mechanical vitality and our trembling obeisance to law and custom have led us to the technological excesses that sometimes harm rather than heal. It is these excesses that gave rise to the AMA report.

If cases like Bouvia's have taught us anything, it is the delicate moral equipoise where, instead of thoughtless benevolence compelling us to press on, we find in deeper care the courage to let go.

How did we come to lose the grace of taking leave and letting go? It began with the emergence of a new way of looking at the person. Since the 17th century, the dominant paradigm of understanding human being and human vitality has been the mathematical and mechanical model. Following Descartes, we have come to view the person as a body-mechanism.

The ingenuity of this commitment and its love of life have led to the miracles of modern medicine where the blind see, the deaf hear, the lame walk, the barren bear, and the dead are raised. The blessings of simulated optic nerve imagery, cochlear implant, functional computerized limb stimulation, in-vitro fertilization, and cardio-pulmonary resuscitation are nothing less than millennial realizations. A new world is dawning.

But this way of viewing humans also leaves us bankrupt when faced with the ultimate decisions of life and death. Indeed, we have come to deny, fear, and abhor death. In these culminating moments of existence, insights of humanistic and spiritual depth are required. What shall we do to serve a better balance?

At one level, we need simply to reassert respect for persons and dissociate from technological, legalistic, and economic imperatives in the way the new guidelines suggest.

This freedom of action was expressed in the case of B. Ross Henniger, an 85-year-old former university president. A New York State Supreme Court judge ordered a Syracuse nursing home not to force-feed Henniger against his wishes. The man's daughter testified that her father wanted to die because of his deteriorating health. She said she had tried to induce him to eat with ice cream, cookies, and homemade soup.

In time, we all turn our face away, even away from chicken soup. We turn it to the wall that for all we know may be a door.

The freedom-enhancing, mania-limiting effect of the AMA guidelines will be good for us, but only if we guard with a goodly sense of humor and humility against one ominous tendency.

We are witnessing the convergence of a growing sense of personal redundancy ("I don't want to be a burden on anyone") with a political expediency ("The old, obsolete, and unproductive have a duty to die").

In this day dominated by the inferior ethics of econometrics, DRGs, and utilitarianism, we must sustain that paradoxical moral genius of Judaism that claims that to harm or kill anyone is to injure the whole human race or to save or heal a single one is to save the race.

Throughout this course of experience, I was developing my own system of conceptual analysis that found expression in two ways. In Project Ten, which became today's Park Ridge Center, I worked to find a forum for religious communions to rehearse and develop anew theologies and ethics about health matters.

This goal found expression, for example, in the book series conceived with Martin Marty entitled *Health/Medicine in the Faith Traditions*.[36] Now reaching some 20 volumes, it explores how Jewish, Reformed, Lutheran, Catholic, Hindu, Islamic, and other faith traditions might reflect and act upon a range of themes in health and medicine, including sexuality, birth, health, pain, suffering, death, etc.

This centering of bioethics and biotheology in concrete religious traditions was not without its critics. I still remember the day I invited Paul Ramsey, my predecessor in theological ethics at Garrett (then at Princeton University), to write the Methodist volume in the series. He was surprised, shocked, and slightly angry. He did not believe there was a "Wesleyan" tradition of belief and practice in medicine (he was quite wrong), nor did he feel it was worth doing.

Ramsey sought, throughout his career, to do philosophical-religious ethics. In the great tradition of his teachers, McIntosh and the Niebuhrs, he believed religious ethics transcended tradition boundaries and had universal and public currency. Although a conservative and brilliantly articulate theologian, he often told me he thought of himself as a religious philosopher, not as a doctrinal (confessional) theologian in the European sense (Reformed, Lutheran, Anglican, Catholic, etc.). In the end, E. Brooks Holifield of Emory produced an excellent "Wesleyan" volume for our series.

Secondly, I now was interested in faith-tradition-based ethics finding a secular currency. Again, I invoke the evangelical-ethical matrix. For

36. Marty and Vaux, *Health/Medicine and the Faith Traditions*.

myself, I sought to develop a systems model of analysis of both death and birth issues.[37] Letting this same borderline deranged, encyclopedic mind develop its labyrinthine schemes, I came up with a list of parameters that I thought bore on the interpretation of the phenomenon of death and dying and contributed to the normative (ethical) task.

In both *Birth Ethics* and *Death Ethics*, I explored biological, psychological, social, legal, philosophical, theological, apocalyptical, and eschatological parameters. In a rule-of-thumb process, I grouped these into three sets—natural, humanistic, and theistic—and held that the former obtained in ethics unless superseded by the next realm. The model is too expansive and too little positivist and analytical to engage in current intellectual work, but I contend that it attends the grandeur, profundity, and mystery of the reality of death.

THE *ANAWIM*

The Hebrew word *anawim* means the poor, the weak, the vulnerable, and the child. Mary's *Magnificat* (Luke 1:46ff.), recalling Hannah's song over Samuel's birth (1 Sam 2:1–10), uses the phrase "the lowly" (v. 52). My sympathies have always been towards the poor, the weak, the vulnerable, and children. The disposition of Yahweh's justice and the inclination of Jesus' love are to the *ptóchos*, the destitute of this Earth. The justice and mercy of God, when formulated as John Rawls' ethics of the "original position," inclines all ethics toward this bias. The applicability of this commitment obviously has profound bearings on medicine. The virtue and wisdom of a society is expressed in how it regards and provides for the sick, injured, weak, vulnerable, and poor in its midst. Today, this vulnerability is most often found in children and elders, especially women. The point of vulnerability is often that of nutrition, disease, and anxiety (depression).

The Christian gospel erupts into the pagan world and radically challenges the existing values about children. The early Christian ethic, animated by Jesus teaching to "allow the children to come" (Mark 10:13–16) and "of such is the kingdom," challenged the prevalent ethic of life on many points: abortion, infanticide—especially selective female infanticide—and child slavery.[38]

---

37. See Vaux, *Birth Ethics*; also *Death Ethics*.

38. See Aries, *Centuries of Childhood*.

I mentioned earlier my sympathy with "let-go" decisions with severely handicapped newborns. While I often took a supportive stand of parents (*e.g.*, Danville's Siamese twin parents), more often, my conservative sexuality-natality ethic came through on these matters. Cardinal Bernardin once lectured at the University of Chicago and praised an essay I had written in the *Chicago Tribune* as resonant with his own views.

THE VATICAN'S CRY OF PROTEST

Chicago Tribune, March 20, 1987

The new Vatican document on "birth science," entitled "Instruction on Respect for Human Life in its Origin and on the Dignity of Procreation," affirms a much-threatened normative value of the natural goodness and sacred mystery of birth. Regrettably, in its desire to preserve the deeply human nature of procreation, it plays down the salutary potential of science to ameliorate incapacity in that same procreative gift. Let us examine the genius and weakness of this Vatican teaching and its bearing on our personal, familial, scientific, and public lives.

To witness the sad spectacle of Mary Beth Whitehead demanding custody of the baby she was paid to bear as a surrogate; to share the anguish of the then-infertile, now-pregnant mother carrying five fetal sacs, three of which must be sacrificed to spare the others; or to hear the new fertility and genetics firms advertise "adopt an embryo" is to realize the moral urgency of listening carefully to the "Instruction."

In a world where a certain disdain of the human body and the natural vitalities and relationships is joined to a gracelessness in accepting any limitation, and when this is accompanied by an almost-manic fascination with the technical, we hear prophetic power in the "Instruction."

When the fetal diagnostics of amniocentesis and ultrasound are used to search, scan, and destroy the imperfect fetus; when embryos and fetuses are used for experimentation; when techniques of "twin fission," cloning, and parthenogenesis are developed as means to improve on the body's own generative and abortive wisdom; and when those women who have been reduced to poverty by an unjust social order are "paid off" as surrogates so that their affluent counterparts do not disturb their careers—in such a world we realize that we are not so much engaged in medical therapy as massive life-denial, perhaps death-wish.

To revise and improve the natural and sacral powers of conjugal love, procreation, and care may be our concession to a double-income, no-kids culture. It may also mean our accession to an existence now devoid of deep feeling in both suffering and joy. The Vatican statement cries out in protest against this dehumanization of life.

But there is virtue in the venture to ameliorate the terrible trauma that marks the human condition and so often flaws birth. There is too little celebration and responsible appropriation of modern birth science in the Vatican document. The teaching does indeed bestow its benediction on diagnostics that safeguard and heal the embryo and fetus. Gene therapies that correct or offset the morbidity of chromosomal defects, insemination techniques to achieve conception where natural conception is impossible, and therapies that repair infertility are welcomed. Beyond this, the statement falls short of addressing the crises of conception, birth, and the responsible raising of children. In its concentration on deviation and perversion of technique, it intensifies the modern heresy focusing on the mechanics of procreation.

We need a more expansive theological ethic of procreative responsibility in an age when population explosion, combined with a diminished resource base, condemns many born into our care to degradation, starvation, and hopelessness; when AIDS and the sexually transmitted diseases threaten those aborning with congenital contamination; when genetic and congenital injury activated by inherited anomalies, environmental causes, and maternal substance abuse condemn many lives to relentless suffering; and when persistent and chronic neglect prompts many to ask the old Greek question "whether not to be born was best." This ethic will necessarily involve thoughtful mating and conception, family planning and prophylaxis, scientifically safeguarded gestation, and careful child-rearing.

How shall we follow the positive and negative lessons of the "Instruction?" Whether of Roman Catholic or another faith, we should all seek to develop a personal conscience wherein we honor the grace of life that has been given us. We also need to honor the generative obligation and claim our part in the transmission and upholding of life. We are the generational bridge to the future for the human community. We must assume that obligation with utmost willingness and seriousness.

We are called to draw life into being, hold persons near with care, and provide them with a usable future. The "Instruction" commends to us the delight of this service. Our procreative calling is not to some automatic necessity but to awesome freedom—to global, not parochial, concern.

The "Instruction" calls us again to consider the familial and extend-ed-familial character of our sexual existence. We are not isolated monads doing our sexual thing in isolation in nuclear units with the pyrotechnics completely severed from "procreatics." Our sexuality is the clue to our com-munality. In family and community, we become ourselves.

Children belong to us all; they are our world. We have common bonds of obligation and nurture. We live in an age of mechanized and privatized birth taking place within an ethos that says "you're on your own" and "don't bug me with your kids"—all combined with an atmosphere of summering contempt and condemnation that decries child abuse while voting down school-tax bills. This ethos is inimical to our baptismal, and even more ba-sic, communal obligations.

In a fascinating way, the Vatican document finally calls not only on the Catholic Church but on the scientific and political realms to heed its teach-ing. Recognizing that our existence is now sociologically shaped by scientific and governmental structures, the statement calls for more rigorous moral assessment of biomedical science and technology. It also argues that gov-ernmental intervention is necessary because "recourse to the conscience of each individual and to the self-regulation of researchers (and, we should add, for-profit corporations) cannot be sufficient for insuring respect for personal rights and public order."

The document deserves widespread and thorough discussion. It raises to new sensitivity the questions of private conscience, family obligation, sci-ence policy, and the church-state issue. We would welcome its provocative stand and carefully ponder its vision and challenge.

Shortly after Cardinal Bernardin died in early November 1996, I wrote the following eulogy from Strasbourg.

Econmium Josephium

In praise of Joe (Joseph Cardinal Bernardin)
On the Occasion of His Death

Father Bernardin was my friend and teacher. In a lecture to the medical school at the University of Chicago, he cited my work as an example of "a consistent ethic of life." I told him I had learned it from him. My positions on social issues—war, poverty, capital punishment—and on biological is-sues—abortion, sexuality, health care provision, etc.—were similar to his. Although we had some variance of view on redemptive suffering and choos-ing to forego further medical treatment, and especially physician-aided dy-ing, no one influenced me more toward a consistent ethic of life. Across our common tenure in Chicago, we collaborated on numerous projects, espe-cially through his resident theologian, Michael Place. We addressed issues such as abortion law in Illinois, which, in Roe vs. Wade, encouraged it for the rich and restricted it for the poor. We always wished that Roe vs. Wade and the Hyde Amendment could have been melded into some kind of humani-tarian synthesis, where adoption could be encouraged and the agonizing choice of abortion diminished. We collaborated on the development of Death and Dying legislation in Illinois, such as living wills, the right to die, directives for end-of-life care, and an issue on which we differed—forego-ing life, sustaining treatment, and euthanasia. The exemplary witness of his living and dying adds strength to his Catholic views of redemptive suffering in faith. In my own view, even his own treatment, the whipple procedure for disseminated pancreatic carcinoma, should be left to the free choice of patient and family, with full information about the unlikely efficacy of the treatment and the severe side-effects. I have learned from Joe, as have mil-lions here in Europe and around the world, the grace of dying well amid the beneficent and ambivalent modern technology, sustained by faith and compassion for fellow humanity.

Joe was a great champion of the poor, the sick, and the dying, and I praise his compelling witness—ethical, eucharistical, evangelical, and ecumenical. He was the major voice in our country and in Roman Catholic Christianity around the world for vigorous social ethics. Like Mother Theresa, there was absolutely no concession to greed, power, excessive free-enterprise, *laissez-faire*, and "trickle-down" economics.

His consistent ethic of life was grounded firmly in the commandments of Israel and the grace of Jesus Christ, which hold human persons to be of inestimable value and the service of humanity as our highest calling. Killing was killing, harming was harming. His ethic was similar to that of Orthodox Judaism in its stringent right-to-life quality.

What was surprising and disarming was its range. He opposed killing of all sorts: American drug culture, cigarette smoking, capital punishment, war, hand-gun availability, cutting taxes and closing inner city hospitals, production and sale of weapons and land mines, and a wide range of things we Americans see as benign concessions to freedom and business. Joe's life and consistent ethic sang the warning song "killing me softly with kindness, killing me softly with his love."

Even more compelling than the *prohibitiva* in his ethic were the *imperativa*: food for the hungry. That he died during his beloved season of thanksgiving and advent was that commingled blue and red, that gift and loss as the liturgical purple gives witness.

Economic development for the poor was a high priority on the Cardinal's agenda. Taking W. Wilson's research on Chicago seriously, he called for vigorous renewal of church, business, schools, hospitals, and culture in the inner-city. He reveled in the rich diversity of Chicago and was loved as his funeral cortege wound through the ghettos witnessed by every citizen. Joe was a throwback to Dorothy Day, Jane Addams, and the church-based, social action movements of the last century. He called on our luxuriant and laid-back city and its suburban communities to wake up, get involved, and share the thrill of seeing the kingdom of God working among the people.

Father Bernardin's witness was eucharistical. Like the Monte Cassino Benedictines of his native Italy, he believed in *ora et labora*—prayer and work. Liturgy and prayer were always at the center of his project. This conjunction of devotion and duty may be his lasting contribution to a generation that has lost faith and, in the process, lost good-works. Our Institute in Strasbourg, France has prepared the landmark document on justification of faith for the world Lutheran-Catholic conciliation. Bernardin embodies the spirit of the document, which is to reunite the Protestant principle of civil protest and evangelical faith with the Catholic substance of celebration and transformation of the world. The commitment of Father Bernardin to morning prayer, silent and personal, has touched us all and encouraged us to do the same. Like him, we would rather stay in bed but we know that ". . . to meet God in the morning is to want God through the day . . ."

I was always struck with Joe's evangelical faith. As a Presbyterian now teaching in a Methodist institution, I see him as embodying the best of an evangelical commitment. His countenance and presence invited faith. He was a God-intoxicated person. Every word and gesture bespoke his Lord. He enjoyed most walking humbly among his people in Chicago as a simple priest. He drew strength from the vibrant faith of the common people. Personal, one-on-one evangelism was the passion of his heart. Here, and in his broader work of theological formulation, diocesan policy, conference-of-Bishop teaching, and influence on Vatican promulgation, he exuded evangelical fervor and winsomeness.

Joe's witness was ecumenical. As exemplified in his funeral at Holy Name Cathedral, his Protestant, Orthodox Jewish, and humanist friends and partners in ministry were very dear to him. He lived out *Christus Praesens* doctrine. Wherever the hungry were fed, the naked clothed, the sick healed, and prisoners visited, wherever children were loved and elders honored, wherever the poor were lifted up, there was Christ *incognito*. All who served were his ecumenical fellows.

As I gaze from my office window at Strasbourg's Ecumenical Institute, I whisper a thank you to God for the life of this holy and gentle man. As the snow gently falls outside and we prepare to return to Chicago to continue Joe's work, the lovely plea of Jean Valjean at the end of "Les Misérables" runs through my mind: "Bring him home."[39]

Finally, the moving words from his memoir, *The Gift of Peace*.

> It is the first day of November, and fall is giving way to winter. Soon the trees will lose the vibrant colors of their leaves and snow will cover the ground. The Earth will shut down, and people will race to and from their destinations bundled up for warmth. Chicago winters are harsh. It is a time of dying. But we know that spring will soon come with all its new life and wonder. It is quite clear that I will not be alive then. But I will soon experience new life in a different way. Although I do not know what to expect in the afterlife, I do know that just as God has called me to serve him to the best of my ability throughout my life on Earth, he is now calling me home.[40]

My sympathies with a natural law, a more Roman Catholic perspective, seemed somewhat discordant with my generally more freedom-con-science-based ethic. In tracing the influence of this more natural ethic, I must point to the natural law dimension of Calvin's ethic. In contrast to Luther's radical antinomian freedom and directionality from the "Word of God," Calvin remained under the sway of the holiness, natural-law, human-reason side of scripture—*e.g.*, the Holiness Code in Leviticus wisdom literature, and even the Augustine, Aquinas development of that tradition. Calvin began his work with Seneca's *De Clementia* and remained a natural-law stoic his entire life.

I had a similar response to the *anawim* tradition so prevalent in the Roman Catholic ethic of natality. When it came to abortion, care of dis-

---

39. Claude-Michel Schönberg (music), Herbert Kretzmer (lyrics), "Bring Him Home" (1980).

40. Bernardin, *The Gift of Peace*, 151.

abled children, concern for poor mothers who were pregnant or were caring alone for small children, I found myself in Cardinal Bernardin's camp. His "consistent ethic of life" firmly opposed to war, capital punishment, and contempt for the poor, as well as abortion and infanticide, gained my support.

Yet in certain baby cases, I continued to argue for reason in "letting go" when the right time had come (an extrapolation of my benign view of death within divine providence). Two dramatic cases illustrated this propensity of my thought. In the Danville case, the twins were joined high in the torso and, although one has survived well after separation (the other died after 30 odd months of excruciating care, including night and day suctioning, etc.), I still support the parents' decision "not to feed."

Danville's Siamese Twins Test Society's Deepest Beliefs

Chicago Tribune, June 28, 1981

When he was a boy, poet Carl Sandburg would visit the circus when it came to Galesburg.

> There out front, as a free show, I saw the man with elastic skin. He would pull it out from his face and neck and it would snap back into place. The spieler, after inviting the farmers in a soft voice to come into the tent to see the Oriental Dancing Girl, turned to the main crowd and let go in a smooth, loud voice. "La-deez and gentul-men, beneath yon canvas we have the curi-aw-si-ties and the mon-straw-si-ties. The wild man of Borneo, the smallest dwarf, the largest giant ever to come into existence and . . . Jo Jo the dog-faced boy, born 40 miles from land and 40 miles from sea . . ." Years later, it came over me that, at first sight of the freaks, I was sad because I was bashful.[41]

Dr. Robert Mueller and his wife, Pamela, a nurse, had anxiously awaited the birth of their first child. The Danville, Illinois couple had trained in natural childbirth, and they were ready for the joys of Lamaze intimacy with the new baby. Their anticipation was heightened when the obstetrician detected two heartbeats and told them to expect twins.

41. Sandburg, *Always the Young Strangers*, 190.

On May 5, twin boys were born, Siamese twins like Chang and Eng in Siam in 1811. Even though the parents were medically trained, they were, like Carl Sandburg, awestruck and horrified. A decision was made to "let nature take its course."

The babies, Jeff and Scott, joined at the midsection with common abdominal organs and genital systems, and only three legs, were left untreated for congestion and pneumonia. This order appeared on their chart: "Do not feed infants, in accordance with parents' wishes."

Then the experience broke into public view and became an issue we all have had to confront. A conscience-plagued nurse sneaked food to the boys. An anonymous tipster brought the case to the attention of the Illinois Department of Children and Family Services. The parents lost a court hearing in which they asked that the state return custody of the twins to them. They pleaded innocent to charges of attempted murder and were released on their own recognizance. Another hearing is set for Tuesday.

Meanwhile, the twins survive at Children's Memorial Hospital. Though the tent is missing, the morbid circus curiosity now in the guise of media coverage and scientific investigation goes on. Like the poet, we witness with sad hearts the spectacle of the helpless infants and anguished parents in this poignant ordeal. Still, we must offer ethical reflection and formulate a moral response.

Across the ages, society's response to such events has been shaped by the ancient emotions of awe and fear. Prescientific cultures viewed exceptional births as supernatural. It was a blessing or a curse, a portent of the future or a judgment of past wrongs.

It was seen to proceed from the hand of God or the natural demons of the underworld. As with animal societies, most primitive societies let deformed offspring die. The instinct at work was survival first.

In our search for understanding and direction in such problematic births, we may attribute them to divine or demonic action, to retribution or premonition, to natural causes or mutation.

I have pondered the why and wherefore and have talked with the Danville family. Through the tragedy of these parents and children, our society gropes for an understanding of life and death, health and disease, normality and abnormality. As in past cultures, our society declares its values and meanings through symbolic events such as this birth. Although today we construe the birth more as an accident than a metaphysical phenomenon, we are forced, like the ancients, to interpret it and make moral decisions on the basis of commonly accepted values. Now, however, there is also the dimension of responsibility. Unlike our predecessors, we cannot innocently plead blind fate or acquiesce to "nature's course." We often know things before they come about and can profoundly modify the outcome of the natural process through medical treatment.

Should we knowingly consent to the birth of a defective child? Do we have the legal right to knowingly proceed with the birth of a defective child? H. Tristram Engelhardt, a leading biomedical philosopher, asks whether there is valid jurisprudential concept in what is called "the injury of continued existence."

The foreknowledge modern technology accords us presents an awesome responsibility. Where knowledge of injury exists, where it is known that harm will only intensify and no amelioration is available, do we, in a sense, become accomplices to the evil if we do not terminate the pregnancy? If the Siamese twins will not survive without profound diagnostic, surgical, and life-support interventions, can we be accused of compounding the affliction if we initiate these measures? Perhaps feeding and warming are basic responsibilities. But what kind of feeding; what antibiotic treatment, resuscitation, oxygen and respiratory therapy? Where on the continuum of life supports do we pass from measures that are ordinary, pain relieving, and life prolonging, to those that are extraordinary, compounding of suffering, and death prolonging?

The Abortion Analogy. As we seek to delineate responsibility in this case, we begin by drawing moral inferences from other areas. For example, we look to personal and public values concerning abortion. If we search for deformity in fetal diagnosis and terminate such pregnancies, can the abortion analogy be used to help decide about defective newborns?

Bill Bartholome, the Texas pediatrician-ethicist, argues no. He points to the danger of our reasoning from the licit practice of birth control to the morally equivocal practice of early termination of any unwanted pregnancy to the questionable practice of selective feticide and neonaticide based on "quality-of-life" judgments. Bartholome argues that this is wrong, not on "right-to-life" grounds, but on the grounds of fundamental justice and equity. To consider some lives qualitatively inferior, therefore possessing less claim to protection, is to assail the basic moral requirement of equality.

While I agree with this logic, I find it morally unconscionable and psychologically unhealthy to discover disease and debilitation and do nothing about it. When we have the capacity of foreknowledge and prevention, we must act responsibly in the light of that knowledge. Selective abortion for fetal disease is an analogy that supports a "let-die" posture in this case. We should do all we can to prevent, detect, and correct birth defects. We must aid the sick with genetic medicine and fetal therapy; sometimes with moral courage, we must terminate those conceived lives that bear profound and grievous injury.

In my view, life begins at conception, and I believe no thoughtful scientist or moralist would argue otherwise. But these questions do not address the real issues. The point is, we have been given by God foreknowledge and power, freedom and accountability. We now possess a terrifying, yet wonderful, freedom; we cannot offer the excuses of fate and inevitability.

It is at this precise point of arbitration over life and death that we must remind ourselves of the irresistible and pervasive malevolence in the heart of man. Our wick is short, our staying power weak, and our capacity to care fragile. We stand, some say, on the brink of an age that will be characterized by constant contempt for others, disregard for the weak and helpless.

Recognition both of what is in the heart of man and the power of the demonic in our world prompts us to be morally cautious in allowing, and certainly in assisting, the death of injured newborns. What do these values mean with reference to the Danville parents?

Life. The case of the Danwille twins occurs at a moment in political history that is characterized by a significant societal value shift. We live in a day of reassertion of "right-to-life" public philosophy. Congress is now considering "life-begins-at-conception" clarification of the Fourteenth Amendment.

The focus on values of right to life and sanctity of life apply also to the Danville family. The ordeal has already altered their lives. In the unlikely chance that one or both of the twins should survive, what will life be like for this family? As we ponder the theme of defending life, it might be proposed that this grievous, monstrous birth is an insult and assault on the life of this family and that self-defense is justifiable. Although this notion must be pursued with utmost care, it is relevant to the discussion.

In discussing this case at the Hastings Institute (Institute of Society, Ethics and Life Sciences), most of my colleagues in medicine, nursing, philosophy, theology, and ethics have felt that the initial decision of doctors and family not to begin life support—even feeding and hydration—was justifiable in light of the jeopardy the birth presented to the family and the drawn-out suffering implied for the children. In sheer ethicometrics, the costs greatly outweigh the benefits, they believe.

One colleague argued alternatively that it was wrong not to feed the twins. The principle of protection of life requires support, although he would find extraordinary measures, resuscitation, for example, questionable. A critical determination is whether the twins are dying. Can they be separated? Can one be saved? The answer to these questions would deter-mine the moral status of particular life-saving or death-hastening actions. He also feels that the ultimate legal adjudication of the case should occur at two levels. One should render decision on the euthanasia principle, the other should consider penalties. Guilty with clemency is a deep religiolegal judgment.

Still others regret that this case ever moved into the public arena. It should have been handled in the confidentiality of the family-medical team relationship, with discussion preceding clear and unequivocal decisions to which all persons involved agreed.

Liberty. Next to the value of life, the most widely invoked topic in medical ethics today is liberty. To whom does the decision to prolong or protract the life of these children belong? Do the parents, the physicians, the state, or the courts have primacy?

We commit most decisions about procreation and family life to the parents. Or, better stated, we challenge or usurp the oversight of the family only in situations of obvious neglect, abuse, or brutality. Parental autonomy is a theme that supports the view that this case should never have passed into the public domain.

Happiness. The final theme that has been helpful in pondering the case is happiness. By this I do not mean the banal, superficial notion of comfort and complacency, but the deeper meanings of felicity, compassion, and blessedness spoken of in the Beatitudes, the charter of human happiness, which have definite bearing on this case. The beatitudes are a rendition of *Akedic* Torah or divine righteousness. As such, it deals with ultimate good and justice.

Happiness is fulfillment that becomes possible in an environment of caring. For parents who, in care, have drawn away and begun to grieve over both the disappointment and the loss of this, their only offering of life to this world, their own flesh and blood, what does it mean to demand that they now reattach themselves or, worse yet, that they are not to be entrusted with this offspring?

Family is the care-giving and life-giving fabric, which patterns, binds, and weaves each of us into a history and a future. It is only within these covenants of family care, where happiness is a prospect because hope, not despair, prevails, that life and liberty are possible. Where children are unwanted and neglected and no nurture is present, only frustration and violence are possible. If we acknowledged this fact, perhaps we would not magnify this singular case out of proportion, but begin to work on the real childhood moral crises of our society, such as illegitimate births, unwed mothers, and unwanted children. If human happiness and well being are to flourish, we must reactivate the intimate communities of caring, such as the churches and neighborhoods, and thus relieve the public agencies that should only be expected to serve those who fall through the cracks.

In conclusion, although life, liberty, and happiness may be helpful criteria to work through this case, an ultimate question mark appears in our moral calculation when we ponder the humanity and plight of little Jeff and Scott. They are human. Like us, they have been given names.

Surely, Siamese twins are to be baptized, either conditionally or absolutely. They possess souls, they bear the divine image. They are ours, they are like us, they are God's heritage, and in His inscrutable will they have transected our lives for a meaning certain, although as yet indiscernible. They are monstrous in the literal sense of that word.

Like the Elephant man, they remind us in our condescension, to ask "whose life it is anyway?" Like those outcasts throughout the ages, they plead to us to hold them, yet do no harm. Whether to save or let die, to probe, to operate, to separate, to engage, or to withdraw remain for all of us to determine in courage and grace.

A RETROSPECTIVE WISDOM?

Reflecting many years later, one twin was condemned to a hellish three years in Misericordia Hospital, suctioned around the clock until he met his inevitable death. The other has survived and leads a normal, healthy life. What do such outcomes say about the decisions of parents, whistle-blowers, legal functionaries, medics, ethicists? In the end, fallibility, forgiveness, hope, and love seem to matter most.

In the Linares case, I offered support in the public forum for the county coroner's view that the baby was clinically dead before he began his months-long season on the respirator. While I regretted Mr. Linares' Rambo-like desperation in extubating his baby with nurses at gunpoint, I sympathized with his moral instincts.

A Tragic Triptych—The Linares case

Chicago Tribune, May 3, 1989

(The baby Linares choked and asphyxiated after he ingested a balloon at a birthday party. He was transported to the hospital and placed on a respirator. After many months of life support, his dad entered the hospital one night, held the staff at bay by gunpoint, and extubated his son.)

I see Madonna and child. The image arises of that archetypal pose we find depicted wherever human art appears—in Africa and India, Byzantium and Renaissance Florence—that primal pose of presentation and protection. But now, instead of an innocent maiden and precocious child, it is a burly young house painter from Cicero cradling his bambino, shielding and safeguarding the limp body of his brain-dead baby, revolver in hand, sobbing uncontrollably. In the background sits the silent, disconnected respirator.

What sort of icon is this? What does it symbolize? What do we see through it? The poignant scene arrests and fascinates us. It is an arche-triptych that rivets our conscience to primal questions of life, death, and responsibility. It evokes awe and fear.

Part of the fear that the scene conveys is that our systems of healing and justice have gotten out of hand. Those noble institutions of medicine and law to which we look for sustenance and safety through this precipitous life have been turned into places of brutality and betrayal. Not that they have turned against society, but rather they reflect our present society's incapacity to know and do the right.

Medicine's rightful role is to restore health and sustain lives, not to perpetuate persistent comatose or vegetative state in the bodies of those who can no longer cry out in pain and protest. Mechanical breathers were created to carry us through vulnerable episodes and out the other side of dark nights of trauma, not to become permanent cyborg appendages to near-brain-dead bodies.

Medicine is the art of conversation and coadventuring, of together seeking life while it is yet given, and receiving death in due time. Such communion or communication does not include leaving messages on phone-answering machines to say that "we are transferring your son Samuel to a nursing home to die." Neither should it necessitate stealing into the pediatric intensive care unit after midnight and holding nurses at bay with a .357 Magnum.

Law and the courts exist to protect human rights and ethical medical practice. They do not exist to disable such practice by posing the haunting fear of litigation or the sorry spectacle of hospital administrators saying they wish the parents had taken them to court for an order to withdraw life support—so that they could have been ordered to do the right thing they found themselves unable to do on their own. As judges and courts, we must adamantly disavow authority over such life-and-death matters. As lawyers, patients, and physicians, we must disavow the craze to sue. How many tortured and insentient brows of sorrow must we see in helpless infants and ancients to call us to our senses?

How can this tragic triptych reform our medical and legal iconography? The Linares family should help us recover the medical *ars moriendi*, the thoughtful and attentive care for dying persons that has so atrophied in contrast to our care for the living.

In an article in *The New England Journal of Medicine* (March 30, 1989), some of America's leading physicians called for a recovery of this lost art. Arguing that "physicians have a specific responsibility toward patients who are hopelessly ill, dying, or in the end stages of an incurable disease," the report contends that "the concept of a good death does not mean simply the withholding of technological treatments that serve only to prolong the act of dying. It requires the art of deliberately creating a medical environment that allows a peaceful death."

When I consult in cases such as that of Samuel Linares, I suggest that when physicians attach a respirator to one whom they suspect is brain dead or permanently unconscious, they must establish a clear covenant with the family that they will also disconnect life support at a certain point when it becomes clear there is no hope of recovery. We cannot be technologically aggressive, morally passive, and then plead, "We're stuck with it."

Cases such as Samuel's show us how necessary it is that some range of decisional freedom be retained for physicians and families. The parade of faces who, in their dying, have refined our conscience—Karen Quinlan and others—has left the moral legacy that right and responsibility require such latitude.

Finally, the Linares case makes it clear that we need mediating structures of ethics between the systems of medicine and law. Like all great academic medical centers, Rush-Presbyterian-St. Luke's employs a splendidly trained and sensitive circle of physician-nurse-pastor-attorney ethicists. The Quinlan case and the President's Commission on Biomedical Ethics pleaded that hospitals use such mechanisms to help physicians and families with hard choices. We need to train such ethics councils, then train providers and patients to call on them. These groups should be called in for consultation, listen carefully, offer concrete advice, and enter their counsel into the chart. This will undergird the physician and alleviate moral paralysis.

If this course is followed, we can diminish the need for desperate gestures such as that taken by Rudy Linares one early morning on the West Side. Let's not make precedent of this case. Letting go too readily could be worse than holding on too tenaciously.

I saw Madonna and child. Now I see the *pietà*. The limp and lifeless body of Baby Samuel lies draped on his dad's sobbing chest. We feel his anguish and the anguish of Samuel's short-lived existence. We need to be instructed by this triptych in our legal, medical, and hospital policies. Perhaps as with the *pietà*, this tragic image will redeem that brief, young life, and ours.

I sum up my views on natality ethics by citing John Dominic Crossan's *Jesus: A Revolutionary Biography*. Here he finds one aspect of Jesus' radical departure from Hellenistic (power domination) and Hebraic (legal obsession) ethics to be his disposition toward children. Citing the dominant child-life culture of the Greeks in the famous letter of the Hellenistic worker Hilarion on June 18th, 1 B.C.E. to his wife just about to deliver: ". . . If I receive my wages soon, I'll send them to you (a concerned husband and father). If you bear a son, let it be, If it is a girl, cast it out (to die)." He then goes on to exegete and expound on Mark 10:13–16: "Notice those framing words: *touch, took in his arms, blessed, laid hands on.* Those are the official bodily actions of a father designating a newly born infant for life rather than death, for accepting it into his family rather than casting it out with the garbage." This passage echoes back to Crossan's earlier caricature of the Hellenistic view of *anawim* (the poor and destitute). The *ptoichos* (those who by "disease or debt, draught or death" had been driven from the land and were literally hand-to-mouth beggars) are "the only ones who are innocent (Matt 5:3) or blessed, those squeezed out deliberately as human junk from the system's own evil operations."[42]

My son Keith, the doctor, has asked me on occasion if I enjoyed trumping the physician on life-or-death decisions. I told him I'm not sure, although I could find two contrary impulses in my religious-ethical system. One the one hand, I was deeply rooted in Judaism, which has always emphasized the divine vocation of the doctor. Ever since Hebrew scripture

---

42. Crossan, *Jesus*, 62–65.

introduced Yahweh as healer ("I am the Lord, your physician"), Judaism has held the highest esteem for the physician. Life-giving, life-sustaining, and-life saving are divine attributes for the God of Life (*L'hayim*). I think that I always esteemed and honored the physician, especially when the profession acknowledged this divine vocation and instrumentality to divine will. The self- appointed arrogance, the "I am a God, don't question my judgments" or the apathetic technician posture sometimes found in physicians was not a genuine reflection of the biblical ethos. Perhaps the noblest biblical document extolling this stewardly virtue is the intertestamental Book of Sirach, chapter 31 (Wisdom of Jesus Son of Sirach).

There was also another stream in the tradition of biblical and theological ethics. It takes off by linking the overweening arrogance I have just described to idolatry and blasphemy in failing to honor God as the source of all life, healing, and death. The critical tradition of which I speak is especially strong in Martin Luther and John Wesley. It resonates with a minor motif in Hebrew scripture that discountenances the magician, soothsayer, astrologer, etc. We humans are not to put our trust in human devices, manipulations, incantations, formulae, etc. We are to cast all of our need, hope, and trust on the Lord. Doctors, other healers, priests—all are mediators of divine therapy. They are to be welcomed as intercessors and instruments of divine grace.

Luther is mightily suspicious of physicians. I've often wished that we could construct a dialogue between Doktor Martin and his flamboyant contemporary, Paracelsus. The latter was an extraordinary scientist, metallurgist, concoctionist, etc. He believed, with Sirach, that the therapeutic potency of the naturals—the minerals, plants etc.—were placed in creation to mediate healing. Luther was suspicious of physicians, both by reason of their arrogating a divine air, but also for their superstition and stupidity. Like Wesley, Luther was a very practical man and knew that proffered cures by bleeding, leeching, scalding, and other various methods were, at best, counter productive and, at worst, murder. A Protestant rationalist-experimentalist rather than an Aristotelian-Galenist, he sought to try new things.

Wesley, like his Puritan forerunners, developed an important experimentalist "Book of remedies" that was widely used in the 19th century. Since Methodist pastors in rural England, among the poor and uneducated in America and Europe, were also the physicians, at worst a critical and, at best, a cooperative position, between religion and medicine has developed within our tradition. Though the focus of my ministry had shifted, I always continued writing on theology and medicine.

The following is an address I gave to an audience celebrating the centennial of Methodist Medical Center in Indianapolis.

THE GIFT OF THE WESLEYAN SPIRIT:
BIOMEDICAL THEOLOGY AND ETHICS

Methodist Medical Center, Indianapolis, September 27, 2007

I remember the discussion well. It was the early 1970s when we were forming the Hastings Center in New York City and the Kennedy Institute of Bioethics in Washington, D.C. About the same time, I was founding what would become the Houston Institute of Religion's Medical programs and what would become the Park Ridge Center in Chicago. Each of these centers, including your great center here in Indianapolis, sought to explicate and activate the cultural beliefs and values that could guide the enterprise of biomedicine and health care.

Faith traditions were a part of this cultural cache of values. David Smith of your Poynter Center wrote the Anglican volume in a series Martin Marty and I edited. At Hastings that day, two Methodist laypersons—Bob Morrison, the head of the Cornell University Medical Center and Paul Ramsey of Princeton—led the discussion. What set of inspirations, they asked, could have guided early 19th-century England—her science and industry, her personal and public health? Could it have been the vision of John Wesley? Yes—the Hastings Fellows agreed—and those strange people called Methodists.

It was an exuberant, yet foreboding, time as we met, much like today: the space program, intractable war in Vietnam, kidney and heart transplants, genetic and birth decisions, abortion, life-extension technologies, Karen Quinlan, when-to-die decisions and the agonies of medical triage. Then, to all this was added the challenges of providing care from this cornucopia of blessing for the sick and poor, both here and around the world. John Wesley, where are you when we need you?

In that ambiguous Camelot/city of Lot moment of the 1970s, so full of glory and darkness—both in knowledge and technology—big global issues in the macrocosm were working their way out in the microcosm of people's bodies. Lasers brought about lethal militaristics and life-saving diagnostics. Communications drew the world together and cruelly accented our alienations. While we tinkled out our little Bach preludes on Schroeder's piano, Linus' black cloud hung overhead. Principles of freedom and self-determination, justice and altruism arose within the issues of environment and energy, Vietnam and Israel, minority, women's and children's rights. All these were all symbolically being enacted in human bodies and clinical decisions—eugenics, Baby Doe decisions and "living-will" policies. We even used military acronyms—MOP + WHOP—to label cancer chemotherapies.

The great bioethics institutes, including Hastings, were created to address these quandaries. Without Wesley, claimed Morrison, the modern age of hygiene, child health, industrial safety, and public health would have been inconceivable. Cleanliness was next to godliness. And the field and street preaching, the "be ye perfect ethic," the manuals of health maintenance and ministry in urban hovels, added Ramsey, all fashioned a guiding theological vision to supply the worldly commitments. To this, my mentor and predecessor at Garrett added virtues learned in his dad's Methodist parsonage in Mississippi: the inestimable dignity of each human being, the pervasive fall that discolored every human thought and action, and uncompromising commitment to justice and care for the sick and poor.

The lawyers, philosophers, and business people at Hastings were skeptical. Even in those days of lingering Eisenhower religiosity, it was clear to most that economic, legal, and technical considerations outweighed the theological. I was not convinced. Had we not learned from Max Weber, who had visited St. Louis in the early century, that it was religious history—the Puritans, Wesleyans, Calvinists and their religious ethic—that decisively shaped scientific history? That parameter, the spiritual/ethical, much more than politics and philosophy, contoured the practical life and death, birth and health judgments that persons made with their families.

Even our post-religious and post-theological at last was realizing its folly and coming to the end of an age of materialistic and positivistic obsessions about to what is really going on in this creation. And I use that word intentionally—for that is the secret of what the world is—the creation. For Wesley, theology is creation, therefore worldly, and the world is graceful, full of Spirit. Spirit defines world, and world is the setting of Spirit. This is Origen's *Logos*, and it is where Wesley starts. We think of the brilliant work of Carl Michelson—closed out so early—a worldly theology. This essay is indebted to him and to Albert Outler's two books on the Wesleyan Spirit.

This leads us to the thesis of this paper. Here, at the dawn of your new Centennial, let me suggest, as we close out one century of care and begin another, that the Wesleyan Spirit can and should continue to invigorate the world with:

- a graceful, incarnational theology;
- yielding an inquisitive and reverential science;
- a realistic appraisal of evil and wrong in a resplendent world;
- a humanistic therapeutics for health care; and
- a sympathetic care and justice for the sick and poor in the local and global healthcare community.

To begin, a few notes on Wesley. His times, his convictions, especially prevenient and public grace, provide foundations for today's challenges. Some of Wesley's most widely read writings were on subjects like electricity, energy, and medicine. His *Valuable Primitive Remedies*, a do-it-yourself healthcare manual, was found on the fireplace bookshelf in most American homes at the beginning of the 19th century. Take, for example, his remedy for the seasonal allergies that get us wired up and worn out in this ragweed season. Forget Claritin and Benadryl—just walk up the mountain and submerge in an icy spring pool and *voilà!* Vasoconstriction, *par excellence*. Among the myriad scholars who have studied Wesley's medicine are my own students, Phil Ott from Evansville and Wayne Martin, one of the circle of Methodist physician-pastors.

In Wesley's time, both the blessing and the bane of the dawning age were being felt. Public health, Vitamin C, better food on the table of what was always thought to be an oxymoron: English cuisine. Hobbes' brutishness and brevity of life—where everyone was at war with everyone—was in full fury. Now suddenly William Blake could dream of a paradise on England's mountains green. We could even build Jerusalem amid those Satanic mills.

Perhaps even that holy lamb of God would come back to Birmingham. But would he be welcome? Were things getting better—really better? Or was the world, as Reinold Niebuhr said, getting better and better and worse at the same time. Would Blake's chariots burn out in infernal chaos or would the blessed green vistas of Dickens' loving concern redeem Scrooge's counting house or Tulkinghorn's Bleak House? Would the mercenary and military spirit prevail in our world, or might a more Moravian mercy and munificence redeem the time? In our day of *Abu Ghraib* on the one hand, and the Lancaster Amish schoolhouse on the other, the choice is stark and the verdict is still out.

The great challenge to Wesleyan theology today is to retain sacred rigor along with secular relevance. As in all mainline protestant traditions, the Wesley boat is cracking in the middle. As pietistic evangelicalism and rampant secularism propel themselves in centripetal fury away in opposite directions from the Methodist tradition, only learned biblical grounding and efficacious practical ministry will call us back and keep us on course. How will Wesley Pavilion at Northwestern, Methodist Hospital in Houston—"the house that Mike DeBakey built"—and this center index that faithfulness and that future?

Incarnational Theology. Incarnational theology anchored in grace is the sustaining wind of the Wesleyan spirit. The heart of such a dynamic biomedical theology is a doctrine of "giftedness" grounded in mercy.

Wesley's conversion—a melding of Aldersgate and the fear-and-trembling decision to step out into the field preaching—was in Outler's words "a conversion from passion to compassion, from being a harsh zealot of God's judgment to a winsome witness of God's grace, from a censorious critic to an effective pastor."[43] His synergistic call to holiness and witness was framed by his Lord's Isaianic vocation "to preach to the poor, to heal the brokenhearted and bring deliverance to the captives" (Luke 4, Isa 61).

In an important new book, Harvard philosopher Michael Sandel claims that genetic engineering now poses a threat as it assaults human dignity and curtails compassion.[44] We not only scope out and mitigate, but now diagnose and treat genetic disorders—eliminating and correcting imagined flaws and guiding life trajectories toward conceived perfections. But our practice of medicine, he claims, is not undergirded by an adequate philosophy of medicine. Here we face another challenging aspect of Wesley's biotheology of the human condition and capacity. We need today an adequate realism of human sin, as well as an idealism of the human prospect. For such a challenge, Wesley is the man. He helped get us into this perfectionist game, and he has the grace-centered theology to see us through.

When Wesley posited perfectionism from his study of the Sermon on the Mount "Be ye perfect—as your Father in heaven is perfect" (Matt 5:48), he was drawing on Origen and the Eastern fathers—anticipating sinless and good beginnings and original immortality—but he also knew Jerome and Augustine, the Latin fathers, who accented our flaws, finitude and frailty. I think that Wesley swayed from one side to the other as he rode along on his horse, reading. And he got it right. Unlike the modern Methodist reactionaries called the "circuit riders" who prompted Halford Luccock to observe "I'd like to see those fat cats on a horse," Wesley and his riders sensed a subtle blending of these apparently paradoxical truths helping us see, as

43. See Outler, *Evangelism and Theology in the Wesleyan Spirit*.
44. See Sandel, *The Case Against Perfection*.

Hans Jonas showed, that finitude and frailty is blessing, that weakness is proleptic strength. If we could only see through appearance to reality, we might see glimmerings of "face-to-face" in that dark mirror. But here and now, we have no abiding city. As Augustine said, we remain the pilgrim people of Haran, Horeb, the Herodium, and *hajj*: Always living in tents, ever besieged, Bedouins ever blessed by the desert's night skies and refreshing oases. We need be as one described in a new book about one of our local heroes—Hoagy Carmichael from Bloomington—he was a little bit at home everywhere, yet still searching.

In a secular version of this paradoxical wisdom, Sandel proposes that we see our differences as gifts—what we could call in the Wesley vision elaborations of divine imagination and creativity—works of providential and prevenient virtuosity. Steroids can make us all Sammy Sosa or Barry Bonds hulks. Growth hormone or cloning can create lots of Michael Jordans—at least in genotype—but *can* they really, or *should* they? Phenotypic uniqueness in the spirit of grace are mysteries of diversification and spontaneity in what C.S. Lewis—after Wesley, who wore his bench for him At Christ Church, Oxford—called the divine Tao.[45] This way of health and life, giftedness—what Sandel calls "persistent negotiation with the given"—even the acceptance of suffering and mortality, is the clue to our humanity and our divinity.

Wesley glimpsed Hebrew and Puritan perfectionism hopefully, not as manic utopianism and cookie-cutter uniformity, but in divine giftedness. My favorite text on this scriptural messianism is the Jewish Yom Kippur *Seder*.

One afternoon, Rabbi Joshua ben Levi found Elijah standing at the entrance to a cave. "When will the Messiah come?" he asked. Elijah responded, "Ask him." "Where is he?" "At the city gate." "How will I recognize him?" "He sits among the diseased poor. All of the others loosen every one of their bandages at the same time and bind them all again. But he loosens and binds the bandages over his sores one by one. For he thinks: Perhaps I will be needed: I must be ready to go at once."

The messianic secret, the secret of the hidden mystery of health and disease, life and death is "With his sores we are healed" (Isa 53, Luke 1).

Today, the vestiges of Hebraic, Hellenic, and Puritan perfectionism have become an inordinate drive for improvement, blaming and suing, wanting and demanding, failing to reach an ascetic rest—Bach's insouciance—*Ich habe genug* (I have enough), and we bring unending vexation to

---

45. See Lewis, *Mere Christianity*.

the world. We need to recover the inherent giftedness of the given in our Sabbatarian heritage—Abrahamic faith—and not be so manic to change the world.

In international life today, the enemies of Wesley's Angloamerica are those we call insurgents, "radicalized Muslims," *al-Qaeda*, the evil wisdom in *Lord of the Rings* (Bk. 5, Ch. 9): "Other evils there are that may come . . . yet, it is not our part to master all the tides of the world, but to do what is in us for the succor of those years wherein we are set." This seems a most Wesleyan sentiment.

Some months ago now, an Iraqi doctor along with several medical colleagues from Saudi Arabia, Jordan, and India led an aborted bomb attack on London and the Glasgow airport. Britain—which wisely refuses any more to use mythic Manichean words like insurgents, "Muslim extremists," "war on terrorism," and "evil empire," and prefers a more Smylie espionage designation of "international criminals"—quickly discovered that this Iraqi doctor had watched his parental home destroyed and his parents killed by the American invasion. As I have tried to show in a set of books on war and medicine, wars against disease, against death, against enemies, are dangerous construals, and we need to discover something of the Semitic, Stoic, and Islamic grace sanctifying the given. Wesley, though so provincial in many ways, was able to look so deeply into grace that he could "look East" to see Tao, to see into Gautama's vision of the old, the sick, the suffering, and beyond, into an active serenity of grace.

To sum up our first point on the Wesleyan spirit of an incarnational theology of grace, I have argued that an *animus* has been released into world history that is formed in the half millennium of theological history from Wyclif to Wesley—a highly creative energy, divine and demonic, thrilling and treacherous. The guiding antidote against the destructive side of the ambivalent energy is *Logos*—incarnational wisdom embedded in Abrahamic, messianic, *Hikmah*—a Decalogic, *Akedic* Tao that guides our believing and living in the way of cross and resurrection, justice and mercy.

Wesley saw this in his brilliant vision of salvation and social justice, of faith and works inextricably united in holistic endeavor. Here, because of the omnisufficiency of grace, amelioration and acceptance commingle. Teilhard de Chardin captures the equipoise: "We must fight against disease and death with every fiber of our being for that is our destiny as living creatures. But when in the course of events death (or disease) becomes inevitable we must experience the paroxysm of faith so that death becomes the falling into a greater life."[46]

Messiah, Hikmah, Wisdom, Way, Truth, and Life. Jesus, recall, came with the awesome prophetic annunciation to give sight to the blind, mobility to the lame, release to the oppressed, and laughter to the brokenhearted—Jubilee.

As Hoosiers in this great company, you celebrate a century of medical ministry and contemplate the next, you will surely reflect on a checkered history: KKK, Hermann Muller, Alfred Kinsey, Baby Doe. There are the great experiments: New Harmony, Mayor Bill Hudnut's Indianapolis. You have Peyton Manning's Colts—unfazed even by the Chicago's Bears. I trust that the Indiana of Dick Lugar and the Bayh family will ultimately join New York, California, Pennsylvania, and Massachusetts in creating your own comprehensive healthcare system—especially at the social justice level—to overcome the seemingly unending inertia at the federal level. Such progressive states will seek human dignity in defiance of Michael Moore's *Sicko* and find a place where a brilliant frontier of medicine is joined to universal health ministry for the "least of these."

Your ministry in this medical center will be crucial as here we pursue Wesley's perfection as human responsibility and care. After the 1970s' Baby Doe cases, and the broader genetics revolution, Daniel Callahan deplored an outcome when "we will indeed have descended into the pit if we make genetic perfection a condition for the right to exist."[47]

The same will hold as I have shown in a series of books for dying well, living well, eugenics, euthanasia, Muller's eutelegenetics, eupolitics, and the rest of utopic manias. The careful and responsible dream is acceptable, indeed obligatory, for any just and good people. Doing good, finding commonweal, involves finding giftedness in all sectors of our existence—not only in church, but also in commerce, industry, education, science, the arts, sports (hello, Barry Bonds and Michael Vick), and international and domestic affairs. In the spirit of Wesley, we can translate grace into custom along the highways and byways of life, thereby redeeming and reconciling the world to its creation.

Beyond a theology of grace grounding the principle of giftedness . . . Beyond the iconic impulse of that idyll of Isaiah 60 where death will no longer seize children or impede living out one's full life . . . Beyond the aniconic

46. Tielhard de Chardin, *On Suffering*, 58.

47. Kevles, *In the Name of Eugenics*, 288.

impulse, which shatters the false idols that seek vitality or death over given life . . . the Wesleyan spirit also bequeaths to us a reverential, indeed enthusiastic theology of science.

There is a desperate need in the world today to renew the puritan covenant of science and technology for the end of the protection and enrichment of human life. Wesley felt this to be the vocation of our primary world institutions: church, business, health care and the state. Calvin had emphasized that human life fulfilled on Earth was the glory of God. And on the Luther side, Bach's "Goldberg Variations" show that what is excellent and beautiful, worldly wise, is much more to be desired than conventional religion.

If we can only be liberated from our faithless and inhuman manias to the hegemonic and security state (the biblically demonic quest for empire), we could then and must then redirect the marvelous divine providence into care of the sick and poor—the messianic mandate—Wisdom, Sophia in the service of life.

If we could significantly counter crime through caring education and esteem for the distraught poor, disease through careful prevention and accessible therapeutics, war and strife through justice-grounded peacemaking, and misery through philanthropy, we could reanimate John Milton's quest, so important to Wesley, of paradise drawn onto the Earth. Then the stellar Bethlehem gift might be realized and the Magi praise out of Mesopotamia, Africa, and Asia be heard again: peace on Earth, good will among all people.

In the next century of your history, and that of this nation and our world, the genetic basis of most disease will become manifest. The subtle connection between nature and nurture will be seen. Not only will vaccines and biologicals cover most infections, but most malignancies will yield to the combination of predisposition control, infection management, and environment manipulation. Then will become clear the biblical solemnity: "God saw all that He had made and behold it was good—very good."

For now, we must counter the blasphemous actuality of our scientific enterprise and its health derivative serving the few exotically and leaving the many in destitution. The plagues of Africa—AIDS, malaria, river-blindness, infant and young adult morbidity and mortality—shake the human fist in the face of the creator who yet pleads "Cain, where is Abel your brother?"

Michael Moore's indictment in *Sicko* is pretty much on target. What Paul Starr called the sovereign profession has become a negligent industry, and the poor, uninsured, homeless patient is dumped, even by the best of providers (*e.g.*, Kaiser, Presbyterian, Methodist) on the streets of Skid Row in

Los Angeles in the middle of the night. Thirty years ago when Starr leveled his indictment, which pretty much insured denial of tenure at Harvard, he showed that it was the Presbyterians and Methodists who cast the deciding votes to turn medical care over to the monopolistic fraternity. Now, the complex of business and law, insurance and pharmacy is diehard committed to keep it that way.

The spirit of Wesley always confounds this usurpation of the ministry of health. What sort of retrieval of his ethos can we make today? It is probably as impossible to recover a church-based health and welfare system that prevailed for centuries as it would be to move in this hyper-capitalist land to a national, universal, healthcare system—which the entirety of the developed world now enjoys. We need, therefore, to find a synergy among private and public endeavors, ecclesial, entrepreneurial, and public efforts.

We probably have maxed out now at near 20 percent of the GNP into health. Great investments continue to be needed in medical research, public health care, and mental and child health. We obviously cannot continue to spend such a great portion of the health dollar on diabetes and end-of-life care—over 50 cents on the dollar.

Our best hope lies in that "enlarged knowledge" of which John Milton and the puritans spoke, where self and family care combines with intimate parish provision (parish meaning every soul in the city, and not the diminished meaning of parish after Hurricane Katrina in New Orleans). To this needs to be added intense public altruism and finally, a resolute rejection of the "American way of death." All this needs to be based on Wesley's "experimental knowledge" joined to exacting social justice and provision for the weak and poor. Such ascetic wisdom bound into communal and global solidarity alone can save us from the present disgrace of our being known in the world as a self-serving, indulgent, materialistic people.

In a moving interview in the July press, Anne Marie Slaughter, Dean of Princeton's Woodrow Wilson School, calls for our nation to repent our errors of judgment and misdeeds against our own and the world's people. Katrina and Guantánamo must end. Rather than portray ourselves as the champions of MTV, "Bay Watch," promiscuity, and family disorder, we need to return to our bedrock values of rescue and refuge to the world's refugees, champions of the sublime values of liberty and equality, rather than privilege and greed. We need to strenuously concur with President Bush who, when seeing the pictures of *Abu Ghraib* did not ask, "How did they get those photos," but said, "that's not who we are." We need to hold him and ourselves to that abhorrence, repentance, and resolve—never again! We need, says Slaughter, to honor the distinguished civilization of Hammurabi, of

Mohammed and Moses, and Jesus, the Christ. We must cease denigrating other peoples as insurgents and enemies who may be home defenders and freedom fighters. We live in one God-given world, where each person and each people is unique and indispensable to the whole, not in Huntington's clash of civilizations where Muslims, or now Hispanics, are enemies to be subdued.

Wesley knew, as Luther his mentor, that loss of humanity was a symptom of the loss of God. When Joel Osteen preaches in his megachurch on how to smile, or T.D. Jakes speaks of success and prosperity, we realize that megareligiosity has become a source of megaimmorality. Nietzsche forecast that religion amiss would devour itself.

We learn that of the 150 of the graduates of Falwell's Liberty University who work in the federal government, 50 percent are under investigation. So, just as cleanliness is next to godliness, godliness is the substrate of morality, and the reverse. Paucity of human justice and love exposes the vacuity of religion. "By their fruits you shall know them" (Matt 7:16).

Doctrine of Wrong and Evil. This leads to our third point of the Wesleyan doctrine of wrong and evil and how this illuminates the phenomenon of biomedicine. On this point, Wesley displays a unique blend of Hebraic-prophetic, patristic, Lutheran (especially Moravian), and puritan influence. He was not a schismatic. He believed he saw the original vitality of Jesus' movement and the primitive church. It was a renewal movement in the English church.

Were he a citizen of our world, I believe he would be listening for the heartstrings of biblical, prophetic, Abrahamic faith. Wrong was therefore, like grace, a cosmic and universally natural and reasonable human phenomenon. Like Francis, he preached to all creatures and all tribes— Mohammedans, Jews, indigenous—even the odd Anglican. Birds, squirrels, and of course, the beloved horses—they were all God's family. His rendering of sin and dissonance within the resplendent creation retains this great secular universalistic currency.

I mentioned my work in Houston in the 1960s, when I was called to develop medical ministries within the Institute of Religion. Many say that the modern movement of bioethics began here with the pastoral and clinical programs with chaplains and nurses in the 1940s. One joy of my job was the liaison with COSTS—the Council of Southwestern Theological Schools. From our position at the center of the world's largest comprehensive medical center with some 40 schools, hospitals, and special institutes, we exchanged wisdom and knowledge with Austin, SMU, TCU, and the other great theological universities of what was then the great frontier of North and Meso-American immigration.

On one of my visits to Dallas, my contact, Albert Outler, called me to his office. He was compiling his massive edition of Wesley's works, and he had come across a sermon that he thought would interest me as a scholar of theology and medicine. It was a sermon on the Garden of Eden. Our primal forebears were delighting in the bliss of creation before the curse of disease, dissension, and death had intruded themselves into paradise. Our first parents luxuriated in the knowledge, the manifold provision all but those strange quarantines: "do not eat . . ." The woman picked the pear—much more succulent and seductive than some coarse and wormy Bramley—so intoned the grave and erudite Oxford scholar, now street preacher. Then Wesley sunnily stops and dramatically isogetes: "His heart and the vessels around it started to clog up." There you have it: the beginnings of atherosclerosis.

Wesley's definition of evil is a breath of fresh air and liberating animation for culture in general and biomedicine in particular. It provides a kind of Arminian antidote to the darker side of Calvinism and the genetic fall of Augustine. The doctrine of hamartiology and theodicy—sin and evil—bears more directly on health and disease, life and death than any other realm of culture. The enterprise of medicine must declare, either explicitly or implicitly, which problems it chooses to confront and which to accept. Take AIDS and diabetes, substance abuse and sexual diseases, for example. Diabetes— a recent epidemic—can be conceived as an inbred and genetic disorder or the result of misfortunate behavior—the diets of the poor and junk foods.

The understanding of causation (*i.e.*, the wrong) influences the treatment options—*e.g.*, screening or behavior modification—and often whether patients are esteemed or disparaged as "trolls." Unfortunate designations of good and evil (*e.g.*, homosexuality) have often stifled medical advance and treated people with injustice, even violence.

The current stem-cell debate is marked by a somber grey mood, which says that if you are going to terminate embryos, by God, you are not going to bring some good out of it for others. Not much better, it must be admitted, than this hyper-Augustinian view is the hyper-Pelagian, which holds that we must bring redemptive compensation out of the horror of global abortion by helping Michael J. Fox and Christopher Reeve.

An honest, realistic, and ethical doctrine of human responsibility is sorely needed today in medicine and health care. The tendency to blame is widespread, especially when it is joined to the right to sue. As we noted earlier, one implication of the doctrine of grace and giftedness is realizing that the given is not necessarily tragic. Our life spans—even our morbidities and mortalities—are not only boundaries and contradictions, but are salutary, even necessary, concomitants of life itself. Hans Jonas wrote an essay entitled "The Burden and Blessing of Mortality."[48] In Calvin and the Puritans, the doctrine of providence has great merit and comfort in its confidence that "each hair of our head is numbered," and "no bird falls from the sky" without God's knowledge and care.

In health care, we need an active, action-inducing theodicy, one that offers the continuing work of prevention and protection, but also acquiesces to an embrace of suffering and death in a cruciform wisdom that Abrahamic faith calls the *Akedah*. Waking one crisp morning at Walden Pond, Thoreau observed that we ought not to think of winter, with its ice and snow, as a problem to be solved.

The doctrine of fall conjoined to the reality of forgiveness yields a fulsome rendering of redemption. Such rich and searching insight will be absolutely necessary to the fathoming of the enigmas of disease in this coming age of biomedicine. The editor of the journal, *Science*, projects that the two dominant diseases in the world by the middle of the 21st century will be AIDS and Alzheimer's—irascible, complex, ever-mutating, defying human comprehension and control. Disease in the future will be more like this, hiding from immunological surveillance, resisting therapy. We have traded the easy for the complicated, the treatable for the chronic and incurable. In the next several centuries, we may isolate and describe the genetic predisposition and environmental stimulus of most disorders. Then what? Will we eliminate the tainted by screening or by designer reconception and the remaking of persons? Will we advance into an era of elective demise, when we each decide when, where, and how we take leave? Or will we revert to the ritual of the migrating peoples? Ice floes and sweeping floods will be frightfully omnipresent in the hot-box future of our own making, a future of socially engineered eugenics and euthanasia—that future so terrifying to artist, prophet, and poet.

For these reasons, I commend the depth and penetrance of a Wesleyan doctrine of sin, fall, grace, forgiveness, and new life as an appropriate ethical theology for the unfolding drama of biomedicine. Supplying much of the impulse of a modern theology of Spirit (See for example, Eugene Rogers and Sara Coakley) and religious life around the globe (especially the Pentecostal and charismatic movements), theology in the Wesleyan spirit avoids the extremes of sin viewed as chronic and inevitable on the one hand, and

---

48. Jonas, "The Burden and Blessing of Mortality."

imaginary as in naïve progressivism on the other. A healthy axiological theology acknowledges our injustices, insensitivities, self-aggrandizements,
and persistent failure in what we do and fail to do. Believing in the ubiquity
and dynamism of human wrong makes repentance, mercy, reparation, and
new beginnings possible.

Especially in health and disease, living and dying, AIDS and liver
failure, behavioral weakness and interpersonal failure, we need to always
proffer Eucharistic grace, forgiveness, and another chance. When the afore-
mentioned Chicago Bears tanked Tank Johnson this summer when he was
stopped late one night on an Arizona highway, supposedly under the influence, they failed to think it possible, because of his past misdeeds, that
his blood alcohol might be within acceptable limits, which it was. But his
career is finished, and beware Barry Bonds, Michael Vick, Tour de France
riders . . . beware the self-righteous, white-steed riders with sword in throat,
mowing down the unrighteous. Wesley's doctrine, though contributory to
a puritan ideology of evil, becomes insidious when only the smile remains
of the Cheshire cat, and Americans especially chide "how wrong of you to
think that I could be wrong." Goodbye, Tank. Maybe we'll just have to live
with another Colts Superbowl.

Humanistic Therapeutics. The next-to-last element of biomedical wisdom
found in the Wesleyan spirit is that of humanistic therapeutics. Teilhard de
Chardin calls this a delicate equipoise between life affirmation and death
acceptance. In my career, I have tried to strike this balance as a faithful response to my mentor theologians of the high middle ages, Renaissance, and
religious Enlightenment: Aquinas, Luther, Calvin, and Wesley. I have always
refused the simplicity of "right-to-life" or "freedom-of-choice" on abortion.
Freedom of choice to abort a female child is as wrong as is demanding the
birth of a child with Tay-Sachs disease. I have simultaneously insisted on the
right to live for handicapped, retarded, and critically ill children and elders
and the right to "let die," and assisted dying for those who feel it is a rudimentary good (as Joseph Sittler says) "to give your life back to God."

I testified in favor of what would become the Roe vs. Wade abortion
decision in the early 1960s. With Fr. Richard McCormick, I supported the
right of the parents of the Danville Siamese twins to withhold treatment,
a decision I honor after watching the weaker twin die after three years of
round-the-clock suctioning at nearby Misericordia Hospital, but one I regret
when I see the stronger son after the separation thriving as a young man. He
wouldn't be here if they had followed my advice and the wish of his parents.
Only the orthodox doctrine of fallibility offers forgiveness. *Peccata mundi*:

the ubiquity and universality of the "sins of the world" and *non posse non peccata* (Luther): "It is impossible not to sin."

I supported the morphine-induced terminal coma in the hypothetical case of "Debbie's Dying"[49] in opposition to the giants of medical conservatism and was honored when the thousands of letters from practicing physicians decisively favored that position. This landmark case revealed clearly that such decisions, far from being "no brainers," were deep ordeals of heart and mind, profound mysteries of good and evil—always entailing uncertainty, remorse, and forgiveness. My briefs on Karen Quinlan and Nancy Cruzan were on the side of the "let-die" judgment though, unlike the politicians, I shared no jubilation but only *mysterium tremendum*—a sense of awe before the solemnity of life and death.

On other issues that show the humanistic commitment to therapeutics, I support Oregon's attempt at public universal health insurance, even with a medical triage component. I welcome the movement of other states in this direction: New York, California, Massachusetts, among others. I honor the comprehensive heathcare systems of England, France, Belgium, and elsewhere, where our children enjoy excellent care without the terrifying fear of "will I be able to pay?" It is hard enough to be sick. The physician-aided dying in Holland, and informally in other, especially Protestant countries, seems worth exploring, and the initial results are promising in terms of not leading to abuse. I have advocated justice and equal rights for homosexual persons, as well as openness in the parish life and ministry of the church.

This generic persuasion grows out of my doctoral research in Germany on Nazi eugenics, euthanasia, and racism, where non-abortion and selective killing displaced therapeutic realism with ideology. That realism of Calvin, Wesley, Barth, and Niebuhr recognizes that we can unnaturally and cruelly prolong the dying process, just as we can fail to accept nature's own wisdom about living and dying at life's beginning.

I have tried to live out this realistic Wesleyan humanism even in my own family. My theology has always been clinical, personal and pastoral, rather than ideological. At the familial level, I approved of the decision of my Great Aunt Edith, a nurse-anesthetist, to give morphine to assist the dying of my great-grandparents when they were decrepit and in intense terminal suffering. I concurred with our physician-son and nurse daughter-in-law's decision to bring to birth our only grandson with XYY.

He's now a strapping seven-year-old, a promising artist like his uncle, and a mean tennis player. I agreed with the decision of our daughter and

---

49. Anonymous, "It's Over, Debbie."

son-in-law in Antwerp to risk a pregnancy, even though she carries in reces-
sive state a serious genetic disease. I even reluctantly supported our other
daughter, even performed her wedding to a diabetic, chronically-indebted,
Roman Catholic chiropractor whose little daughter Aislinn Moira we baby
sit with delight as I write this essay. In case you wonder about our granddaughter's name, her dad is Irish, and we all carry at least five lethal genes.

There you have it: the theological profile and the personal confession
of one who married into a Methodist family, who after decades of work
in the medical world has been privileged to close out his career teaching
in a Methodist seminary. As I now also study and write as a Fellow of the
Center for Advanced Theological Studies at Cambridge—where Catholic
and Anglican, Puritan and Wesleyan movements had their beginnings,
struggled, and to this day exert their vital and transforming spirit into world
history—I am increasingly aware that one of the Earth-changing spiritual
gifts of this heritage, which we all share and seek to perpetuate, is the gift
of science, medicine, and concomitant beliefs and values to guide their
expression and their utilization as life enrichments in our world. Humane
therapeutics, what I have called biomedical realism, seeks the equipoise
found in the wisdom of Qohelet, the preacher: there is a time to be born and
a time to die, a time to pick up sticks and scatter them, a time to laugh and
a time to weep, a time to win and lose, to succeed and fail. For we live inescapably, if we think about it, as surely as in Garrison Keillor's Lake Wobegon,
"where all the women are strong, all the men are good-looking, and all the
children are above average."

Social Justice and Community Solidarity. Now, we move onto Wesley's
final destination. Although an innovator, with Luther of the modern, personal soul, and individual religious experience, at his strangely warmed
heart, he is the champion of social justice and community solidarity. Along
with Wesley's impact on world history through its peculiar impact on
Angloamerica, his lasting impact is being felt in the conjunction of salvation and social justice. This balance and complement is sharply challenged
in contemporary biomedicine. Your great city is a microcosm of the world,
exactly like Chicago, Calcutta, or Beijing.

Although much better than Freetown, Kinshasa, or Khartoum, here
some children are provided orthodontic braces and private schools while
others are malnourished and without hope . . . all in the same city. In
Chicago, like Indianapolis, a white citizen in the suburbs will live 10 years
longer than his black counterpart in the ghetto. The white citizen will have
50 percent less incidence of tooth decay, back pain, cancer, hypertension,

heart disease, diabetes, and so on. And the gaping gap is growing to the point of becoming intolerable, at least between the top and bottom billion. Wesley's contemporary, Thomas Jefferson, though a racist, chauvinist, and gourmet, said, "I tremble for our nation when I remember that God is just. His justice cannot sleep forever."

Illness, especially illness that is preventable, bends you over and breaks you down. That is what touched Wesley's heart: persons, the dignity and glory of God in the world, broken, humiliated. In health care it is so severe. I remember leaving the hospital, day after day, seeing scared men and women with their hurting kids, waiting forever at the pharmacy line, a life-line of hope, only to learn that their medicine was not on the approved list—and they would stumble into the dark Chicago night in despair.

In health care, the alienation of rich and poor seems most pronounced and most unconscionable. Today, it appears that this discrepancy in health care can only become larger and more daunting. As technologies advance, fewer and fewer have access. Sophisticated heart and stroke therapy, genetic and prenatal choices, even the daily things like asthma, clean-air maladies, and diabetes seem to spiral out of control. Basics like access to wholesome foods—once near-at-hand in rural societies, now elusive in urban settings as are exercise and leisure. All these salutations of life more and more elude the poor. China may send fish and food, but this will diminish as quality controls and China's own affluence and appetite increase. I guess that antifreeze-laced toothpaste at least keeps your choppers from chattering in winter.

Wesley's answer of providence and justice was several-fold: it involved parish and neighborly solidarity, elymosenary relief both official and private, and prevention of harm, lifestyle enhancement, and sustenance and provision for those who fell on hard times (especially the biblical designates: widows, orphans, and refugees).

At its origin, Wesleyan economics accepted the capitalist surge and trickle-down flow of resources. Hear Wesley's words: "Earn all you can, save all you can, give all you can." Warren Buffett and Bill Gates are quintessential Methodists and Presbyterians.

But goodness-of-heart philanthropy is only a partial answer. We must also have the social welfare apparatus that Jews and Muslims, Catholics and Protestants have always advocated. Wesley, following Calvin, believed that the poor deserved our protection and provision. Our wealth was not our own, not our deserving. It was in part wrested from the poor and the indentured and was ours only in the sense of stewardship. When puritans and liberals—Locke and Jefferson—change the creed from the "pursuit of property" to the "pursuit of happiness," adding the French revolution's equality of all, it is a philosophical and cultural advance.

Regrettably, because of distorted theology, idolatrously corrupted, we still believe that we own and deserve what we earn, and we believe its even more insidious form that the world owes us our living and no one can take it from us. Yet in deepest truth, we know that we possess nothing, take nothing with us, and that the entire meaning of resource is to honor and serve the neighbor.

The most profound expression of the Wesleyan spirit of liberty and solidarity is found in Luther's dialogue with Erasmus in *The Freedom of a Christian*: "The Christian is the perfectly free Lord of all, subject to none." Ride on, Amen! But wait. There's more: "The Christian is the perfectly dutiful slave of all, subject to each." So where does it all end? We'll see about that—that's the offense of the spirit of Wesley and the gospel of the Lord he served. It's the essence of Torah and Tao. We close with *Neilah* (closing of the gates), the final service of Yom Kippur. The Messiah has been found at the gate, sitting with the sick and the lepers. Here at the membrane of time and eternity are Lazarus and Dives and Abraham:

> The sun is low, the hour is late; let us enter the gates at last.
>
> When a man begins life, countless gates stand waiting to be opened. But as he walks through the years, gates close behind him, one by one.
>
> Remember the unopened gates. Open them before they are locked.
>
> The gates do not stay open forever. We walk through the years and they shut behind us.
>
> And at the end, they are all closed, except the one final gate, which we must enter.
>
> Today I shall come, says Messiah, if only all of you would listen to my voice.

Before it is too late, let us open the gates that lead to blessing and beauty, enter the gates of Torah and tranquility, go through the gates of kindness and compassion. These are the gates to the eternal in this life. Friends, at this moment of remembrance and resolve, let us enter these gates.

PART FOUR

The Search for Synthesis

Ministry in a Faith-Conflicted World

HERITAGE AND HOPE

OUR SOJOURN IN CHICAGO proved lasting. Although we moved twice (to Hyde Park, then Evanston), and although we were short-listed candidates for chapel dean at Princeton and Chicago and seminary dean at Pittsburgh, we remained in Chicago. My own theological and pastoral interests broadened, as I was able to serve two congregations as interim minister: Church of Christ (a Japanese congregation) and the now predominantly African-American Second Presbyterian. The great privilege of preaching at Second, with the exquisite Tiffany glass and the professional quartet that included two winners of the Metropolitan Opera Competition, inspired my preaching skills and broadened my horizons.

The following sermon was preached at the 150th anniversary celebration of Second Presbyterian Church. Abraham Lincoln's widow and son belonged to the church. The train drawing his casket back to Springfield in 1865 passed by the throngs near the church. I tried to capture such heritage and hope in the message.

HERITAGE AND HOPE

Second Presbyterian Church, May 31, 1992

Psalm 127.1–2, Matthew 16.13–18, Hebrews 3.1–6

Chicago 1992—like 1942 or 1892 or 1842, for that matter—seems to be the best of times, or is it the worst of times? Chicago 1992:

- The roof of an underground tunnel collapses, spilling millions of gallons of river water into the basements of Chicago's great buildings, causing perhaps $1 billion in damage and losses.

- The Bulls and Blackhawks are still in the running for world championships.

- At Old Wrigley, the Cubs are nestled customarily near the bottom, and at new Comiskey, the Sox are poised, as expected, near the top.

- The city with broad shoulders dismantled huts for the homeless under the Halsted tracks, as it plans for a third airport, a gambling casino, and property tax caps.

- And here on the South Side, in the shadow of this dazzling and desperate megalopolis, a company of Christians gathers and dares to confess Christ before the city and resolves to live in renewed faith and hope into the second half of its second century. Our predecessors in these pews 50, 100, 150 years ago would be shocked and surprised to see Chicago today. They'd be shocked at the casino, racetrack, and riverboat gambling, they'd be horrified at Lotto's blasphemous advertising slogan, "the odds be with you." They were more candid about the psychology of temptation and piety than we are in our "live-and-let-live" age.

But, I think, they'd be pleased to see us here today . . . Afro, Asian, and Euro Americans—young and old, rich and poor. We have achieved a diversity that Presbyterians have always believed in and hoped for, but seldom achieved. That congregation that more than a century ago applauded the abolitionists and contributed to the underground railroad to aid escaping slaves applauds us today from the clouds. They gathered here in front of the church and grieved with President Lincoln's widow and son, members of this congregation.

A goodly heritage . . . a godly hope. Our foundation and building is secure, our future is sure and promising, no misplaced piling or leaks over our subterranean tunnels. Christ has cleared the pits and entered paradise. Built on this bedrock, we seek today to renew a good confession. Our scriptures ground us in the truth about confession and congregation.

Psalm 89 is a kingly psalm. Is the record of a commemoration service, such as the one we celebrate today. The people recall God's mighty acts of deliverance and covenant. They pledge renewed faithfulness and righteousness. I will sing thy steadfast love, O Lord, forever. With my mouth, I will proclaim thy faithfulness to all generations. Righteousness and justice are the foundation of thy throne. Steadfast love and faithfulness go before thee. Blessed are the people who know the festal shout, who walk in the light of thy countenance, and who shout and jump as the song and dance goes—our sister act and our brother act. "The church with Psalm must shout," wrote George Herbert, "no door can keep them out. Let all the world in every corner sing— my God and King."

Confession and profession: faithfulness is saying and doing good word, God Word.

Psalm 127 is a warning: Unless the Lord builds the house, they labor in vain who build it. Activity, even hyperactivity, without Word, is quixotic, beating at the wind. How often the church has become frenetic in self-occupation and self aggrandizement, while a world hungry for gospel and help goes wanting. "But didn't we cry Lord—Lord didn't we sing the right thing." "He who does my father's will, will enter the kingdom." Words without love and work are noisy gongs or clanging cymbals (1 Cor 13).

The faith we have inherited and share with our Hebrew forbearers is that given us at the opening of the Bible. God willed and created, and it was good.

Confession. Intention. Action.

When we move to the New Covenant, the New Testament, the New Confession, the note is the same. In the beginning was the Word and the Word didn't just sit there; the Word became flesh. Intention, action, Word, will, work. Truth is in order to goodness, contends all noble religion. It is the keystone of our book of order, "By their fruit, ye shall know them."

Take Peter's confession: there is generality and specificity in all confession. Who do men say that the Son of Man is? That's the question to the philosopher? To the politician? What in general is your worldview? What are your family values? Waiting for Perot, perhaps we say, "I have principles, but no programs." But who do you say that I am? Now this hits home. You know we are *Rocky* 2? We mark today the glorious threshold of summer; our children are now graduating, or commencing from nursery and grade school, from high school and college, from graduate, professional, or trade school.

For many, it is a moment of introspection, confession, and profession. In houses of worship, it is a time of *mishpatim* and confirmation. It is a time for many of our sons and daughters to stand up, take a deep breath, not look back, and say to the world: "this is who I am. This is who I want to be. I want this loyalty to mark my life." Just saying the words in front of other people seems to tie it down. We become what we confess. We damn or bless ourselves with what we believe in our hearts and confess with our mouths. Word is conformation. Autonomically, we say the creed, the Lord's prayer, even the Lord's supper. We utter our eternal benefit: Jesus is Lord! The words make it come true. Unless we were "Big Tuna Accardo," everyone here has been called forward at some time to make confession.

- Will you say a word to this young person?

- Will you teach this class?

- Will you pray at our dinner?

- Will you lead worship?

Confession is one of the most awesome phenomena of the human spirit: it changes us. And like Peter, we're on the spot and we think it and we say it and suddenly, perhaps even to our own surprise, it is so. "You are the Christ. The Son of the living God," and, as we say it, it is confirmed within us, and we are conformed to it. We become Rocky too! You are Petros and on this rock (*petra*), I will build my church, and the gates of hell shall not prevail against it.

Confession of life is always made against threat and adversity, against the powers of death. There is an ominous stillness and secrecy in this scene in Matthew. He charged them strictly to tell no one that he was the Christ. The trek to Calvary had begun. Jesus, says the Epistle to Hebrews, is the high priest of our confession. He is the sacrifice that seals our pronounced loyalty in life and death. Dietrich Bonhoeffer, who wrote a commentary on Matthew called *The Cost of Discipleship*, said that "when Christ calls a person, he bids 'him come and die.'" Martyrdom was in the air when our parents of the Heidelberg confession asked and answered: "Who is your only hope in life and death? My only hope in life and death is my faithful Savior Jesus Christ."

Anticipation of cross-like Nazi gallows pierced the sky for his friend Bonhoeffer when Karl Barth wrote the Barmen Declaration. It was the sign of the confessing church of Germany and now has an honored place in our Book of Confessions. We confess the truth that Christ, not the state, not the church, is Lord.

This brings us at last to our sermon text, "fight the good fight of the faith." "Take hold of the eternal life to which you were called when you made the good confession in the presence of many witnesses." Timothy is calling the church, its leaders and its members, to faithful confession amid the maze and morass of the demonic—that is, all that breaks and kills amid the ordeal, the apathy, the antagonism, the adversity. Fight the good fight of faith. Take hold of life—remember and sustain your good confession.

The cloud of witnesses—those who witnessed your confession—they watch over you. Your heritage is your hope. Our confession is a private, a parochial, and a public matter.

In those enigmatic words to Peter, Jesus speaks of confession as a personal, secret, quiet, non-coercive kind of witness. Tell no one. Let your manner of life attest your words, go into your closet when you pray. Theologian Carl Michaelson, whose life was taken from us so early, spoke of our confession not as a hammer, as in a Cecil B. DeMille movie, but as a gentle hint, a clue to the world as to what we've discovered life can mean. The church has a confessing ministry to its own and to the world. We have an intramural and extramural commission. This is nicely summarized in our Book of Order in a passage called "The Great Ends of the Church." This should be read on landmark occasions such as this:

> The Great ends of the church are the proclamation of the gospel for the salvation of human kind. The shelter, nurture and spiritual fellowship of the children of God; the maintenance of divine worship; the preservation of truth; the promotion of social righteousness; and the exhibition of the kingdom of Heaven to the world.

From these scriptures and sacred text, let us consider in conclusion three aspects of a good confession. These are qualities of faith, which honor our heritage and enliven our hope:

- we make our confession before the demonic and death;
- before a disbelieving world; and
- before the generations.

We make our confession before the demonic and death. "Where Christ erecteth His church," wrote Richard Bancroft in 1600, "The devil in the same churchyard will have his chapel. But the yawning gates of death and hell shall not prevail against the rock of a Christ confession." In the wake of Memorial Day this week, as the caverns of violent death opened again in Sarajevo, in the Gaza Strip, in Haiti, WFMT played Benjamin Britten's "War

Requiem." This magnificent oratorio was composed for the rededication of Coventry Cathedral. When you visit Coventry, you still see the shell of the old Cathedral destroyed by Nazi bombs. The 1940s, like the 1990s, were times when the demonic was ever-present. Now in the power of Coventry's confession, a new stark and dramatic sanctuary has risen from the rubble. Like the Kaiser Wilhelm Confessing Church in Berlin, also constructed next to the shell of its bombed-out predecessor, the Confessing church rises toward eternal life amid the rubble of human violence and death. We confess against the dread of death. She lay dying with cancer, a young mother— sheer and bitter tragedy. Leaving young children behind and a husband who loved her dearly. The pain, the nausea, the indignity; this was the end, it's over—no, not quite. Her last words: "I am baptized—Christ is my Lord! I will lay me down in peace, for thou Lord makest me dwell in safety." With His own blood, he bought her, and for her life, He died. The winter is past, the pain is over. Flowers appear on the Earth.

Before a disbelieving world. Our confession is made before the demonic and death. It is also made before a disbelieving world. God seems to have abandoned 20th-century humanity to its folly. We can grow genetically engineered super tomatoes, but not citizens. We can jimmy a satellite back secure onto the Shuttle Endeavor in deep space, yet we can't secure and heal a sector of Los Angeles. The world is caught up and condemned in its pretense and its obliviousness to need and injustice. A suburban church would not let its kids come to Comiskey Park a few weeks ago. It feared racial and gang violence. A North Shore Presbyterian spoke for thousands recently when he said: "No more taxes, no more AIDS, no more unwed mothers, no more dying—no more city."

The city can be Jacques Ellul's House of Dereliction—but Simon and Garfunkel were right and that North Shore geek wrong. "I guess the Lord must be in New York City;" "This is where God is," pleads Martin Scorcese in *Mean Streets*. Some would say of us what Jonathan Swift said of St. Anne's, Dublin: "A beggarly people; a church without a steeple." But God has placed our lives and our church, even with its blown-down steeple, here in the city, and we bless you from north, south, and west, who have come to show solidarity with us. The world betrays its unbelief by its poverty of heart and soul.

Before the generations. Finally, our confession is made from generation to generation. We pause today with thanksgiving for 150 years into a remarkable heritage. We thank those women and men, those youth and children, all who made a good confession, who kept the faith, who built the church, who came back from fire and sword, who made the coffee, spread the table, planted the tulips, ran the rummage sales, prepared the meals, tutored the children, comforted the bereaved, visited the sick, welcomed the visitor, invited the friend, offered the handouts—all in the name of the good confession, Jesus is Lord. In every gesture of care:

- they insured that the gospel was sounded in word and music;
- that the faith and life was conveyed in dedicated teaching;
- that pastoral care was provided; and
- that authentic Christian behavior was exemplified.

We also pledge our faith to generations to come. To our children and the children of this city, and to the persons who are making their lives in our part of the city: the young adults, the singles, the mothers and children, those struggling to make it through the day, those struggling to make a living. We pledge ourselves to renew this city, to renovate its buildings, to enhance its beauty, to make our streets smart and safe, to strengthen family and community, to provide love and care in the neighborhood, to sustain a sense of prayer for all people where God can be known, worshipped, and served. In sum, to seek a lovely and sustainable world for generations to come.

And our most solemn and sacred trust is to be true to Christ and to Christ's future. Let us pledge with all the strength within us to present Him as Lord to future generations, and to that end, we will teach and pray, worship and sing, reach out and love, work and march, all to a good confession. "Lord, knowing that unless you build the house, we who build it labor in vain. Unless you watch over the city, we stay awake in vain." We would be building now those temples still undone! Amen.

My own mind was also expanding in an attempt to synthesize not only science and theology, but worship, music, liturgy, the arts, literature, film, indeed all aspects of culture. The following meditation was offered seven years earlier at Grace Lutheran Church in River Forest during the performance of Bach's "Cantata 93."

WER NUR DEN LIEBEN GOTT LÄSST WALTEN
(CANTATA #93)

Grace Lutheran Church, Sunday Feb. 17, 1985

1 Peter 3:8–18

The ambulance carried an 18-year-old black boy into our emergency room. He had pulled a knife on an old man as he carried home his groceries on Chicago's west side. Unexpectedly, the old man pulled out a gun and shot him in the head. He died the next afternoon at the University hospital. That same day on the northwest side, a 76-year-old man buried a pocketknife in the arm of a 19-year-old girl as she, at knifepoint, sought to relieve him of his watch and money. Two old men now join Bernie Goetz, the New York subway vigilante, as our newfound heroes. In the words of a rather bizarre film, *Network*, they were "mad as hell; they refused to take it anymore."

We wonder how we will respond to the ravages of human malevolence, to inevitable sickness and suffering, to uncontrollable natural evil? Do we resist, resign ourselves, or take some intermediate posture? If we follow Niebuhr's prayer, how do we know what things can be changed, cannot be changed, and where do we find appropriate courage, serenity, and discerning wisdom to know the difference? These questions pressed in on the mature, 46-year old Johann Sebastian Bach in 1731 when he composed the *Cantata Wer nur den lieben Gott lässt walten*. Bach wanted to express both the daily trauma of our existence and the underlying trustworthiness of God. To express this distress and hope he was persuaded by Picander to use both modern free verse and the traditional chorale cantata form. Before him, he had two texts prescribed for the fifth Sunday after Trinity. A rather astute theologian, Bach knew the mysterious synergy and momentous power that was often found in the juxtaposition of lectionary texts. In the gospel for the day Jesus says to Peter: "Launch out into the deep water and let down your nets!" Peter answers, "Master, we have toiled all night and come up with nothing. But at your word we will fathom the depths again." The night was followed by morning. The empty hold was filled. The yield was abundant.

The second text was more difficult. Set against the background of the violent persecution in Asia Minor in the first century, the Epistle from First Peter says in sum: As you suffer for the right, you are drawn into the depths of Christ's passion. In that anguish, you will participate in the joy that was set before him, enabling Him and you to endure the cross. Live therefore in mercy, sympathy, and gentle submission, a patient example to your persecutors. Don't live in aggressive retaliation to the wrongs of life, yield to Christ who did not resist evil, but overcame evil in His good cross.

Two passages: both baptismal texts in the life of the early church. Peter, the frustrated fisherman, letting down his nets into the depths of Galilee's sea; Peter the Apostle, about to be let down to his death in inverted crucifixion, planted deep in Rome's soil under Nero. The toil of life, the torture of death, and all the tragedy in between—Bach lifts it all, the baptismal drama of life and death—into the illuminating and fortifying presence of *Christus Victor*. The one who suffers on in victory for the regeneration of this, his world.

Bach also had before him the Luther Bible texts of Psalm 55—one of those whining songs of complaint about the persistence of woe . . . "They rise against me . . . lie in wait for me . . . stalk the city like dogs to jump and devour me . . . Lord consume them in your wrath . . . have the last laugh . . . You are my strength . . . my defense"—In these Psalms as in the book of Job, evils are personified as enemies who conspire against us and attack us. All the evils of life are enemies with faces: violent thugs, rapacious merchants, belligerent nations, negligent landlords, faithless friends, misunderstanding family members, bad genes, cruel circumstances, degrading poverty, icy blasts, malignant diseases, meaningless deaths. We cry out to the Lord, our avenger: Expose them Lord, bring them down. "I won't take vengeance into my own hands, I promise . . . but only if you're sure that you will heap burning coals upon their heads." "Damn you, you'll pay for this" . . . so natural, so satisfying.

Remember how the embattled Job exulted "I know that my avenger liveth and He shall stand at last upon the Earth." Handel understandably preferred the mistranslation "redeemer." Can you imagine a soprano rendering the gentle aria, "I know that my avenger liveth?" Anyway, I'm afraid the avenging Lord is not the avenger we crave. He's not Mr. T., the A-Team, Dirty Harry, or Rambo. He doesn't attack our enemies. He doesn't even show them up. He doesn't obliterate the pain of life. His Word is very much out of step with the modern theodicy. You know, "Why did God do this to me?"

"Why do bad things happen to good people?" All these arrogant theodicies are based on gods Kierkegaard called "ludicrous twaddle." Our little systems have their day. Identify cause, impute blame, and demand recompense. His Word . . . be still . . . wait his leisure . . . suffer God to guide you. Psalm 55 concludes "Cast your burdens on the Lord. He will suffer for you." Of course, fight back when it is seemly . . . do your own part faithfully. As Mahalia Jackson says, "Don't ask God to bring the mountain to you when your feet and legs are in good shape." Above all, trust in him all your ways.

Victory over evil is moral response, not passive resignation, nor violent re-taliation. In Gandhi's word, it is *satyagraha*—love force.

In the Cantata after this first statement of Neumark's classic hymn by the choir, we have the recitative, one of the most powerful passages in the Bach repertoire. Here, Bach asks where release and rest is to be found. When neither fresh dawn nor gentle evening can satisfy our tears, our only joy is *Christlicher Gelassenheit*, letting go to the leading on of Christ.

A number of us in this congregation, indeed the congregation itself, is active in "Project Ten: Health Medicine and the Faith traditions." We recently had a letter from a North Dakota physician who belongs to the Hutterite faith community. This small religious group has their own philosophy, in-deed practice of medicine. This doctor explained why his community could not accept modern Western medicine. Why? *Gelassenheit*, he said; you re-fuse to let go. You fight, you attack disease and death . . . you refuse to give up, to give over, *Gelassenheit*.

You know giving up is one of the loveliest Christic words in our vocab-ulary. In crucifixion, Christ gave up his life. Giving up has become an ugly, chicken word to us. Yet Bach poses it as a magnificent and strong virtue. *Er trägt sein Kreuz mit Christlicher Gelassenheit.*

In this passage, that primitive chorale is joined to free-flowing verse to express the grip of inescapable circumstances, the plaintive wandering of abandon, all undergirded by the ultimate constancy and security of God. In Albert Schweitzer's words we have *cantus firmus* and gay insouciance, liter-ally, carefreeness. Then follows the tenor aria and the women's duet and the theological contrast of two moments, two hours. The hour of trial—*kreuzes stunde*, the hour of joy—*Freudestunde*. God's grace does not abandon us in our hour of need—He knows us intimately: our every thought, every need. He knows what is happening to us; He does not allow affliction to over-whelm us, he sends his help. *Er kennt die rechten Freudestunden.* At exactly the right moment—the *kairos* moment, his appointed time—he leads us through. As Paul wrote to the church at Corinth, "God is faithful, and will not let you be tested beyond your strength, but with the testing he will also provide the way out so that you may be able to endure it" (1 Cor 10:13).

That God allows suffering may be offensive to the theology of some. It certainly is offensive to those who worship the indulgent god Jane Russell called the "cosmic sugar daddy." But if God is really the one Jesus showed us, then all reality—history, politics, and natural day-to-day life process—is cruciform in its inner direction. This means that time and space are the environment for creation's straining and suffering toward redemption. God himself intimately participates in the vicissitudes of life.

Nothing befalls us, said my teacher Helmut Thielicke, that has not been allowed to pass the eyes of Christ and come on through to us. All that happens to us is therefore purposive.

I think we can go beyond this and say that God is in the midst of our lives, stirring up crisis. He is redeeming each of our lives day by day. He is renewing his creation, and that involves disruption and pain. Scripture, from the psalms and prophets to Peter, teach us that God is a refining fire, a shaker, an overturner. Falling into the hands of the living God is trouble, not rest. Crisis, in the biblical sense, means opportunity. God is breaking down our securities in order to break through, to bring new creation and genuine comfort.

The deepest meaning of our texts and the Cantata is that God, through Christ, is doing something in this world. His dealing with us as persons, churches, and nations, drawing us into turbulence and tumult, is, of course, is the meaning of baptism. All the great crises we face today ought to be seen in this light: God disturbing the comfortable orders of our lives: racial tensions, poverty, drought and famine, international relations, ecological collapse, nuclear holocaust.

This is the theology of Lincoln's Second Inaugural (note the resonance of this passage with the scripture texts and the cantata):

> If we shall suppose that American slavery is one of those offenses, which in the providence of God must needs come but which, having continued through his appointed time, He now wills to remove, and that He gives to both North and South this terrible war, as the woe due to those by whom the offenses came shall we discern therein any departure to those divine attributes which the believers in a Living God ascribe to him? Fondly do we hope . . . fervently do we pray—yet if God wills that it continue until till the wealth piled up by the bond—man's two hundred and fifty years of unrequited toil be sunk, and until every drop of blood drawn with the lash shall be paid with another drawn with the sword, as was said three thousand years ago, so still it must be said: The judgments of the Lord are true and righteous all together.[1]

Words of vengeance, violence, some say, but down deep were words of gentle resignation, *Gelassenheit*, magnanimity, and peace. In this spirit, in the tenor recitative Bach takes violent geophysical images to show the stillness deep inside. He creates a tempest around Peter, the rock. Like the night the storm came up on Galilee, master rescue us, lest we perish . . .

1. Abraham Lincoln, Roy Prentice Basler, and Carl Sandburg, *Abraham Lincoln: His Speeches and Writings* (Cleveland: World Publishing Company, 1946), 792–93.

peace be still . . . Peter is always at the eye of the storm. The song trembles with thunder, storm clouds and heat, wind and rain, even the convulsion of death . . . at the silent center of the whirlpool is stillness, calm, serenity. The peace of Christ.

If the winds and waves are under his sway, if the heights of the heavens and the depths of the seas and all that pass through obey his will . . . if even the sparrow's fall is comprehended, the fishes catch is surely Christ mediated and then turbulence is nothing less than his call, suffering his appointed hour, and sickness, his glorification. Elijah discovered at Mount Horeb, God is not the wind, not the fire, but underneath, throughout, within. He is the still small voice.

Six years after Bach's death, another composer was born, one who restored the vision of a caring God after the assault on belief wrought by the Lisbon earthquake of 1755 in the same way that Bach had restored belief devastated by the black death of the late middle ages. Mozart heard the truth of Bach's message and knew the same inner secret of life. That is why he and his contemporary Mendelssohn sponsored the revival of Bach and Handel, those two geniuses born in 1685, that *annus mirabilis* whose tercentenary we celebrate this year. Karl Barth called Mozart and Bach two of the church's great theologians. Why? Because beyond immediate and ultimate evil, which Whitehead called cosmic discordance, they heard a divine harmony. "Mozart," writes Barth, "had heard and causes those who have ears to hear, even today, what we shall not see until the end of time—the whole context of providence. As though in the light of this end he heard the whole harmony of creation to which the shadow also belongs, but in which the shadow is not darkness, deficiency is not defeat, sadness cannot become despair, trouble cannot degenerate into tragedy, and infinite melancholy is not ultimately forced to claim ultimate sway. Thus the cheerfulness of this harmony is not without its limits, but the light shines all the more brightly because it breaks forth from the shadows."[2]

"Break forth o beauteous heavenly light and usher in the morning . . ." Both Bach and Mozart allow the shaft of divine light to penetrate this shadowy world. Although Hindemith argues that Bach was never able to penetrate through the veil because of confinement in the musical forms of his age, he lifted those Earth-forms to such perfection that he achieved his own stated life purpose, "to create harmonious euphony to the glory of God and for the instruction of his neighbors." When he heard Mozart's serenade for 13 wind instruments, Salieri cried, "I was frightened—it was the voice of God."

2. Karl Barth, *Church Dogmatics*, III/3, 297ff.

"God needed Mozart to get himself into this world." And Bach—allow him now in this Cantata to get God into your world. Bach's final word is about God getting into our world with story and salvation, melody and harmony: "sing, *Bet Und Geh Auf Gottes Wegen*." Amen.

RETURN TO MINISTRY

I suppose it was inevitable. The return to the church and some form of ministry was encoded from those Pittsburgh forays into civil rights, those Watseka, Illinois pastoral routines, the pioneering medical work in Houston, Texas for which James Gustafson once complimented me as one of the many theologians doing ethics in whom one could still feel a theological imprint. In Chicago, especially with Project 10 and my increasing work in the church, I was able to synthesize theology and public life, the evangelical and the ethical.

In the summer of the year 2000, we were living in the Latin Quarter of Paris, and I was continuing to craft these memoirs. One night, I am alone while Sara dines (and films) with a Northwestern colleague. I am torn whether to go up to the ancient Romanesque Cathedral St.-Germain des Près for a concert where the Mussorgsky Choir of St. Petersburg was performing the Mozart Requiem. I need it! I have just passed an older woman who sits just down our street Rue Dauphin. She is a *clochard*, and I've watched her for two weeks. She sits all day and sleeps in the rough. Reminded by pastor on Sunday, I struggle to see God in her wretched, hopeless face. Although I am startled to tears. Her ragged dress is torn and pushed up around her scrawny legs. She is dying, I think. The exquisite *laissez-faire* of Paris permits no one to intrude. She lies on cardboard sheets right outside an upscale dress shop. I wonder if her time has come. With Mozart I pray *requiem aeternam and lacrymosa*. The *mystère de la vie, y de la mort*.

SEMINARY

My early retirement (age 55) from the Medical School and move into theology came when Garrett-Evangelical Theological Seminary invited me to join the faculty and start an Ethics Center in the fall of 1993. Furtive earlier attempts to reenter the religious profession (Princeton, Union-

Richmond, Pittsburgh, and Chicago) only convinced me further that this was where I belonged. Upon arrival, my agenda was clear. I wanted to formulate a foundation of theological ethics for the great public and personal social issues of our day. I had become persuaded by philosophers like Tris Engelhardt and Alasdair MacIntyre that a secular ethic was impossible. With Engelhardt, I agreed that the substance of ethics had to come from particular normative traditions. Procedural ethics (formalism) were possible from philosophy and law, but not goodness and right, justice and love. Where he and I differed was whether there was a compelling universal ethics of substance. I thought so; he did not. I then set out to explore the parameters of a root-religious ethic that grounded Judaism, Christianity, and Islam. Such an ethic would then likely resonate with the Asian faiths and secular philosophies as well. My *Akedah* book (*Jew, Christian, Muslim*) ultimately would test this possibility.

The ethic of the Hebrew tradition that Jesus also promulgated was my starting point. Here, in addition to sublime philosophy and theology, were found principles and concrete rules for agriculture, commerce, health care, and domestic life. I was not convinced with Luther or Paul that Jesus rejected these or their exquisite summary in Decalogue law . . . "no other gods," "do not kill," etc. Now with a twofold agenda of an inquiry into the religious foundations of ethics in my scholarly work and teaching an outward application, through the Center for Ethics and Values, venturing into the practical fields of business ethics, health care, political ethics, war and peace, etc., we could begin to make some small contribution to this compelling cause of the late 20th century. Could the parochial be united with the universal? Could the evangelical translate into the ethical?

I found appealing the claim of Philo and philosophical and mystical Judaism of the eternal and universal quality of the law. The Christian, especially Catholic tradition, had called this natural law. Especially when it came to the domestic and house code, the rules of birth, life, and death, of sexuality, marriage, murder, rape, and theft—these matters were handled with exemplary goodness, justice, and humanity. Idealist, utilitarian, and other pragmatic schools of thought could not come up with such compelling and nuanced ethics for the everyday life issues.

Autonomy, non-maleficence, beneficence, justice—the formal ethical categories—were just that form awaiting substance. Matters of temple and priestly regulation were not immediately applicable to present-day questions, except for the teaching about food, hygiene, and purity. Even these matters seemed to possess powerful currency to today's concern. In the beef crisis in England, the HIV pandemic (especially in the U.S. and in Africa), and the starvation crisis in Somalia and deeper Africa, we see the immediate relevancy even of the "ceremonial" ethic of Israel.

World law, such as it is, the laws of just war and war crimes, laws of the seas and environment, of international trade and development, of civil rights, universal laws of humanity and genocide, prisoners, and world trade could only rightfully be grounded in Hebrew Noachic and Decalogic statute.

Evanston and the Ethics Center offered everything that was needed. First there was (here and throughout Chicago) the critical mass of first-class biblical, historical, theological, and ethical scholars. Second, we had been able across the years to forge associations with churches, parishes, and synagogues across the city that would be the laboratories for the work of the Center. Finally, a cadre of wise and dedicated layperson-business leaders—among them Jerre Stead and David A. Shotts—would extend our vision into the world of business ethics and help us develop the significant funding base required for solid work today. Our hope at the center was to undertake helpful research, develop conferences on major issues in bioethics, business ethics, and just-war issues. We also sought to prepare publications for further creative work in numerous areas of ethics and values, with the *Dying Well, Living Well,* etc. series.

A grant from the Kellogg Foundation enabled us to undertake our first project on "Dying well in the late 20th century." On another program pathway—"Religion, war and peace"—we held conferences on Korea, Armenia, Bosnia, and Kosovo. As the millennium turned, Brent Waters joined Steve Long and me to offer invigorated and concentrated leadership to the center. Brent now continues as director, guiding a superb program focused more on the internal life of the seminary, theological, and bio-scientific issues.

The opportunity for a short sabbatical leave in summer and fall of 1996 added to our previous international and Middle East exposure and enabled us to lay further background knowledge behind my agenda of work. This travelogue is an account and analysis of how this adventure, seen against the clash of civilizations, cultures and creeds, shaped my research in the new millennium.

AN INTERPRETIVE TRAVELOGUE

Holy Land Pilgrimage, 1996

We hadn't planned it this way. We just took off from Strasbourg, six weeks before term there began. We accepted a longstanding invitation from Millie and Dimitri Vasilides to visit their hotel on the Greek Island of Samos. If the Apostle Paul had stopped there (Acts 20), why not Ken and Sara? We then took the boat across to Turkey. After a week there, we flew on to Israel for two more. During that time, I reread the book that I have most consulted since seminary (next to the Bible), *Christianity in World History* by Dutch mission-historian Arend van Leeuwen. I offer this short review on his sweeping questions of the meaning of theological history as I experience anew the places and times of the concourse of biblical faith beginning in Palestine/Israel, then in Asia Minor, Greece, Italy, and out to the edges of the world.

I want to trace a story with you. This story, many feel, has something to do with the meaning of God's work with this world. It is the story of Bible geography, history, and theology—the faith journeys of the biblical traditions. We will hang this story on places in Greece, Turkey, and Israel, working back in time. Some of the specific places are: Macedonia, Corinth, Athens, Samos/Samothrace, Patmos, Ephesus, Pergammon, Troy in Asia Minor, Byzantium/Chalcedon (now Istanbul), Bethlehem, Nazareth, Capernaum, and Jerusalem.

These towns and cities are only signposts in a broader story that involves the countless villages and mountains, seas and rivers, fields and plains that is the biblical landscape.

I want also to share with you the meaning of the ideas, beliefs, values, and concepts that arise as Hebrew faith becomes Jesus' Aramaic storytelling, Paul's Hellenistic theology in Greece and Asia Minor, and eventually the Muslim saga. We will follow the story all the way through to John's mysterious vision in Revelation regarding cities like Ephesus, Pergammon, and Megiddo (Armageddon) and Islands like Patmos. Why and to what effect does the biblical mind confront Syria and Anatolia, Greece and Italy?

Ideally, we would start with Italy or even Spain. Here is where the Christian testaments' historic trail ends, depending on whether the Apostle Paul died with Peter under the Nero persecution in Rome (c. 64

C.E.), or whether he lived to be an old man having completed his vision to carry the gospel to Spain (Rom 15.24, 28).

We begin one step back in Greece. One could go back to China, India, and Africa, but we find our normative source of being and meaning in the world more in the Greek Islands. The Hellenistic *oikumene* (household) was the theater where, under the *Pax Romana*, what Paul calls the fullness of time (*pleroma tou chronou*) (Gal 4.4) was made ready. The Greek language and its thought forms and the Greek theology and anthropology were both confirmed and confronted by an Aramaic and Hebraic message of a messiah. Was Jesus the Aramaic *Masa*, the Islamic *Mahdi*, the anointed King in the Davidic line (Hebrew: *Mashiah*), or was he the Greek *Christos* or *Sophia*, as is already designated in the Gospels? Did Paul (and Peter) do right by taking the gospel to the Gentiles, even the Barbarians? Had Jesus' intention been to go only to "The lost sheep of the House of Israel" (Matt 10.16)?

GREECE

It was approximately 49 C.E. when Paul embarked from the port of Troas, just South of Troy in Asia Minor, heading for Macedonia, Northern Greece (Acts 16). Paul, after his transforming Damascus road experience, had preached and healed around his home in Tarsus (Eastern Anatolia) and in Antioch, now Syria. His first missionary journey had taken him to Cyprus and Southern Asia Minor. The Second Journey worked the West Coast of Asia Minor, the interior Western cities (Phrygia, Galatia, etc.), and the circle through Greece. In Acts 15, a showdown council had occurred in Jerusalem where the legitimacy of Paul's understanding of the gospel, continuing limited obligation to Jewish law, and his mission to the Gentiles was affirmed.

Now Paul is confronted one night (Acts 16.9) by the visage of a man from Macedonia saying, "Come over and help us." After overnighting on the Island of Samothrace, they (Paul, Silas, and Timothy) sailed for the Greek mainland, landed, and preached in Neapolis and Philippi. Searching for Diaspora Jews along the Gaguitis river, he finds there Lydia and her family, from the Island of Thyatira, a wise businesswoman selling the valuable purple material so famous in that region. They were God-fearers (though non-Jews, they knew and honored the monotheism and ethical monolatry of Judaism), and the Lord opened her heart to give heed to what Paul said . . . she was baptized, along with her household, and she said, "if you have found me faithful come to my house to stay" (Acts 16.14, 15).

A church is founded. In fact, some 10 or 12 years later, Paul writes (probably from prison in Rome) to the church at Philippi, including "the bishops and deacons (1.1) (*episkopos* and *diakonos*)." What has transpired in this short decade to bring about this development?

Just as Jesus found good soil for the Word in and around Capernaum (although not Nazareth itself, a few miles away) and animosity in Judea and Jerusalem, so Paul found friendly soil out among the Gentiles, and hostility in Jerusalem. Jesus, James, and Paul meet their fate and were assigned to their deaths in Jerusalem.

Why is it that the true picture of God and the right way humans ought to live (monotheism and ethics) find their way into the world through Abraham, Moses and Sinai, David and Isaiah—through the corridors of the history of Israel? Why then does this *visio Dei* and *via Dei* move from Israel to Asia Minor, Greece and the hinterlands of the world (eventually Barbarian Europe)? Why does Byzantine Christendom leave behind Israel in Diaspora, in near extinction, and why does it leap across Arabia, where Mohammed would fill the vacuum of law and gospel (*Taurut* and *Injil*) with Islam? In my view, the gospel way ("the law of Christ," Romans 1) is inescapably Hebraic. To de-Judaize Christian theology is to disavow the biblical heritage and distort its theological and ethical structure. The Word of God and life for the whole world enters through this pathway. God willed that "the Way"—a Hebraic, universal, and novel conviction— take flesh in the Hellenistic *oikumene* during *Pax Romana*. How can we respond to this enigma of history? What is the *Heilsgeschichte*, the history of salvation? Yes there was vital Christian witness in places like Syria and Persia, Ethiopia and India—no place has been left without a witness—yet the dynamic thrust is westward ho! Greece brought to the gospel, as the Apostle John would show, meanings of the Hebraic religious revelation through what Jesus embodied as the (1) way, (2) truth, and (3) life (John 14.6). Let us explore dimensions of reality in light of Greek ethics, philosophy, and theology—tagging reflection onto the Greek cities of (1) Thessalonika and Corinth, (2) Athens and (3) Philippi.

THESSALONICA AND CORINTH

Thessalonica and Corinth were two great cities where Paul founded churches and where monumental ethical crises in ethics were faced. Here too, Christian faith confronted the full excellence and limitation of the Platonic (Pythagorean) theology and the Aristotelian ethic. What was that system and how did it contribute to the church crises that occasioned Paul's letters to Thessalonians and Corinthians?

On arrival in Thessalonica, Paul immediately went to the synagogue where he preached and argued from the scriptures "that it was necessity for Christ to suffer . . ." (Acts 17.2). Here, we see the beginning of what Paul would later (to the Corinthians) call the Gospels' offense "a stumbling block to Jews and folly to Greeks" (1 Cor 1.18ff). Incited to resentment, the locals co-opted some riffraff to attack Jason's house and haul him and "some of the brethren" before the city council. The charge was leveled: "those who have turned the world upside-down have come here also" (Acts 17.6).

Equanimity, moral balance, and civic peace were supreme values for the Greeks. The noble virtue of *isonomia* (equality in law) is present when Zeus rules the *polis* and Themis (right) and Dike (justice) are his consort and daughter. The classical idea of liberty (*eleuthera*) involved taming the inner soul and the outer world into exquisite balance and equipoise. Already, we anticipate a dissonance with that worldview deemed derivative of Hebraic-Christic Torah and gospel. The Hellenistic peace and excellence of life is a human construct combined with the *Pax Romana*, which included stoic serenity and natural law. This concept was posited on the basic premises of sheer human power and all-sufficiency.

We learn more about the confirmation that caused the trio to skip town abruptly in the earliest New Testament writings: the two letters to the Thessalonians. Paul draws on the Greek philosophical and ethical heritage to address matters like civic responsibility, marriage, and community life. Written perhaps as early as 49 C.E., Paul calls on the congregants to be "imitators of Christ," "free from idols," "example to all the believers in Macedonia," "pure and blameless in conduct," poised for "the day of the Lord."

To those whose hope for Christ's immanent return has led them to drop work and just wait around, he counsels civic responsibility, "Those who don't work shouldn't eat." The Word and way of God is wisdom and power (*theou dunamin kai theou sophian*). (1 Cor 1.24)

How does Greek virtue and ethics more generally resonate and contrast with the life of Christ-participation and obedience called for by Paul? Greek virtue was to control the passions by the inner citadel of contentment.

Overriding love (*philadelphoa*) for fellow humanity constitutes the noblest *eros* in Pythagoras. The Christian community is commended to faith and love (*pistin kai agapein*) for one another and for all (*pantas*). Sobriety and watchfulness undergirded by expectant (hopeful) work for righteousness is the heart of piety (*eusebia*) in both schools. A universal piety, always there, has been designated valid for all.

There are also peculiar features to the Christian ethic. The Greek acts from reason, the Christian from fear of God and awareness of the impending wrath of God. Put more positively, it radiates from the "love of God" and the "desire to please God." As the modern philosopher Wittgenstein would say, "We are to embrace the two-fold virtue that comes from wisdom and the fear of the Lord." The Christian ethic, like the philosophical, blends piety (relational devotion to God) with justice (humanitarianism). Now, however, rightful being and action is grounded in the being of God, just and benevolent, and the sheer will of God. There is no emphasis on reason or calculated benefit. In Thessalonians, in fact, Paul defers from speech and act that flatters or pleases men (1.5).

At Corinth, also we find an ethical dialogue among the values of the Hebraic, Aramaic, and Hellenic mind. Paul, we surmise, did not feel quite at home with the Greek philosophers at Athens. As we will see later, the critical philosophical mind resonates with the prophetic in one sense—that of the iconoclastic—but critical reason enthroned to ultimacy leads only to sophistry, skepticism, and relativism. Paul had heard a transrational, transempirical word. Paul's mind and spirit was inflamed with the gospel of Christ's salvation and the drama of redemption in this passing world. For him, philosophy offered no release from sin, not even the noblest Socratic virtue. I think he was more stringent than God at this point. For him, Christ alone brought forgiveness and new life. So he passed on quickly to Corinth, 60 miles west of Athens. A great city in antiquity, its population is estimated at half a million in the first century of the Christian era. The channel of Corinth and the Isthmus made it a lively center of trade.

An important event in Corinth was the conversion of Crispus, the leader of the synagogue. One wonders whether the moral vision of life in Christ, with its strong Judaic tenor, had appeal for this synagogue president who also, we can assume, held out strongly against the licentious values and practices of the surrounding culture. Though brought to the authorities on false accusations, Paul was never brought to trial because Gallio, the proconsul (brother of Seneca the philosopher), found no breach of Roman law (Acts 18).

Paul's letters to the Corinthians are some of the loveliest and most powerful texts of scripture. The first letter is written about 54 C.E. from Ephesus, addressing several matters of dispute about proper Christian behavior. Two prominent issues were in the realm of human sexuality and concern for the disadvantaged.

The introit to the first letter contains Paul's theological reflection about Judaic and Greek convictions and commitments. The Jews sought a sign, that is, they demanded concrete righteousness according to classic Deuteronomic standards of fruitfulness, rewards, and punishments. The Greeks, on the other hand, sought wisdom. Both the scribe and the debater of this age were going the right way, but not all the way in their search for virtue and wisdom. Christ crucified, the power of God to salvation (and forgiveness of sins) to all who believe was the capstone of God's way and truth.

To both Jews and Greeks, Christ is the power and wisdom of God, for God's weakness is stronger than human strength and God's foolishness is wiser than human wisdom (1.24, 25).

The spiritual and ethical life of humans is a search for power and wisdom, which is for a self-mastery and self-understanding of life. Paul contends that these qualities are not human artifacts or achievements, but gifts of divine grace. It is looking away, rather than living "the Way." As long as humans seek to impress (sign) and fathom (wisdom) reality, they do it their way and fail to yield to the overarching authority of God. Sin is simply egocentrism. In the crucified One, we meet that inversion of human aggression and intelligence that is way and truth.

Corinth was a licentious place. On the great mountain, Acro Corinth, stood the temple of Aphrodite, the epitome of that disorienting *eros*. Here, Paul sketches the contours of the Christian existence, which draws away from the idolatry and immorality, the disrespect and injustice, of our pagan background to "new life in Christ Jesus" (1 Cor 1.30, 6.11–20,

7.17–24, 12.12–13). Building on pagan (stoic) ascetic and austere discipline, he counsels the community "to bring all thoughts captive to obey Christ" (2 Cor 10.5). This way was now extolled as life's joy, meaning, and fullness.

Jesus has come into the world, so Paul unfolds in his elaborate theological Christology, to restore human life in the cosmos to its lost innocence and goodness (Rom 8). This original righteousness, depicted in the first Adam before he went wrong, is now re-embodied in this second Adam, Christ. He is the new Abraham, the pioneer of faith and the new Moses, the recapitulator of "the Way." Taken by the Holy Spirit into His life through the forgiveness of sins and obviation of the fall, a new existence, both primal and *Parousial*, begins.

In the Corinthian correspondence, Paul sets forth a new Christology of love. The inflamed primitive *eros* of the Aphrodite cult and the Hellenistic-Roman dispensation only sought to appease the fertility and orgiastic deities and fates in their caprice. Since these ultimacies and norms are unreal after the gospel, such beliefs and practices are erroneous and destructive. Now an excellent theology of the body, of marriage, of love, and concentrated benevolence in service to the world is offered in Christ as the culmination of all that was sought and yearned for in the 1000-year Corinthian ethos. This expectancy that went back to Aristotle, Plato, and Socrates, to Pythagoras in his penetrating musings, to Homer and the brilliant Mycenaean epic emerging in pre-history Cyprus, Crete, and the paradisal Islands of the Mediterranean was now culminated in a vision of life and love that would forever change the world:

> And I will show you a still more excellent way.
>
> If I speak in the tongues of men and of angels, but have not love, I am a noisy gong or clanging cymbal. And if I have prophetic powers, and understand all mysteries and all knowledge, and if I have all faith, so as to remove mountains, but have not love, I am nothing. If I give away all I have, and if I deliver my body to be burned, but have not love, I gain nothing.
>
> Love is patient and kind. Love is not jealous or boastful; it is not arrogant or rude. Love does not insist on its own way; it is not irritable or resentful; it does not rejoice at wrong, but rejoices in the right. Love bears all things, believes all things, hopes all things, endures all things.
>
> Love never ends; as for prophecies, they will pass away; as for tongues, they will cease; as for knowledge, it will pass away. For our

knowledge is imperfect and our prophecy is imperfect; but when the perfect comes, the imperfect will pass away. When I was a child, I spoke like a child, I thought like a child, I reasoned like a child; when I became a man, I gave up childish ways. For now we see in a mirror dimly, but then face to face. Now I know in part; then I shall understand fully, even as I have been fully understood. So faith, hope, love abide, these three; but the greatest of these is love. (1 Cor 13:1–13)

"Love is patient and kind." The disdain, indeed contempt, for the weak and poor was a fatal flaw in the Corinthian and Hellenic philosophy of beauty, symmetry, and excellence. The sound mind in the sound body, so extolled in archaic and classical art, statuary and literature, is again challenged by the theology and derived anthropology and axiology of Christ crucified. Paul is writing (1 Cor) from Ephesus (16.8), waiting to return to Jerusalem for Succoth. Here, with Diaspora Israel, he will reenact the Decalogue, now intensified in meaning by the Holy Spirit's invasion of the world at Pentecost. The meaning is the same, whether it be at the Lord's supper (the commensurable sacrament where rich and poor, poor and destitute are joined in enacted new life and sharing (*koinonia*), at resurrection (ch. 15) or in the offering for Jerusalem (part of the crucial ethical arrangement in Acts 15); the poor and needy are held dear in that which we, "set aside and store up on the first day of the week" (16.2).

While on this point, let me share my view *en passant* of the accord reached in Acts 15. I think Paul is reticent to tell the whole story here or elsewhere, and since he exerts enormous sway over Luke (his traveling companion) and the other evangelists who finally record the gospels, we get a biased rendition of the event. As for my bias, I accept the view of my faculty colleague Robert Jewett, who has completed his *magnum opus*, *The Hermenia Commentary* on Romans.[3] Jewett believes that the spiritual requirement of gospel inspiration to the western edge of the empire (known world) was reciprocal with the ethical requirement of poor relief back to Palestine. Salvific righteousness and ethical righteousness were joined hand-in-hand. Acts 15 seals the deal. The evangelical and the ethical have sublimely fulfilled each other.

3. See Jewett, et al., *Romans: A Commentary.*

ATHENS

If the Greek "way" is confronted at Philippi, Thessalonica, and Corinth, the Greek "truth" is confronted in this brief appearance at Athens. The glorious city of Pericles and Plato, of Aristophanes and Aristotle, seems as foreboding to Paul as Jerusalem was to Jesus. But just as Jesus set his face to Jerusalem from his verdant and beloved Galilee, Paul knew he must go to Athens.

Paul arrived in Athens alone, having left Silas and Timothy in Berea. Agitated at the pagan spectacle that greeted him in stone and sun, he entered the synagogue and *agora* and argued with any who would be engaged. The Stoic and Epicurean philosophers heard him adjudicating religious matters.

Athens was a complex city, like Jerusalem. Though its past glory had faded—though glorious democracy and debate had deteriorated to near tyranny and cynicism—still it remained a cosmopolitos with a noble tradition of philosophical and religious inquiry. The text is remarkable:

> So Paul, standing in the middle of the Areopagus, said: "Men of Athens, I perceive that in every way you are very religious. For as I passed along, and observed that objects of your worship, I found also an altar with this inscription, 'To an unknown god.' What therefore you worship as unknown, this I proclaim to you.
>
> "The God who made the world and everything in it, being Lord of heaven and Earth, does not live in shrines made by man, nor is he served by human hands, as though he needed anything, since he himself gives to all men life and breath and everything.
>
> "And he made from one every nation of men to live on all the face of the Earth, having determined allotted periods and the boundaries of their habitation, that they should seek God, in the hope that they might feel after him and find him. Yet he is not far from each one of us, for 'In him we live and move and have our being'; as even some of your poets have said 'For we are indeed his offspring.'
>
> "Being then God's offspring, we ought not to think that the Deity is like gold, or silver, or stone, a representation by the art and imagination of man. The times of ignorance God overlooked, but now he commands all men everywhere to repent, because he has fixed a day on which he will judge the world in righteousness by a man whom he has appointed, and of this he has given assurance to all men by raising him from the dead."

Now when they heard of the resurrection of the dead, some mocked; but others said, "We will hear you again about this." (Acts 17, 22–32)

Paul first appeals to local beliefs and customs, reading their own inscription and later quoting their own poets. But his heart and mind are provoked within him at the idolatry and intellectual insolence. He concludes his message with a condemnation of idolatry, of ignorance (once overlooked) and announces with a John-the-Baptist fury and impending judgment the call for repentance and the ultimate decisive confrontation of Jesus' resurrection from the dead. The listeners were outraged or amused, but a few were ready to hear more . . . "We will hear you again about this."

Herodotus found the genius of Greece in four elements:

- the literary form—the epic of Homer;

- the religious form—the Olympian Pantheon;

- the political form—the *polis*; and

- the intellectual form—Greek philosophy.

All of these epistemic and ethical forms (movements) have endured with great power into the modern world. The discipline of "natural philosophy" as the instrument of a search for truth may be the noblest achievement of Greece. How does the confrontation of Paul with the Jesus gospel (especially with the folly of crucifixion and resurrection) square with that achievement?

Boldly indifferent to religion, Ionian philosophy in the seventh-century B.C.E. pioneered an empirical and theoretical brilliance that would lay the foundations for natural science for millennia to come. Thales and Anaximenes, Pythagoras and Democritus opened windows in the search for truth and reality. Pythagorus, first in Pythagor, Samos, then Athens, and later in Persia and elsewhere, probed the formal structure of reality in music, theology, and mathematics. Thales had two great insights: all is water and all is restless. Black-hole theory and the entropy principle have improved little on that.

But what about these contradictions to common sense and cause and effect? What is this "babbling" (Acts 17.18) about redemptive suffering and saving resurrection? The conflict with philosophy, I take it, occurs on two fronts. On a third front there is, I believe, broad agreement.

Greek philosophy, which fundamentally dissociates theory from practice, idea from appearance, and form from matter, cannot accept that the Holy could suffer or that the dead could rise. Though idealist and mystic thought abounded in Greece, it could not accept a profound co-mingling of spirit and matter which would allow Job to sing "Though worms destroy this body—yet in my flesh, I shall see God" (Job 19.26).

A major critique of my personal philosophy, theology, and ethics is that I seek truth and right in historical events. Philosophers, in the linguistic tradition especially, see this as the fact-value confusion—trying to root values in facts. The critique has great force. It is dangerous to anchor normative values and reality designations in supposed natural facts and historical events.

Throughout human history, many subjective and inaccurate discernments have been called truths and goods. For this reason, philosophers since Plato have posited another realm, one beyond time and space, an eternal or ideal realm to ultimately found facts and values. Empirical philosophers (Aristotle, Hume, even Kant) have facts and values anchored in the perceptual and emotional apparatus. My view reflects, and indeed borrows this rational iconoclasm, but is finally swayed by the fact that historical faith (Judaism, Christianity, and Islam) arises from concrete times, places, persons, and deities. Concrete faith claims that the eternal has chosen the material dimension for manifestation and redemption. In my life's work, I have chosen to affirm and analyze that epistemology, metaphysics, theology, and axiology.

HEBRAIC HELLENISM

Breaking from its Elusian and Delphic past, Greek thought is now unable to accommodate mystery. Not only is the generic realm of miracle and spirit rejected but the particular contradiction of the messianic resurrection; savior of the world, dying God, eternal Holy Spirit, all in thorough-going Hebraic materialism, is incomprehensible—sheer folly. The Greek can only puzzle with the Hellenic Pilate when he asks Jesus "what is truth?" to his affirmation "who is of the truth hears my voice" (John 18.37, 38). Transacting grace, beyond yet within, known reality is beyond mind and unmanageable. Exactly the point!

Beyond the offense of redemptive suffering and saving resurrection, the Hebrew-Christian ethic finds great commonality with the high

justice and moral piety of the Greeks. The insight that truth is in order
to goodness can only come as Hebraic and Hellenic wisdom are pooled.
We wonder what contact there may have been between 1500 B.C.E. and
the first-century C.E. between these two cultures. Was Egypt a possible
mediator? Manuscripts may have been lost in the Alexandria fire that
could tell us so much. Perhaps some new caves near Qumran or some
Nag Hammadi manuscripts from Egypt will one day open up this intriguing story.

SAMOS, SAMOTHRACE

On the Isle of Samos: Living one month in Pythagoras' home town, on
the tyrant Polycrates' wall, from where he was lured, then crucified across
the sea near Ephesus (522, 21 B.C.E.), one recovers the glory and power
of that Aegean Age. Persons from Samos migrated to the ancient Island
of Thrace and gave it its new name. Paul stopped there on his way to
Macedonia (Acts 16.11) and "touched" at Samos (Acts 20.15). When you
ponder the mission of this energetic, embattled, and so efficacious apostle,
you can only wonder what effect, if any, your life has had and is having.
Here are two islands, I've seen them both (visited one for a long stretch).
Paul supposedly just "touched" by both. Was there time for lunch? Did he
meet any islanders? Did he disembark at Samos City or at Polycrates' old
wall at Pythagor?

Did he know of Pythagorus or his students, Socrates, Plato, and
Aristotle? Surely a learned Greek, albeit a zealous Hebrew Pharisee, would
have heard of these; after all, he knew the lesser poets. "No man is an
island," wrote John Donne, yet we are all islands and we are all ships passing in the night. Jesus was once pressed by a crowd. Someone "touched"
the fringe on his robe. "Who touched me?" he asked (Luke 7.39). Was it
the Jewish phylacteries or tassels that often contained the ten commandments that she reached for? This would explain Jesus' retort "power has
gone out." Pentecost healing, as much as the Sermon on the Mount and
its commensurable setting, is the counterpart to Sinai in the Christian
testament. "Who touched me" . . . "She was made whole and her hemor-
rhage ceased." What was this? A reversal of nature? An intervention? A
miracle? We wonder. Was what happened believed, or did the belief occur? Scripture declares mystery.

There is an island today just off the coast of Turkey. It is just an out-cropping of rock, but underneath is the proverbial iceberg. Greece recently planted a flag on the stone, and Turkey responded with the fleet, as did Greece. This was just before the July 1996 crisis in Cyprus, where some Greeks ran over into United Nations "no-man's-land" and were killed by the correspondingly violent Turks.

Just an island, he "touched" by. "He will not fail or be discouraged till he has established justice in the Earth and the islands wait for His law . . ." (Isa 42.4).

PATMOS

I'm still trying to put them together in my mind:

- Megiddo (Armageddon) on Esdraelon Plain, the ancient fortress and stables of Solomon's empire;

- Ephesus, Smyrna, Pergamum, Thyatira, Sardis, Philadelphia, Laodicea; and

- Patmos.

A summer pilgrimage to these places puts a historical/geographical bearing on this heartland of the evangelical/ethical aspect of Christian belief: The Book of Revelation.

Like Samos, just off the coast of Turkey, Patmos looks across to the coast town of Miletus on Asia Minor. Tradition holds that John, the be-loved (and youthful) disciple was an evangelist in Asia Minor and was brought to trial in Rome during the persecutions of the Emperor Domitian (81–96 C.E.). He was exiled to the Island of Patmos where, tradition has it, he meditated in a cave half way up the mountain. Here the Apocalypse was to unfold. The revelation begins with prophetic—pastoral counsel—condemnation and commendation (the two-fold ministry of Decalogue and prophet) to the seven churches of Asia Minor, perhaps congregations where John had worked: Ephesus, Smyrna, Pergammon, Thyatira, Sardis, Philadelphia, Laodicea. John is then ecstatically transported up to the throne (Ezek 1.26–28) where the four creatures (evangelists?) and 24 el-ders praise the Lord on the throne. There near the throne is the slain lamb who holds the seven seals. At this point, an elaborate apocalyptic vision unfolds, which is the Johannine theology of history dealing with the pres-ent and immanent tribulation that Christians face and the cataclysmic struggle that will ensue until the "Kingdoms of this world become the Kingdoms of God and of his Christ" (11.15). What we have is a searching pondering of the life of the Spirit in the world imparting meaning under God, cast in terms of a symbolic rendition of history.

The first vision unfolds as the first four seals are opened, revealing the four horses: white, red, black, and gray. After the divine conqueror white horse (*cf.* Rev 19), red represents the peacetaker war horse, the black horse the scales of justice, and the pale horse, death (diseases, famine, and war). The following three seals reveal the martyrs in white robes, the impending eco-catastrophe (earthquakes, etc.) and the great announcement that God is protector against the "destroyer" of the Earth. Then seal seven discloses more calamities on Earth, announced by seven trumpets. Then unfolds the apocalyptic epic that sketches the history of the Earth and the final cataclysmic battle of good and evil. Did these visions actually happen? Apparently only to those given to see. How then do they become the substance of parochial faith and universal truth?

From the heavenly temple with the Ark of the Covenant, containing divine presence and commandments, Word goes out to destroy the "destroyers of the Earth:"

- A woman with child attends the great war in heaven when the rebellious beast (dragon) is cast out (11, 12).

- The beast is given power to assault God and good, with the power of blasphemy (13) and to incite immorality and injustice, war, etc.

- The lamb begins to form His redeemed community, who assemble on Mount Zion with the lamb (19). The great Hallelujah Chorus announces the final conflict.

- The dragon. who has been bound for 1,000 years, is released. and final conflict begins on the Plain of Armageddon (16.16).

- The Gog vs. Magog battle ensues.

- The book concludes with the lyric vision of chapter 21—the new heaven and new Earth, no longer needing sun nor moon, the new Jerusalem with its 12 gates.

One's mind is driven not only to Handel's epic "Messiah," which so deeply shapes the transcendental-historical consciousness of post-18th-century European culture, but also to the treasure of art and literature, films, and worship that have been infused with this vision. Augustine's *The City of God* is obviously patterned here on its portrayal of an earthly and heavenly scenario. Dante's *Divine Comedy* and Milton's *Paradise Lost* and *Paradise Regained* profoundly translate the images and worldview. What does it all mean?

Second Isaiah, writing from another exile, this time in Babylon (597–539 B.C.E.), attempted to outline the whole cosmic drama of God's dealing with the world (Isa 40–55). Cyrus the Persian, in this saga, becomes a kind of pagan messiah (44.28, 45.1), indicating that the writing finds historical setting when he defeated the Lydian King Croesus (547 B.C.E.). Daniel offers his saga, probably taking final form during the persecution of the Jews under Antiochus IV Epiphanes (c.167 B.C.E.). And now, John of Patmos.

All three visions are obtuse, lyric, and fantastically imaginative. Yet they all offer the same vision. How do we fathom the meaning of historical patterns in this world that is not only created by God but also visited by God, at Sinai and Nazareth? This same God kept in touch with his world indirectly through the living faith of patriarchs and prophets, priests and preachers. And these seers!

Our post-modern, post-William Blake age shrinks from panoramic visions and meta-historical cosmologies and histories. But unless we are alone in some cold cosmos, "an accidental collocation of atoms" as Bertrand Russell says, the tale bears telling.

Even the poor attempts of one such journeyman as now shares his story with you shows that he has been touched by apocalypse. It prompts me to try to tell the broad and comprehensive narrative and elucidate a view of history and nature superintended by the judging and saving God known in Christ. It forces my mind into patterns persistently evangelical and ethical. Just as the occasion to visit Greece and Turkey takes one back to the sacred texts from Thessalonians to Revelation, the whole biblical narrative drives one back to Palestine and Israel. Here our travel diary ends, for here the story begins. I conclude that natural and supernal, temporal, and eternal are mysteriously conjoined in the reality (history) of God.

ISTANBUL/BYZANTIUM

Before we leave Turkey one must briefly comment on Istanbul/Byzantium. It was here in Constantinople—the Emperor Constantine's city—that a development of history occurred that would preserve and universalize, but also severely compromise, the history of Israel and the story of Jesus. Now an Islamic city in a state that seeks to consciously embody Islamic law and ethics, yet remain staunchly secular, Istanbul and its sister city Chalcedon became the seats of Christian thought and culture. Beginning early in the fourth-century C.E., Judaism, at once an historical movement and a nation, had been scattered into diaspora by the Jewish wars with Rome 66–70 C.E., which culminated in the mass-suicide at Masada.

While Jewish Christianity went underground in Jamesian and Ebionite faith (eventually to reemerge as Islam), Gentile Christianity flourished and transformed the middle and Western world through the Bishop-cities of Constantinople and Rome. Rabbinic Judaism meanwhile would endure until, and even after, the founding of the state of Israel in the absence of a concrete place on Earth in theological thought, spiritual convictions, the endurance a diaspora people and in the brilliant ethical traditions that stemmed from the Babylonian and Judean (Jerusalem) Talmud schools.

EGYPT/SINAI/CANAAN

Since my work has always been in ethics, and since I have always sought to ground my own ethics in the biblical story, I begin with Egypt, Sinai, and Canaan as a geographical-historical locus for tracing this ancient Near Eastern axiology. The archaeologist Schliemann decided in the 19th century to find the ancient palace of Priam (c. 1200 B.C.E.) and began the magnificent exposure of the ancient city of Troy. When you visit this marvelous study on the northeastern coast of Turkey, the moving saga of *Iliad* and *Odyssey* moves from fantasy to history. The Bible recedes into more remote recesses of history and prehistory. We can attach some known places to Abraham, and his visage becomes historical. The garden of Eden, birthplace of Noah, and numerous accounts from the priestly (fifth-century B.C.E.) and preceding Hebrew testament texts are like the "land of Nod" literally, no place. Ararat is the ancient name for Armenia or Eastern Anatolia, though efforts to find the Ark, even by the Astronaut Jim Lovell, have been disappointing. Babel may be the Babylonian *ziggu-*

rat (from Akkadian *ziqqurratu*), and the story of Shem, Ham, and Canaan may have transpired on the Palestinian Plain. We'll never know.

Was Abraham an historical figure like Moses, or one mythic like Adam, Eve, or Noah? The patriarchs can be more precisely located in time and place. Terah, the father of Abraham, is identified with Ur of the Chaldees, which has been excavated. The *ziggurat* stands poised dramatically to the southeast. Terah seems to have begun a trek typical of today's bedouin. It may have been to find a better place to live, better sustenance for the herds. In any case they migrated west of the Euphrates, perhaps to somewhere near Haran. Here some six centuries later, Joshua would look to that "beyond-the-river" where "our fathers worshipped other gods" (Josh 24.2). The third dynasty of Ur (2050–1950 B.C.E.) is roughly concurrent with Abraham and Hammurabi.

Terah made his way into the land of Canaan. Though he died in Haran (Gen 11.22), Abraham seemed compelled by his father's mission and some other, more mysterious, impulse. We eventually find him west of the Jordan near Schechem at the historic "Oak of Moreh" (Gen 12.6). This site may have been at the foot of Mount Gerazim, near Jacob's well. Here a well-traveled woman would say to Jesus, ". . . our fathers worshipped on this mountain. . ." Close at hand is Herod's temple where John was imprisoned and Herodias' daughter danced. Abraham probably continued to migrate down the Schechem-Jerusalem route (Bethel is en route), down into the Negev and to Beersheba and Hebron where he began to settle. Archaeology tells us of numerous invasions and wars occurring in the region at this time. The Kings of Elam, for example, made war on the Kings of Sodom and Gomorrah, southeast of the Dead Sea. One can still see here pillars of salt and the brine, fire and brimstone, caustic events. Abraham's offered sacrifice of Isaac probably did not occur at Mount Moriah (today's temple mount in Jerusalem) or at Mount Gerazim. The ascent Ramet el-Khalil, the old hill top sanctuary of Hebron, may be a good bet.

Here at the mosque, revered as the sight of the tombs of the patriarchs, the *Akedah* (sacrifice of Isaac) probably occurred. Here also, Dr. Goldstein from Brooklyn opened fire one afternoon during prayers, killing 30 Muslim Arabs.

Things get more concrete through Ishmael, Isaac, Jacob (Israel), and the sons, especially Joseph who is sold into slavery in Egypt and becomes a precursor of the great Exodus of all the "Children of Israel."

EXCURSUS: ABRAHAM

One of our new doctors at Strasbourg will present her work in the near future: "Abraham in Luther and Kierkegaard." What a seminal figure Abraham is in the history of faith and of humanity.

- He moved out from cultural stasis to divine call.

- He began to sense a uniform deity from the pluriform theological environment. In this sense, he was like the Egyptian Pharaoh Iknahton. Elolam, El Addai now became El, Elohim, and slowly focused into Yahweh.

- A near contemporary of Hammurabi, he sensed the primacy of righteousness and justice in the divine. It therefore became a human requirement.

- We find in Abraham, therefore, the shadowy beginnings of Israelite law and ethics, which expresses so many influences of Mesopotamian and Egyptian spirituality and morality.

- The Yahwist and Elohist (J and E) writers of the Pentateuch both place Abraham at a threshold position in the consciousness of God and in the elucidation of an ethical faith.

- In Hebrew and Christian testament, Abraham and Sarah are paradigms of faith.

- The faithful willingness to sacrifice Isaac (*Akedah*) informs the gospel writers and Paul as they seek to interpret the death of Christ.

- To this day, we seek to fathom the meaning of Abrahamic faith and the religions that proceed from that faith: Judaism, Christianity, and Islam.

- *Aqedah Yisaqh* (the binding of Isaac) tradition continues to serve as a guiding metaphor in the Christian traditions' interpretation of the theological meaning of Christ's death and Islam's travail. The *Akedah* heritage of biblical reflection is one of the most meaningful symbols creating centuries-old dialogue opportunities between Jews, Christians, and Muslims.

Beginning in Genesis 37, we have the account of how the children of Israel happen to be in Egypt. Was it famine that brought about the migration to this great food-producing region? In Genesis 37.25, we see Joseph disrobed and sold to a traveling band of Ishmaelites who trudged him along with their gum, balm, myrrh, and other products bound from Arabia to Egypt. While in Egypt, the Israelites took so seriously the "be-fruitful-and-multiply" mandate that they grew great and numerous, so much so that they became a threat to the Egyptians.

Was Tutankhaten (1358–1349 B.C.E.) the Pharaoh who "knew not Joseph," or was it some predecessor or successor? It may have been Ramses II (1301–1234 B.C.E.). The Hebrews may have been co-opted workers building the city that bears his name.

The Exodus is the pivotal, formative event in Israel's faith. When conjoined with the Sinai theophany and receipt of the covenant, it founds the faith and ethic of this people. It is also a deep spring, along with Athenian democracy, of human freedom and human rights. Whether the sea of crossing was the Gulf of Aqabah (the sea of reeds) or the Red Sea, whether Sinai was Jebel Katerin, El Asi (the volcanic mountain of South of Aqabah), whether the occupation of Canaan was an invasion or an interior uprising, these constitutive events are the landmark in human spiritual and ethical history.

Moses, wrote Martin Buber, enabled us to see God not only as a terrible and awesome force, but also as the face of a friend. This will become known as the God named Yahweh. Though a totally disarming and demanding visage, God now becomes personal and moral. In the remarkable experience of seeing and hearing the word (theophany), we sense God's love, justice, and will capsulated in a disclosure of "way" (*Weg Gottes*). Ancient perceptions that animated acts of appeasing and cajoling some capricious deity now were transformed into leading and following. When Jesus says "follow me," or "learn from me," he places himself firmly in the tradition of Moses.

The second half of the second millennium B.C.E. is an epoch of great migrations in Western Asia, Central and Southern Europe. Migrating tribes such as Achaeans, Sardinians, and Lycians overwhelmed Greece, Italy, and the Aegean world. Indo-European peoples were changing the landscape of Europe. Egypt waxed strong and weak as Hittites, Philistines, and other "peoples on the move" contended in Western Asia. The conquest-of-Canaan narratives occur against this historical sweep.

Kathleen Kenyon conducted the masterful excavation of Jericho in the 1950s. The foundation of the original city, dated about 7800 B.C.E., makes it the oldest city in the world. Today, it is a center of the Palestinian authority, and Jews, Christians, and Muslims hope again that the "walls will come tumbling down" (including Israel's Berlinesque Wall). Since there is no evidence of a sudden wall-collapse, we may infer that the story speaks of a desolate mound, left after Egypt conquered and destroyed the city c. 1550 B.C.E. This confirms that walls are built or torn down in slow evolutionary fashion.

Since I came to Garrett in 1993, I have taught the course on "War and Peace" several times. In *Ethics and the Gulf War*, I explored the conquest of Canaan as the prime instance of Hebrew holy war. Christian crusades and Islamic *jihad* are also rationalized on these foundations.

Against the problematic history of these events, especially in light of the systematic destruction of Palestine and Bedouin communities by Israel since 1948, I have come to affirm the ethical legitimacy of holy war and crusade as a fight for the "way of God," a defense of that "way of life" against those who would destroy it, a broader extrapolation of the will of God for history in terms of the achievement of freedom and democracy. There is a truth and a right, a holy resistance of tyranny and oppression, which includes a rejection of physical war. Human war-making is most often an exercise of national aggrandizement, co-optation of the resources of another people, or sheer malevolent, racist belligerence: France and America in Vietnam, Russia in Chechnya, China in Tibet, Israel in Palestine, and America in Iraq.

The fall of Ai, the genocide of the Amalakites, the fall of Gideon, the cities of Shephelah (Josh 10.28–43). and the devastation of Megiddo (11.11) must be seen as an unfortunate equation of military ambition with divine will, or a romantic retroprojection of glorious conquest (like the American extermination and concentration of the Indians) that now, during the period of state establishment, should be remembered with shame and forgiveness, not patriotic fervor.

Reflection on the age of Kings and Prophets shape a history of mingled obedience to God in personal and public life, with declension in faith and resurgent idolatry and immorality. The sublime message of the psalms, about the true devotion and action that pleases God, or the ecstatic vision of Isaiah and the Prophets, of a kingdom of righteousness that will one day end the warring traditions of the world, is set against the landscape and history of biblical Israel.

SOLOMON IN ALL HIS GLORY

It was in a sermon on Solomon at First Presbyterian in Evanston that I first noted an intriguing thought of a scholar who claimed that, at the peak of his power, King Solomon had all of the resources to create a global empire. He chose not to, but rather established a secure, magnanimous, and convivial state in Israel. If he had chosen the route of a conquering empire, would he have changed the course of history, perhaps denied the sequel empires of the Assyrians, the Persians, Alexander the Great, Rome? Would this historical power, as this author conjectured, have countered and made impossible the rise of Islam? Could the tiny core of religious Israel, centered in Solomon's great temple in Jerusalem, have been the epicenter of some expansive, religiously pluralistic empire? Or would history ever after have to wait for one who would come to restore the kingdom of his father David—some Messiah? Some *Christos* (anointed king)?

As Sara and I trace back one of our family lines—my mother's: the Shoup family—they rise from the misty bogs of Germany and Pennsylvania with the names Jacob, David, and Solomon . . . the legacy lives on.

Adonijah was to be David's successor. He was actually crowned king, until Bathsheba heard of it. As so often happens in scripture, the ill-conceived was installed via trickery. Bathsheba prevails on the senile David and has Solomon crowned. Solomon emerges monarch in a cortege of great men: Benarah, the commander; Zadok, the priest; and Nathan, the prophet.

A man of peace, Solomon divided his kingdom into twelve regional jurisdictions and developed an impressive military force. When the 1928 excavations of the Oriental Institute at the University of Chicago uncovered strata IV at Megiddo, the full extent of this *Wehrmacht* was seen. He supposedly had 40,000 teams of horses for the war chariots. At Megiddo today, the horse stables and chariot stalls are clearly seen. Solomon struck a contract with the King of Tyre to obtain building materials and skilled labor for his building projects, including the Jerusalem temple. Thousands of Phoenicians were employed felling and dragging the cedars of Lebanon and other lumber. In addition, they quarried the blocks of stone in the mountains adjacent to Jerusalem. Sol's fleets in the Red Sea and chariots on Megiddo plain were impressive to all the world.

The Acropolis at Jerusalem, including the temple on the northern side, was constructed on the beginnings of the David wall on the old Jebusite fortress site. Solomon's temple was a "long house" worship center in the Assyrian mode. At the center of the temple, was the throne (Isaiah 6), perhaps the ark and the protruding rock, now the great black rock in the Muslim *es-Sakhra*, the dome of the rock. Abraham was believed to have set up the rock here which had been preserved since the flood. This mythic legend places this sacred place within the contours of ancient ontocratic traditions, where the "navel of the Earth" was the naturalistic juncture of contact with the gods. Melchizedek, the mythical first priest had his altar here.

Abraham sacrificed Isaac here, all the prophets worshipped here. It was the apex of Jesus' transfiguration and ascension. Mohammed also ascended from this point. Solomon's temple draws together all the preceding and subsequent threads of this elaborate mythic/historic tradition.

BETHLEHEM

The city of David is now the focal point of grave tension between Israel and Palestine. The wall is a blight on the "little town" that "silently—how silently" bore the "wondrous gift." Rocket-launching Israeli helicopters frequently strafe the environs of Bethlehem. Sitting near Rachel's placid tomb and the cut-off highway to volatile Hebron and the Negev, the primarily Christian and Arab city, Bethlehem, is now being cordoned off by Israeli settlements, road shuntings, property confiscations, and harsh policies of interdiction and check points that prevent Palestinians, for the most part, from entering Jerusalem to get to work. The bus bombings— during the administration of Prime Minister Rabin and Netanyahu in the late 1990s—are the stated reason for these repressive measures. Under Sharon (2001), the confrontation had reached ominous proportions.

We visited Father Mitri Raheb, director of the Christmas Lutheran Center in Bethlehem. He is one of the most impressive theologian-political leaders in present-day Palestine. Along with Dr. Naim Ateek, formerly at St. George Anglican Cathedral and director of Sabeel, an international study-action center in Jerusalem, and Elias Chacour at Ibilin, now Haifa, Raheb is creating an impressive center of thought and activity for the entire region. His *Habilitationschrift* at Marburg, he is building an international educational center to foster inter-religious dialogue between Christianity, Judaism, and Islam. If any force can bring about peace, it will be this conjunction of the great Abrahamic faiths.

Who can forget the three men of faith at the Camp David agreements: the Baptist Lay Preacher and President of the United States, Jimmy Carter, flanked by Menachim Begin and Anwar Sadat, both men of towering faith and ethical vision. Even subsequent Camp David summits cannot completely fail with this inspiring founding inspiration.

In the south of Bethlehem are the shepherd's hills. On my fist visit to Bethlehem in 1965, I remember riding a donkey and camel out on these haunting hills, where shepherds still watch their flocks.

The Church of the Nativity is a most moving site. Eusebius called it the "mystic grotto." Undestroyed as so many biblical sites were by Moslem conquests and subsequent conflicts, Bethlehem was left unscathed (especially after Constantine's mother Helen's Basilica crafted the frescos in Arab dress). The cave and sacred rock floor, where Joseph and Mary were lodged when the Inn was full, still moves millions of pilgrims to tears. We, too, were happily oblivious to Dominic Crossan's point that there actually was no census or return to hometowns to be taxed. Even if such a cumbersome trek was ordered, it is not recorded until 6–7 C.E., after Herod's death (4 B.C.E.). We'll stick with Ray Brown's thoughtful exposition of "The Birth of the Messiah."

The old Constantine church is thus one of the oldest in Christendom. The same trip south of Jerusalem was the occasion for a meeting with an extremely forward-looking rabbi in Tekoa (Amos) and with the impressive study center at Tantur. This center now straddles the Israeli checkpoint on Arabs coming up into Jerusalem. We were pleased to find a wide open underground railroad through holes in the wall at either side of Tantur.

The facts of the nativity are always troubling. My teacher John Hick of Princeton fell under the censure of the New Brunswick Presbytery while I was in seminary. He did not disavow the virgin birth; he merely questioned whether it was an essential doctrine. Recent Jesus scholarship has generally agreed that this notion is an overlay of the later developing high Christology and is superimposed back on the birth narratives. Basing much of my rapprochement theology on Jesus' brother James' life and letter further complicates the virgin birth.

One delights in cardiologist poet John Stone's short masterpiece, "The Virgin Mary." It contains just two words: "She wasn't!" Crossan, Sanders, Vermès, and a raft of Jesus scholars hold this view. I have never found the virgin birth such a sticking point or, for that matter, that important. Was Jesus born in Bethlehem or Nazareth, was Miriam his genetic mother and Joseph his biological father? On the one hand, the gospel writers strive to establish biological lineage. On the other hand, Jesus transcends genetics and ethnicity. The "man for others" is, from the outset, a Savior for all people. There is good reason to sustain the paradox of both truths. This seems to be the point of the old Roman Nicaean and Chalcedonian creed: "fully God and fully human."

I once had my high-school students in Mount Lebanon reenact the manger scene. You are Joseph, you—Mary, you—the cow, you—the wise man, the shepherd, the star, etc. What is happening? Tell it as you see it. I was amazed at the creative theater and theology. The mystery of Bethlehem will forever enchant the world. At Advent, I always pull off the shelf the meditations of my professor at Princeton, Paul Scherer. He captures the existential grip of these historic-transhistoric events.

My teacher Thielicke, like Luther, was haunted by the *kleines Kleckerdorf*, where eternity "came down the staircase of time." Lutheran eyes have a special view of Bethlehem. I envy father Raheb there in the old city. Perhaps we in the West view *Weihnachten* too much through German eyes. *Tannenbaüme*, snow, *Stille Nacht*, Saint Nikolas. I need to remind myself that Jesus and his parents were probably quite dark, like a lad named Jeshua I met 30 years ago in Nazareth. He was as black as our African-American friends. No Sallman's "Head of Christ" here. Jesus, his family, and company were Jews and Palestinians. They spoke Aramaic, the *lingua franca* of this area of the world since after the Persian Empire.

Tradition intertwines with this scant history in lovely ways. From St. Helen's church to Shepherd's fields, from Luther's God slipping down the back staircase of the world to an old priest I heard once in Saint-Dénis, France in a 10th-century chapel. He sat alone in the church with a restless catechumen—together they sang a simple *chanson de Noël*: *Il est né le divin enfant* (he was born the divine child).

NAZARETH

The church of St. Joseph is also quite moving among the plethora of hyper-hyped holy sites. You will be shown and told on Patmos, for example, of the 70 icons St. Luke himself painted. Like the American radio religion hucksters chronicled by Bill Martin at Rice, you can always buy (for a few shekels) splinters from the cross (or the Ark around Ararat), holy water from the River Jordan in Coke bottles, or as one venturous televangelist advertised, autographed pictures of Jesus!

The Franciscans have been stewards of this beautiful church built over the remembered sites of Mary's visitation (Luke 1.26ff.), Joseph's workshop and, we can assume, the home where Jesus grew "in wisdom, stature, and in the favor of God and people."

A recently uncovered door lintel has stimulated much discussion throughout Israel. It suggests that Joseph may not have been a peasant carpenter (*tekton*, J.D.Crossan), but a skilled, and perhaps affluent, artisan. Crossan claims that even artisans were below the peasant class, just above the destitute. Crossan would delightfully argue this new discovery away in his inimitable Irish way, the way he did when I asked him if Jesus were a rabbi and whether the tassels on his robe (*e.g.*, the menstruating woman) may have contained *tephilim* (phylacteries) of the Decalogue. Jesus, in Crossan's view, was fairly critical of—and distanced himself from—the ritualistic, even legalistic, features of the rabbinic and priestly Judaism of his day.

The earliest Christian pilgrims came to this small town, where people tilled the hillsides or practiced domestic trades. An ancient well, such as Jacob's well at Sychar (Samaria), still flows and supports a very ancient tradition, as the well where Mary and her neighbors drew water. As one stands on the high point of Nebi Ismail west of town, you can look north and see Sepphoris, where our colleague Dennis Groh has excavated. At the deeper vista towers the magnificent Mount Hermon with its snowy crown, even in summer. When your pilgrimage moves you further east to Capernaum and Beatitudes mountain, you can see why the Nazareth vista may well have inspired Jesus as he said "a city set on a hill cannot be hid" (Matt 5.14).

One cannot help conjecture on the silent years of Jesus' childhood and youth. Numerous apocryphal gospels and later devotional writings romanticize this *terra incognita*. Did he capture and release birds with his hands? What of the documented synagogue and temple presentations? What of his slights on the family (the wedding at Cana, the trip as a 12-year-old to Jerusalem)? This present century of research, with its recovery of local history, culture, and first-century Judaica may enrich the picture.

To me, all the evidence points to an observant, highly studious, and devout *bar mitzvah*, one who practiced the rigors of scriptural examination and application much as some young Orthodox scholars I met in Jerusalem (although without the caustic edge). For Jesus to know what he knew and say what he said, he must have been deeply schooled in the faith. He seems to be joyous, life-loving, sympathetic to the poor and sick, young in spirit. Something of the ascetic, Essene-like John the Baptist, something of Hillel, the wise and learned rabbi, is felt.

Crossan is, of course, correct in saying that Jesus was an itinerant Galilean peasant, even a wandering cynic philosopher. What this means is most difficult to reconstruct. My bias lies with Géza Vermès, E.P. Sanders, M. Goodman, and the Jewish scholars of the New Testament. One must sympathize with the faith and ethic of Israel to understand Jesus. His is a three-fold mission of teaching, healing, and feeding the hungry. The picture of a historic person is not near so strong for me as one who was fully conversant with and obedient to God his father. This concentrated piety focused his will on that of His father to the point that his own biography (even his teachings and actions) recedes in importance to that calling wherein he was Lord and Christ. When Peter offers his confession at Caesarea Philippi, just north of Nazareth and the Sea of Galilee (Mark 8.29 parallels), it seems quite natural to me that Jesus did not deny or demur that he was Christ, nor did he affirm and applaud. He accepted it as fitting and the best that this blessedly expressive companion could offer—a response fully human and divine. The ministry around Tiberius, Capernaum, and Galilee is much different in terms of Jesus' self-expression than the final *Sukkoth* pilgrimage to Jerusalem, where he would become caught up in a divine destiny and faithfully resigned to his father's will that would entail suffering and death. Easter morning, to me, then is a rendezvous with the pastoral bliss of Galilee, overshadowed by the cross of Jerusalem, wherein we glory. This all before Palestinian bombing and Israeli blundering destroyed the Holy Land.

CAPERNAUM

Capernaum was Jesus' home base. Nazareth was too provincial and inhospitable, Sepphoris too cosmopolitan, perhaps. Here, at Capernaum, we find a beautifully excavated and designated place that rings true in the same way as do Megiddo, Masada, and Troy. On the broad horizon, we have the Sea of Galilee, the pastoral scenes where Jesus called the two pairs of brothers, Peter's house, Magdala, Gennesaret, Nain, and other idyllic scenes. The synagogue ruins of Kefer Nahum have been beautifully restored and kept under Israeli authority. The foundations of Peter's house and the principal contemporary buildings of the early first-century town are now well displayed. On the brow of the hill, you can almost feel and hear Jesus preaching by the lake, the Sermon on the Mount, the fishing by night, the withdrawal to a quiet place.

As of old, Apostles heard it by the Galilean lake, turned from home and toil and children, leaving all for his dear sake . . . "Jesus calls us . . ."

Jesus' ministry around Galilee prospers. Although he seems to warn against broadcasting the "messianic secret" of Mark 7.31–37, and although some detractors have already come up from Jerusalem (Mark 7.1), his words and good works are well received. "The poor," (Mark 12.37) "heard him gladly." But when Jesus turns "his face to Jerusalem," after Peter's confession lets the messianic secret out of the bag, the encounters become increasingly antagonistic. Violations of the law are surmised and concocted. His great deeds are seen as threatening and blasphemous. The singularly righteous one of history becomes a hideous sinner.

What contributes to this vivid contrast between the Galilean (Capernaum) and Judaean (Jerusalem) ministries? Géza Vermès focuses the ministry of Jesus as teacher in his activities of charismatic interpretation of scripture and the sharing of proverbs and parables These ministries, he contends, were fully within the normative traditions of Israel and provoked little opposition. It was the messianic designation (that couldn't be muted, "the very stones will cry out"), the teaching of kingdom, that posed a threat to Jewish and Roman authority. The controversy over the law, according to Vermès, incited opposition and eventually, crucifixion.[4]

One gesture of his love for all people that became more provocative in the Judaean environs was his association with disreputables. The diminutive Zaccheas was a despised tax collector. Was he up in that lin-

---

4. Vermès, *The Religion of Jesus the Jew*, 46–75.

den tree that still stands in Jericho? Mary of Magdala came from Galilee, but her association with Jesus intensifies near Jerusalem. His association with sinners, lepers, and outcasts, although consistent throughout his ministry, became problematic in light of the purity obsession jaded by the corruption and contempt for the poor of the Jerusalem temple establishment. In this sense, Jesus' cleansing of the temple in the last week of his ministry is doubly ironic. "Who was this unclean one to cleanse the money changers?"

What is the ethical significance of Jesus' association with sinners? Is it related to the high theological doctrine of Paul that, for us, became sin to rescue the rest of us trapped in that status? He came, after all, to call sinners, not the righteous. The healthy have no need of a physician (Matt 9.12). Like any person of moral acuity, Jesus was put off by the self-righteous, ostentatiously pure, disdainful hypocrites. The self-effacing publican (despised one), not the Pharisee, goes down from the temple justified (Luke 18.10). Yet what was the ethical breach of:

- the publicans and tax collectors (Matt 9.11, 21.31, etc.);

- the winos and gluttons (Matt 11.19); and

- the promiscuous and adulterous (John 8)?

- to say nothing of the lepers (Mark 14.3) . . . and what was the attraction?

I've come to feel that two distinctive features of Jesus' self-disclosure rub against embattled and defensive Judaism, even while they recover and restore emphases of the historic faith. The affinity with sinners (the lost, sick, and alien), the doctrine of repentance and forgiveness of sin, and the ingathering of the world are aspects of the universalist destiny and commission of Israel.[5] *En garde* Judaism sees this as strange, but for the *avant garde*, they are as old as the Abrahamic venture, desert sanctuary, and David's Psalms.

In my view, Jesus knew (and came to reinstate) the authentic meaning of Decalogue, Torah, Wisdom, and prophesy—the substance of Paul's "gospel of God" (Rom 1.1)—which often was lost by the channels and champions of official Judaism.

Conventional morality and, even worse, churchly (parochial) morality always exaggerates the evil of sins of poverty, circumstance, and even

---

5. Liturgy for Yom Kippur.

necessity, and downplays structural evil and the inhumanity that grows out of disdain for common people. The cache of criminals that seemed to be welcome in Jesus' presence were not upright folk; they had gone and done wrong and they knew it. They were also "close to the kingdom" because of this experience. Having been destitute and derelict heightens the sensation of grace. Forgiveness, repentance, and new life are acutely perceived by the needy.

Paul the Apostle was such a chief of sinners (1 Tim 1.15). Although he, on occasion, boasted of his "former life" as an inquisitor Pharisee, one zealous for the law, he knew that he had sinned gravely against the Christ and his followers. He had killed, falsely accused, and blasphemed all in one mighty assault on God's will and way. Yet this same alienation and intensity of wrongdoing drew Paul dear and near to the risen Christ, and the same zeal given then to a righteoused sinner was now unleashed in a mission that would transform human history. It is the same story with Peter, the Emperor Constantine, slaveholder John Newton, and Watergate conspirator Charles Colson. We might say that one in whom sin becomes acute is near salvation. The Lutheran ethical tradition and the repentance tradition of Baptists and Pentecostals understand and exploit this insight.

JERUSALEM

Jerusalem "killeth the prophets . . ." (Luke 11.50 and parallels). Actually, the evidence is scant that any prophets were killed at all—although two of the world's greatest prophets, Jesus and Paul, received their death sentences here. Yet Jerusalem, even today, is a *High Noon* showdown kind of town. At the same time, we believe that in one day, the Isaianic Zion peace will flow in rivers from this city of peace. In the meanwhile, only blood flows, as all the animosity and violence of the world seems to drain its *Akedic* mystery into Zion. We met a lovely, although frightfully naïve woman, while we were at St. George's (Anglican) Cathedral during our last stay in Jerusalem. When we asked her how long she was staying, she said, "anywhere from one night to forever." She went on to share how she never felt such peace as she found in Jerusalem. I don't believe she had talked with any terrified Arab Palestinians who couldn't get through Israeli Army checkpoints to go to work in Jerusalem, or with frightened Jewish soldiers who (with the rabbi's supervision) had to scrape flesh off buildings after the bus bombings in 1996. A metaphor for Jerusalem is the Wailing Wall. It is not the exuberance of Abraham Heschel who, when I was with him in Toronto at a meeting when the six-day war gave Israelis access to the Wailing Wall, collapsed in tearful joy. I'm thinking of another afternoon, when some crazy Arab kids up on the ramparts of the Dome of the Rock started dropping stones on the bobbing Orthodox faithful at prayer along the Wailing Wall. After the machine guns were silent and the screams faded, dozens of Palestinians were dead—that's Jerusalem.

When David made his covenant with the Elders of Israel at Hebron, he was 30 years old (2 Sam 5). For seven years, he ruled here before capturing Zion from the Jebusites and establishing a reign there of 33 years. He built the city, we are told, from Kihon, the water source (south wall) inward. After further victories over the persistent Philistines, he finally transferred the Ark to Jerusalem. This was placed at the Millo, a platform on the north side of the city in a palace that was built by the Phoenician artisans from Hiram of Tyre.

In Kathleen Kenyon's excavation of the city, the old Jebusite walls (1500 B.C.E.) were further defined, in some places 27 feet in width. Solomon would enlarge the city, and as we noted, erect an impressive temple along with palace and administrative buildings, where now is the Temple of the Rock.

When the Muslims conquered Jerusalem in the seventh century C.E., their central mosque was placed on this holy site. From 1000–587 B.C.E., Jerusalem was the religious and political center of greater Israel, then Judah. In 587 B.C.E., Nebuchadnezzar and the Babylonian forces captured the city. Beginning in 516 under Zerubbabel, then Ezra and Nehemiah, a smaller temple was rebuilt. Antiochus Epiphanes profaned this, but the Maccabeans purged and restored the temple. When Herod the great became King of Judea in 40 B.C.E., he fortified city walls, constructed powerful foundational structures, and stabilized the temple, which was completed in 19 B.C.E.

When Jesus spoke from the Mount of Olives (Luke 24.2) that there would not be "one stone left upon another," we have both a glorified view of the beauty of Herod's temple across the majestic Kidron Valley and an *ex post facto* retrospect from after the 66–70 C.E. destruction of Jerusalem, where this masterpiece was literally left in rubble by Titus' armies.

On September 24, 1996, they broke through the tunnel. It will eventually connect the Jewish old city sites (*e.g.*, Western wall) with the Eastern

Christian sites at the lower *Via Dolorosa*. Now, like the tunnel at Megiddo and the old water temple in Istanbul, we will have a dramatically lighted, musical, Disney-theme-park-like tour along part of the pediments for Herod's temple and the actual street where Jesus carried the cross. One can only wonder if Jewish workers ever think of the cross of oppression that Jesus carries for today's Palestinians as he carried it for Europe's Jews two generations ago.

Although the project has been underway (under the temple mount and other Muslim sites) for 30 years, the government of Israel spoils holyland sites. Everything is cordoned off, and texts are slanted toward the official religio-political line. Some say, jestfully I hope, that tomorrow's pilgrims to Bethlehem will be helicoptered or tunneled by the army through militarized zones. The old days, when I rode a camel or donkey from Jaffa gate or Damascus gate south to Bethlehem, are long gone.

Protests, perhaps renewed *intifada*, are threatened by Arafat and now *Hamas* or *Hezbollah* and perpetually feared by Israel. Colin Powell, under President Bush, made some headway. Blacks understand the Palestinian and the Israeli plight. The summit convened by President Clinton in the bimillennial year has failed. In our experience, the Arabs, Palestinians, and Christians are now mute and subdued after 50 years of constant humiliation, oppression, and wholesale confiscation of their centuries-old lands, along with abrogation of most other basic human rights.

That Israel, with Holocaust still fresh in their souls, could in conscience visit this quasi-genocidal oppression ("be rid of them") on these aboriginal Palestinians is the ironic tragedy of the 20th century. Global messianic peace will remain remote until this peace is achieved. As we inch into the 21st century, hope and peace and a two-state solution seem remote. Zionist nationals, Zealots, Christian fanatics, and Muslim suicide bombers conspire to make Jerusalem a *dar al-Harb* ("war-place"). God help us . . . send us justice and peace!

My first visit to Jerusalem was during Easter week in 1962. On Palm Sunday, thousands of pilgrims, led by the Franciscans, wound from Bethany around the Mount of Olives and up to the (now walled up) Golden gate, where Jesus made his strangely called "triumphal entry." At home, Sara and I always play on Palm Sunday an old Caruso rendition of "Les Rameaux" (the palms).

My own picture of this complicated event, where Jesus seems to accede for a moment to the expectations of the zealots, comes from E.P. Sanders.

> The Gospels offer us an event prior to the temple action which, were it the unvarnished truth, could well have led to Jesus' execution: the entry into Jerusalem. The claim to be king is explicit only in Matthew and John, who quote Zech. 9.9 (Matt 21.4ff.; John 12.15) and say that the crowds cried not only "Hosanna" but also "Son of David" (Matt 21.9) or "King of Israel" (John 12.13). But if Mark and Luke also portray Jesus as riding on an ass, and plenty of those in Jerusalem would have remembered the prophetic passage, especially if Jesus' followers cried "Blessed be he who comes in the name of the Lord"(Matt 21.9/Mark 11.9/Luke 19.38; quoting Psalm 118.26 [LXX 117:26]).

> Is the story true? Perhaps it is. Jesus was executed as one who claimed to be "king of the Jews." The entry and the execution fit each other precisely. The Romans were not slow to act when sedition threatened, nor, were this a large demonstration, would they have needed a Jewish 'trial' in order to urge them on. Perhaps the event took place but was a small occurrence which went unnoticed. Perhaps only a few disciples unostentatiously dropped their garments in front of the ass (*cf.* Matt 21:8/Mark 11.8/Luke 19.36), while only a few quietly murmured "Hosanna."[6]

I regard the passage as being one of the most puzzling in the Gospels. If it happened at all, surely the disciples were in on the secret and knew that Jesus was claiming to be king. We have seen previously that they very likely did have this understanding, and also that they knew that he was to be a special kind of king. The expectation of a new world order (whether "in the air" or in a new Jerusalem), in which Jesus and his disciples would be the chief figures, but which would not be established by human might, seems to me the best explanation of the puzzling passage about "triumphal" entry. Jesus and his close followers understood that he was entering as "king," but there was no large public hue and cry about it. It fits into Jesus' last symbolic acts: he entered as "king," demonstrated the destruction of the present temple, and had a meal with his disciples that symbolized the coming "banquet."

6. Sanders, *Jesus and Judaism*, 306.

Jerusalem holds the key to the whole structure of Christian theology. The theology of kingdom (eschatology) hangs on to the biblical history of this city from David's seizure of Jebusite Zion, to Jesus's bizarre reign from Golgotha, to John's ecstatic reminiscence (of days when he followed Jesus or that day by the "skull" when he was given care of Jesus' mother) now projected into "new Jerusalem." Somehow, I believe, the mythical and the political intertwine in this place. For now, we're at a tragic impasse, due largely to belligerent Israel's misconstrual of biblical Judaism, bombastic Palestinian Islam, and perhaps most treacherous of all, the American Zionist Christian right with its dispensationalist Darby theology. On this bed of theological chaos, America has sent forth her globe-threatening geopolitics.

Ethics and law devolve to this place. Is the temple custom, the Levitical code, the kosher ritual, the Mosaic Torah, the Essenic Decalogue, or the Noachic foundational law still normative? Or is some, even all, of this historically derived wisdom now obsolete? Is the saga of Jerusalem, the destiny of Jesus, and the story of Israel somehow a universal story? Is the God, Yahweh, enshrined on that throne called the Ark on the Millo platform by David, is this the God of all nations, of time and space, of all reality?

Is Jerusalem the sacred mountain from which ultimate justice and peace shall one day proceed and to which all nations shall process (Isa 2), or is it amount of arrogance and violence, the profanation of making an altar of stone for the unseen God who will not be confined by human construction (Exod 20.26)? The "gospel of God" (Rom 1.1), as completed and propagated, is the assurance of the former eschatological/earthly vision. The following two sections of conclusion sketch that initial and secondary process.

THE COMPLETION OF THE GOSPEL OF GOD (ROM 1.1)

The theologian ventures reluctantly into the domain of the Bible scholar. But when that theologian is presently at work on a novel hermeneutics of discerning the substance of the Christian *kerygma* in its consonance or dissonance with Judaism and Islam, he may discover something that might interest the biblical field. This has been my experience in the season of work I presently undertake, exemplified in two books: *Ethics and the War on Terrorism* and *Jew, Christian, Muslim*.[7]

Although it is always being reinterpreted in every time and place, the consolidation and completion of the "gospel of God" occurred during the life and work and also in the death, resurrection, and spirit-disclosure of Jesus. It appears to be related to the surmounting of five challenges: *Jesus' witness, Peter's ignorance, Paul's obstinance, James' allowance*, and *the apostles' progress*. These challenges, which interpenetrate the prior and later Abraham faiths of Judaism and Islam, also clarify the character and content of that gospel.

FIVE CHALLENGES

The formation and formulation of the Christian proclamation seems to have been predicated on the successful transaction of five "close-in challenges" during Jesus' earthly appearance. Although inheriting a rich milieu of Hebrew scripture, Greek philosophy and mystery, and Roman peace and civilization, these inducements or corresponding obstructions within the enfolding cultures do not appear to have been decisive in the concourse of that gospel. The real challenges that seem to have had the power to abort or launch the entire project and, in fact, successful transaction of which would precisely define and richly elaborate the very substance of that witness, had to do with individual persons. What Paul and Mark simply call the *euangelion* (Rom 1.16, Mark 1.15), Paul and Peter call *euangelion theou* (Rom 1.1, 1 Pet 4.17), and Paul and Luke call *kergyma* (1 Cor 1.21, Luke 11.32), becomes the substance of the faith and witness of that nascent movement we call Christianity: That he cried, "Jesus Christ is Lord (*kurios*). God has made him both Lord and Christ; this Jesus whom you crucified" (2 Cor 1.19–22).

The "gospel" was similar to other divinities. The "Word of God," for example, was known and basic to the prophets. The "Way of God" was as fundamental as Torah. The "kingdom of God" was a profound physical and spiritual realm. Most importantly, this designated "gospel" was not some elusive philosophical concept. It was flesh and blood, life, and death. It "mattered"—it was all that mattered.

The word *gospel*, or proclamation, was also a simple, secular phrase. It could be the "good news" brought by a messenger or shouted by a

---

7. See Vaux, *Jew, Christian, Muslim* and *Ethics and the War on Terrorism*.

watchman on the wall. Still far distant the runner bringing "glad tidings" can be. Even if my hunch is overdrawn. that these several encounters seal "the forming gospel" and save it from oblivion, they certainly do clarify its character and substance.

In efforts to find rapprochement among the Abrahamic faiths, first I must offer hesitancy about my own approach. At times I have come close to calling the "gospel" the synergy of Torah and *Akedah*. In one sense, as Jesus said (Mark 12), Torah and *Tanakh* are the whole thing —just as Decalogue encapsulates the entirety of human response to God and responsibility to the other. *Akedah* (Abraham's willingness to offer his son—actualized by God the father sacrificing Jesus) weaves together all motifs of the faith. These dimensions come close to constituting the "gospel of God." But that simplicity causes the danger of being reductionist: how shall we then describe that unique, yet universal, substance called the "gospel of God?" The gospel is more than "law" and "rescue," separate or compounded. The gospel is the whole mystery of redemption—the meaning of God within creation.

JESUS' WITNESS

At the outset of his written "gospel," which is a potent and moving force in and of itself and a major testament of evangelism, Mark observes that hearers in Capernaum were "astonished" at Jesus' teaching, "as from One with authority" (Mark 1.27). This incident might well be joined with Luke's report (Luke 4.16–22) of Jesus' first *midrash* proclamation at adjoining Nazareth, where he rises in the synagogue to read scripture: Isa 61.1–2, 58.6; Mark 1.27; Luke 4.16–21.

> . . . The spirit of the Lord is upon me anointing me to . . .
> bring good news to the poor: *ptokoi*
> bring healing to the brokenhearted: *aikmalotois*
> bring release to prisoners of war: *aphesin*
> bring sight to the blind: *tuphlois*
> send out the oppressed: *tethpausmenous*
> announce the jubilee year: *eniquton dekton*

And they marveled at his eloquence . . . "Isn't this Joseph's son?" (Luke 4.22).

A remarkable scene—a turning point. We can imagine his father Joseph there and Mary, his mother. She very likely became an eventual reporter and interpreter of "the gospel." And his siblings—perhaps James, his brother, would become a crucial promulgator of "the Way" at a later decisive juncture. We witness the glory of the performance—like a splendid *bar mitzvah*. We don't know whether it was "his custom" to read the scroll regularly or merely to frequent synagogue. The shock and surprise may suggest that this was his first *halakhah*, and one might find audacity in his response—"today these words are fulfilled in your hearing" (Luke 4.21).

Still the dark clouds gather. "Isn't this the kid next door . . . the carpenter's son?" We know the synagogue at Capernaum stood close to Peter's home, where he cared for his mother. Was he there? Could he ever guess how later events would unfold, how he would be enlisted and then placed in the dock himself?

In all the confrontation-encounters we will recount, Jesus is found hammering up against his world that does not recognize, understand, or receive him:

> Good news . . . to them who were afar off . . .
> . . . He came to his own and his own did not receive him. (John 1.11)

He is a prophet in Jewish tradition. He knows that the world is protologically and eschatologically potent and good. He evokes that kingdom. The first challenge he faces is the most abrupt. Perhaps it shouldn't be so startling. Some commentators have noted that each *bar mitzvah* throughout all ages must consider the possibility that he/she could be the messiah. All it would take was this perfect concord with the will and way of God. Embedded in the very notion of the law is that it can (and might) somewhere, somehow, be followed by someone. Jesus' bold assertion in this sense is perfectly understandable and acceptable.

Yet in a larger sense, Paul is perfectly Jewish-Orthodox when he cries in Romans 7.15, "For I do not do what I want, but I do the very thing I hate." Rabbi Kahane, or other messianic pretenders across the millennia, have been unmasked for who they are: fanatics or fools. Jesus is saying, unequivocally: "This is who I am and what I'm here to do." So, in this early challenge, Jesus is confronting a powerful impediment to the full establishment of God in the world. Or, put positively, what he is laying down in that teaching moment is a *sine qua non*—a foundation stone of the gospel. What is it?

Initially, we must recognize the immense difficulty of successfully communicating such a profound message. Just transecting space and time from eternity is the longest journey imaginable. The history of the Jews—Abraham, Moses, and the prophets—shows the divine complexity and human perplexity involved in successfully communicating even the simplest message: God is . . . God loves us and God's world . . . God seeks our fellowship . . . God wants us to live God's "way." To this, the "gospel" message adds other immense obscurities:

> . . . that we have been thrown out of natural association (sin/fall);
>
> . . . that this estrangement requires suffering sacrificial love and death (atonement); and
>
> . . . that, to make things right, this reconciliation will be proven by a most elusive verification (resurrection).

Now, how do we get there from here? What is the concourse of "filling up" of the gospel? Initially, Jesus' witness at the outset of his ministry in Capernaum/Nazareth anchors the "gospel" in Jewish experience. The messianic day has arrived, when God will consummate his purpose with His people Israel and the world. All that the prophets (*e.g.*, Elijah, Elisha) anticipated and inaugurated; all that Moses received, delivered, and carefully nurtured; all that Abraham first saw and answered; all this is now made crystal clear. Israel's day of fulfillment has come.

Jesus casting his lot with John the Baptist and receiving John's baptism has gone before. This, too, is thoroughly Judaic as "the lamb of God—who takes away the sins of the world" (*Akedah*) submits to this cleansing and healing—for his own death preparation and for the subsuming of humanity's crisis of sin and death. For Jesus' work to work, for it to be efficacious—so that it "saves to the uttermost"—he must be *Akedic* (suffering-servant) and Decalogic (new Torah) messiah ("anointed one"). He thus self-claims charism (anointing) to undergird the gifts he brings to people. For the "gospel" to be embarked and set sail on its course, it must be rooted and anchored in an absolute necessity that this "message" embraces and "pertains to" Jews and Muslims, the children of Abraham, and through these irascible children, the stars and sands of all humanity. How and when that will be worked out rightly remains beyond our ken.

All we know is that to slip into an anti-Semitic and anti-Islamic "gospel"—Gnostic, Marcionic, and syncretistic—is now and forever, wrong!

Second, the gospel begins locally in Jesus' hometown. Like the Hebraic love of God and neighbor, it begins in one's house, then with the next-door neighbor, then on to Jerusalem, Judea, Samaria, and the world. The hometown crowd is familiar and skeptical (Mark 6.7).

Skipping over the proximate neighbor and heading west toward Europe—leaving Arabia bereft of Christian witness—may account for the phenomenon of Islam, if indeed this movement arises from the "Ebionite" (poor, Jewish-Christian) group who were forgotten by the Hellenistic church and if the rapid-fire leap of Christian evangelicalism to the far occident—Italy, Europe, and Spain. In Paul's ministry, this meant "passing over" Arabia, the near-orient and even, in some sense, Africa. Then to move on to the confusing, circuitous concourse of "the gospel"—all the way down to the great global mission phenomenon of the 19th century and the universal history of today. Why it went like this is still an historical enigma to fathom. That Africa and Asia seem to be emerging as epicenters of the Christian movement, that the plantation of nation Israel in world history is the eye of the storm, and that Islam is positioned in vivid confrontation to Jews and Muslims is illuminating. But the "gospel" crisis at Nazareth-Capernaum (Galilean outposts, away from Jerusalem) goes deeper and bears another challenge. The gospel is from, to, and for Israel—yes, but it is also through Israel for the whole world. It comes to the near and dear and to the "far off," also dear.

It must liberate, save, heal, and fulfill Israel and, at the same time, rescue the world. Abraham's seed is the distant sands and stars of the coastlands. The fall, flood, and foolish tower of Babel are world-wide. Though Hebrao-centrism is offensive to the universalist, so also universalism is offensive to the Hebrao-centrist. The necessarily provincial (down-home) is necessarily planetary (cosmic). An immovable object—yes, almost—but it is met with an irresistible force: the gospel to Israel and the nations, the gospel of God. This impediment will threaten to trip up the passage of proclamation again with James. But, for now, we're still on the move, although folk are murmuring and grumbling.

PETER'S IGNORANCE

Another way to phrase the five hurdles to a competed, victorious race for the "gospel" accomplished is:

- Jesus' synagogue presentation;

- Peter's Caesarean confession;

- Paul's Damascus persecution;

- James' Antioch concession; and

- The disciples' worldwide proclamation.

In this set of headings, the emphasis is on the actor, as well as the act and the achievement—much more than my other list, which accented the impediment or roadblock. Peter's confession is fully elucidated by Mark's "gospel," which reflects the close association with the man called Peter (*i.e., Rocky*). Jesus and his disciples set out for the villages of Caesarea Philippi. On the way, he asked his disciples, "Who do men say that I am?" They replied, "Some say John the Baptizer, others Elijah, and yet others, one of the prophets."

"But you," he asked, "who do you say that I am?" Then Peter answered, "You are the Messiah" (*mesha* in Aramaic and *Christos*, anointed, in Greek). Then he ordered them not to tell anyone about him.

He then began to teach them that it was necessary for the Son of Man to undergo great suffering, be rejected by the elders, the chief priests, and teachers of the law, then be put to death and be raised again three days later.

He spoke of this very plainly.

So, Peter took him aside and began to reprove him. But he turned around, looked at his disciples, and reproved Peter with the words, "Away with you, Satan; your interests are those of men, not those of God." Then he called the crowd to him, as well as the disciples, and said to them, "Anyone who wants to be a follower of mine must disown self, take up his cross, and follow me. For the man who wishes to preserve self will lose it, but if a man will let himself be lost for my sake and for the proclamation, that man is safe. What does a man gain by winning the whole world and losing his true self? What can he give to buy back that self?" (Mark 8.27–38; parallels Matt 16.13–28; Luke 9.18–27)

Note first the *dramatis personae* of the three scenes:

- Jesus and the disciples;

- Jesus and Peter (aside);

- Jesus and the disciples; and

- Jesus and the crowd and disciples.

A conviction is being established with one man (remember Matthew's elaboration of Peter's confession—"on this truth I will build my church," etc.), on behalf of the apostle's band, including the crowd (the world, all who will hear this proclamation *euaggelion*). This ultra-local mode of association with the world—Abraham, Moses, Jesus, Peter, Mohammed—is God's way of the ultra-global.

Again, it is a confrontation—and there is anger and disappointment. Peter almost gets it, but not quite. That he got enough of it proved decisive in the course of the proclamation into the world. This is the turning point of Mark's (Peter's) *euaggelion*. Now Jesus' face is set steadfastly toward Jerusalem. Green Galilee yields to parched Jerusalem. Tranquil Capernaum becomes treacherous Jerusalem.

We are interested in the adversarial nature of this moment, the potential for setback. Is Peter the good-hearted, blunder-busting, vacillating friend and protégé of the Messiah, or is he at that moment the instrument and voice of all the resistance the world can muster? "Get behind me, Satan!" These are pretty harsh words. We'll settle, as did his Lord, for his ignorance and reluctance, given the subsequent nobility and reliability of his witness. (Feed my sheep.)

Here, we are up against one of those cryptic, mysterious moments in the saga we trace. The main story is the historic proclamation, the prophetic, messianic assertion of the kingdom we noted in the first scenario. Now we meet "the Man," "the Son of Man." Walter Wink's *The Human Being* is the latest and best treatment of the enigma of "the Son of Man."[8] We know that something suspicious is up when Jesus pledges the disciples to silence: "He ordered them not to tell anyone about him." The assault on the success of this kingdom is, as Paul describes it, "principalities and powers," other kingdoms. The journey producing salvation is most delicate and precarious. It involves the clash of civilizations, but inviting and embracing, not hunting and hurting, this blessed provocation.

8. See Wink, *The Human Being.*

The first impediment, "ignorance" or misunderstanding, is evoked in Jesus' question. This instance is also strange and inverted, since pupils always ask the teacher questions in rabbinic practice. But here, Jesus asks, "Who do people say I am?" He was taken for John the Baptist. As with John, he was thought to be a re-appearance (redivivus) Elijah, even Jeremiah. Then Peter offers an awesome word, perhaps on behalf of a caucus of disciples that he seemed to lead, you are "*Christos*," "*Mesha*," the anointed One, the Davidic King-Messiah.

This culmination also gives a temporal quality to the establishment of the gospel. When Jesus "set his face to Jerusalem" (Luke), it was a sign that the "hour" had come. Following this confession, when the disciples sought to hasten or rush in the kingdom, they had to be reminded, "my hour has not yet come."

There seems to be a precise, inexorable timing involved in the inauguration of the gospel. What we may have here, theologically speaking, is that there is a time for "confession" and a time "to remain silent." There is a time to act and a time to wait.

Albert Schweitzer was provoked by the timing issues in Matthew 10, as here in Mark. "Some here will not taste death before the kingdom comes in power." Jesus says that before the disciples have visited all the cities . . . "the Son of Man will come." But, it doesn't happen. Schweitzer would recast his entire Christology on these malpredictions. The issue seems to be that "the times" are in "God's hands." Not even the Son is given to know when the kingdom will be restored to Israel (Acts 1.7). God has everything ready and coming in "due season." We must be ready, waiting, receptive, and cautious in "bringing it on." God's action lies in profound reciprocity with our reaction, but we are not the arbiters.

The "stumbling block" or impediment to belief (and therefore confession and proclamation) is the *Akedic* element—*polla pathein*—suffering in order to resurrection. The *Akedic* sequence is clearly tracked. "The Son of Man will be:"

- betrayed (handed over) to the priests and scribes (human action);

- condemned to death (religious act);

- delivered to Romans (civil act);

- mocked, spit on, whipped;

- killed; and

- after three days, be raised ("I have the power to lay down my life and raise it up," John 10.18).

This path of sorrows (*Via Dolorosa*) is too tough to take, not only because it requires us to look on this good, perfect man being tortured and executed, but because we are then called to follow suit: "take up your cross and follow me."

Peter's ignorance, vacillation, confession, preaching, and eventual championing of Jesus in his martyr death, was vicarious for the disciples, the crowd, even us. He is *homo representans*. He stands in our stead. The cosmic resistance that surfaces there in the villages around that great Roman seaport, and the rock-hard enduring "proclamation" that "seeps in" there and follows through to Thursday, Friday, Easter, and Pentecost, secures gospel for the world.

PAUL'S OBSTINANCE

Apocalyptic Battle of God. Paul comes onto the stage of gospel history a few years after the death and resurrection of Jesus, but his writing precedes and influences the Gospels. Although he seems ignorant of the life and teachings of Jesus, we sense that he greatly influences the "gospel" formulation of those events. The Jerusalem and environs mission is underway. The small company of Christians is seen as a menace. One Stephen—evidently a Jewish proselyte or Hellenistic convert—is singled out for persecution (stoning and death) for blasphemy. The whole ghastly ordeal, trial and execution, is superintended by one Saul of Tarsus. The gospel is off and running, but this resistance is formidable. Will the movement break down and disappear? We remember the counsel of the Sage Rabbi Gamaliel, "If this (movement) is man-given, it can be stopped, but if it is of God, nothing we can do to stop it." (Acts 5.39)

So, can this revolution be thwarted? Maybe so, except for one apostle, called late in the game—Saul, one untimely born, to be Paul. The formulation of the substance of the gospel owes more to this person than any other. The road to the Damascus incident reported in Acts 9 is remarkable, colored as it is by Paul's extraordinary experience, reported by the sagacious historian, Luke. The preaching of the gospel is hitting up against some high-powered resistance. Almost like the Jewish Holocaust in and around Munich, there was a desire to eliminate every last one, in this case, of the Christians "still breathing threats and murder against the disciples, Saul . . ." The Roman Empire was magnanimous and could live with a diversity of sects. Even the liberal Judaism of the 30s and 40s—Hillel and Gamaliel and their schools—explored a wide range of interpretations and texts. Saul from Tarsus was trained somewhere in this system. But the mission was more radical: it would become something like the College for the Purity of the Faith, the Spanish Inquisition.

The narrative reports an actual wrestling match that is going on between the zealous Javert the hounding hunter—Saul of Tarsus—and the risen Jesus. This ascended one is not sitting back on the deity throne, as in Psalm 87, but down there on the dusty horse path road north from Jerusalem to Damascus. Not yet overseeing a firm establishment church, but still a touch-and-go witness, we find him tripping up and dismounting the aggressive terminator-would-be of the gospel.

I follow my Princeton teacher J. Christiaan Beker in his *Paul The Apostle*, who sees post Damascus Road as an apocalyptic battle of God for a gospel hold in the world, being waged by Saul-become-Paul.[9]

- You have heard no doubt of my earlier life in Judaism.

- I was violently persecuting the church of God and was trying to destroy it.

- I advanced in Judaism beyond many among my people of the same age, for I was far more zealous for the traditions of my ancestors.

- But when God, who had set me apart before I was born and called me through his grace, was pleased to reveal his Son to me so that I might proclaim him among the Gentiles . . . (Gal 1.13–16).

- Last of all, as to one untimely born, he appeared also to me. For I am the least of the apostles, unfit to be called an apostle, because I persecuted the church of God. But by the grace of God I am what I am, and his grace toward me has not been in vain, so we proclaim and so you have come to believe (1 Cor 15.9–11).

9. Beker, *Paul, the Apostle*, xviii.

- ... circumcised on the eighth day, a member of the people of Israel by the tribe of Benjamin. A Hebrew born of Hebrews; as to the law, a Pharisee; as to zeal, a persecutor of the church; as to righteousness under the law, blameless (Phil 3.4–6).

- Meanwhile, Saul, still breathing threats and murder against the disciples of the Lord, went to the high Priest and asked him for letters to the synagogues at Damascus, so that if he found any who belonged to the Way . . . he might bring them back to Jerusalem. Now, as he was going along and approaching Damascus, suddenly a light from heaven flashed around him. He fell to the ground and heard a voice saying to him, "Saul, Saul, why do you persecute me?" He asked, "Who are you, Lord?" The reply came, "I am Jesus, whom you are persecuting" (Acts 9.1–9).

- All the Jews know my way of life from my youth, a life spent from the beginning among my own people and in Jerusalem . . . I have long belonged to the strictest sect of our religion and lived as a Pharisee . . . I was convinced that I ought to do many things against the name of Jesus of Nazareth, and that's what I did in Jerusalem; with authority received from chief priests, I not only locked up many of the saints in prison, but I also cast my vote against them when they were being condemned to death. By punishing them often in all the synagogues I tried to force them to blaspheme . . . I also pursued them to foreign cities with this in mind. I was traveling to Damascus with the authority and commission of the chief priests, when at midday along the road . . . I saw a light from heaven, brighter than the sun. Saul, Saul, why are you persecuting me? It hurts you to kick against the goad. ". . . I am sending you to open the eyes of the Gentiles—that they may turn from darkness to light, from Satan to God" (Acts 26.9–18). Saul's companions did not see this Damascus-road drama, and Paul himself does not dwell on it. Yet it is a most decisive episode in emergence of the Christian movement.

The gospel for Paul is not a subjective experience, but the over-whelming and overriding triumph of God over the forces of what would thwart or defeat the gospel. His formulation of the "gospel of God" (Rom 1.1; 1 Thess 2.2, 8, 9; 2 Cor 11.7; Rom 15.16) is identical to the "gospel of Christ" (Rom 15.19; 1 Cor 9.12; 2 Cor 2.12, 4.4, 9.13, 10.14). The gospel is a message of vindication of Jesus and the victory of his "Way." His death and resurrection is of cosmic significance. Paul's vow to impede those he found in "the Way" now becomes an irresistible ardor for that "Way." This very pedestrian event portends planetary significance.

As Caravaggio's "Rembrandt-like," dark-and-light, dramatic paint-ing of this scene illumines, we encounter here a life-shaking and Earth-shaking shock flash, throw-downturn about. This is Elijah and Baal's prophets contending amid the lightning flashes. It is two titans embraced in a death-lock. Something and someone has to give. Or is this the typical hyperbole we always hear in conversion stories? Was Saul really that bad? Was he so adamant against Jesus' gospel? Was he secretly drawn to it, and was his resistance a kind of transference? Whatever, this sequence of texts portrayed the event as a *Götterdämmerung*—a showdown of whether this nascent movement will succeed or be cast aside. It accomplishes more than adding the new "Gentile" dimension. As time and events will provide, it turns the Christian faith away from Judaism and toward the Hellenized "God fearers"—Gentiles and a small company of Jews who will resist their own traditions at great peril. A small "particularity" party poses a new "universality."

The episode speaks to me of how spiritually unsatisfying main-line second temple Judaism was in Paul's day, and how ethically bankrupt were the thousands of surrounding salvation cults. The skeptic could say that the strategy of God became to bring on Orphic, Dyanisian, Mithraic, and Gnostic "enthusiasm" to Israel, as well as genuine justice and piety from Israel to the morally and religiously floundering Roman and Hellenistic world. Saul/Paul would become the mediator. Even more, the episode reveals the hunger for God found not only among the poor people "of the land" to whom Jesus appealed but the cultured folk in the Hellenistic cities to whom Paul would speak.

Pauline scholar Charles Raven offers an interesting angle in his book on Teilhard de Chardin: "St. Paul took up the task (of gospel formulation after Peter's confession) when having been disappointed by the failure of Jesus to escape the accursed death he had his consequent repudiation challenged on the Damascus Road."[10]

Raven's speculation that Saul had hoped that Jesus would "escape" the dreadful cross, just as Socrates' disciples had hoped he would skip out of his house-arrest and avert the hemlock, parallels the elements of Peter's confession and attempted dissuasions: faltering faith, abhorrence at the prospect of suffering (including his own), "I will show him what he must suffer for my namesake" (Acts 26); and misguided triumphalism.

Paul's little world of heroic (non-*Akedic*/non-messianic) Judaism, and perhaps Jewish-Christianity itself, was shattered. He may have let his heart be tempted by the Davidic restorationism and even militant retributionism of the Zealots in Jesus' company (Judas, Simon the Zealot). But this turnaround, this facing and exposing of Jerusalem, was a journey he could not join. Perhaps he was embarrassed, even endangered here in the house of his learning. He knew these high priests and the High Priest well. This theory is posited on a chronology where Paul shares some overlapping years with Jesus, a point that is extremely controversial:

- Jesus' Ministry: crucifixion and appearances (27–30 C.E.);

- Saul's rabbinic training in Jerusalem with Gamaliel/Hillel (28–33 C.E.);

- Saul's persecution of the Jerusalem Christians, Stephen's stoning (33 C.E.);

- Saul's conversion and call (39 C.E.);

- Killing of James, son of Zebedee, under Herod Agrippa (4–44 C.E.);

- Jerusalem council, Antioch Dispatch (c. 52 C.E.);

- Paul's first missionary journey (c. 52 C.E.);

- Letter to Thessalonica (49 C.E.);

- Death of Peter, Paul, James (62 C.E.);

- Jewish wars (66–70 C.E.).[11]

10. See Raven, *St. Paul and the Gospel of Jesus* and Raven, *Teilhard de Chardin*, 163.

11. See Jewett, *A Chronology of Paul's Life.*

Pondering the possible chronologies enables us to see why Saul was a man who had to be dealt with. Jesus could not go around him. The concourse of the gospel (for the world) must go through him. He was chosen from his mother's womb. Here is the focal point of the crisis scenario we find in Paul's Damascus Road experience: Whatever the crisis that went on in Paul's life, was it hope and disappointment? An erroneous reading about the inauguration of the messianic age? A faulty reading of Torah requirement and obedience as this pertained to salvation? Here, in Jesus' culminating days—especially at the point of crucifixion, resurrection, return appearance, ascension and Pentecost (was Paul there?)—in Saul's soul, as in Augstine's, three centuries later, everything came to a climax. Saul had to be confirmed in his way or cast-down and corrected. Amazingly, it made all the difference to God and to the ascended Jesus. The man had to be confronted and, like the hound of heaven, brought to submission, and Paul (Galatians 1) knew it, "He who set me aside from my mother's womb . . ."

It only remains now to characterize the "gospel of God" as we have it from the "*en christou*" mind and heart of Paul, which was precipitated by this crisis/confrontation.

Here I follow St. Augustine, Princeton mentor Beker, and Chicago colleague Bob Jewett[12]on what seems to be the four decisive resolutions in the gospel proclamation worked out through Paul's life and work beginning on the road to Damascus.

- The "New Being" is the *sine qua non* of the gospel.

- This is enacted against the cosmic background of the new creation and the apocalyptic age to come.

- The "crucified One" is the initiator and receptor of the New Being.

- His "Way" is the "gospel of God" or "law of Christ" (Galatians) is now the response of thankful life, not a precondition or requirement of salvation.

Augustine on Paul's Conversion. Everyone knows the decisive starting point of faith in Augustine's confessions. It ensues in the paradigm of Paul's conversion. In the midst of a profound existential and ethical crisis over

12. See Beker, *Paul, the Apostle*; Jewett, et al., *Romans: A Commentary*.

his dissolute and aimless manner of life, he beheld "the dignified figure of chastity and continence" and began to "weep bitterly." He flung himself down under a fig tree, as tears welled up like a river, and he heard a child singing in a neighboring house: "Pick it up—and read." He remembered how Antony had heard the words, "Go and sell your possessions and give the money to the poor: you will have treasure in heaven. Then come, follow me" (Matt 19.21)[13] He took up the book of Paul's epistles, which he had been reading, and blindly stuck his finger on the page. Rather than the proverbial "Judas went out and killed himself" and "Go thou and do likewise," he fingered Romans 13.13–14 (perhaps a clue to Paul's then Damascus upheaval).

> Not in dissipation and drunkenness, nor in debauchery and lewdness, nor in arguing and jealousy, but put on the Lord Jesus Christ, and make no provision for the flesh or the gratification of your desires. Then, overwhelming peace came over him, ". . . the light of certainty flooded my heart, and all dark shades of doubt fled away."[14]

Paul's plight was misbelief and misdirection. He was set in his mistaken mind and ways. As is obvious from his autobiographical texts in scripture, he thought he was right, he pursued it with vigor and ended up kicking Jesus in the balls (groin?). This guy had to be stopped in his tracks.

Now one might get away with mistaken concepts or a theology that is slightly askew. But when you are fighting zealously for your own "way" and this "way" was certainly not the "way" of Israel or of Gamaliel, Hillel or the great Pharisee schools—trouble brewed. This was the belligerent defensive "way" of the corrupt Jerusalem priesthood and theologate (scribes) sternly rejected by the Pharisees, the Essenes, and Jesus himself. This was the mafia Luther derided as "priests and theologians," these were the immoral cabal who killed Jesus, James and desiccated the poor. This was anti-Torah, anti-Decalogue, anti-Akedah, and anti-God. Yahweh—of old—and his Christ—had to do battle—ambush this "loose cannon" on that Basra (Damascus) road and set him on "the straight path" (Torah).

13. Athanasius, *Life of Antony*.

14. Ibid.

Augustine again preaches on Paul's conversion in Sermon #279.[15] This, he writes, is making ". . . the preacher out of the prosecutor, by striking and thereby healing, by slaying and thereby bringing to life—the lamb slain by wolves makes lambs out of wolves." Where is the great preacher when we need him in these days? Saul was a ravenous wolf. He went out with his warrants "breathing and panting slaughter." For Christ to "live in him" later on, he would have to kill Saul now. "Saul, why are you persecuting me? It is hard for you to kick against the goad." "The head in heaven was crying out for his members still located on Earth."

"I will show him what he must suffer for the sake of my name" (Commandment 3). But listen to who has done . . . and is still doing the suffering, and the changed Paul will eventually sing to the Romans: "The sufferings of this time are not worthy to be compared with the future glory that will be revealed in us" (Rom 8.18).

Paul, in the aftermath of Damascus, now a conveyer of the gospel—the proclamation sees the unequivocal centrality of the new being—the new creation. It sings throughout his letters. And the vitality of this new creation is the gift of the crucified One. Paul discovered with Peter that the One "despised" (Isa 53) will receive the accolades of the ages. One dishonored will be honored throughout time and eternity.

In identifying the Apostles' indispensable formulation and articulation of the "gospel," Augustine sees the clear message of not living "not to offend" nor of living "as the code requires," but of being like David, another irascible follower, "a man after God's own heart." In sermon 278 (414 C.E.), Augustine again ponders Paul's conversion and call. In this remarkable sermon, he joins Paul's experience to the Lord's prayer, honing in on the "forgive us . . . as we forgive" couplet.

Paul's conversion experience was one where God's forgiving mercy had to "pump out the bilges of his soul." The cesspool was full and stopped up with the accumulated "bilge" ("I count it all [the credits of righteousness] as shit"). The stoning of Stephen reverberates in the mind. We may wonder again if Paul had a hand in (assenting at least) in the death of Jesus. Now we come to this goading and undermining the progress and success of the gospel.

From this existential dimension, Paul (via Augustine) reflects on the whole trajectory and terror of the ethical life. The worst thing a sick man

---

15. Augustine's Sermons, Sunday, June 23, 401 C.E.

can do is fool himself that he is well. The gate of new life is repentance, forgiveness of sin and "believe the gospel" and . . . "follow me." To be renewed and well, the doctor's diagnosis must be accepted and the prescription be filled and taken.

Paul has his condition in clear and retrospective view. He isolated the proscription and prescription at every point.

"I was a blasphemer, persecutor, and inhumane man" (1 Tim 3.16). He might have said, "The reason Jesus struck me down, and healed me was that I might be a vessel of divine diagnosis and therapy for others (wow!) for the Gentile world."

You begin to be well (whole and new) by following the prescription of the law. The crisis of faith is the crisis of behavior which hurts others, hurts yourself, and even kicks God in the teeth. "There are two commandments and two kinds of sin."

You sin against God and/or other human beings. This is the resistant and recalcitrant life that goes "its own way." It kicks others around and defiantly attacks God's self. Salvation (healing) is to realize that "you are not your own." You were bought with a price. You must glorify God in your body, your life.

Augustine is a bodily theologian. He is like a Jew or Muslim finding the concourse of the gospel, not in flesh "gone haywire," but in "putting on the Lord Jesus Christ" and living in, through, and out of that body. Living "the Way" is to die to "the flesh," putting aside and away the furious life of self-affirmation and self-justification, and letting the Word, Way, and Will of God have its say and sway within us.

Beker sees the stages of Paul's clarification and consolidation of the gospel in a similar way. It is not that his subjective conversion has become a new norm for Christian experience, nor that some intra-psychic restoration has become the new meaning of Judaism. The gospel is simply the announcement that God has created a new state of affairs, honoring the sacrifice, redeeming work, and victory of His Son Jesus. This new reality concerns every person, community, nation, and history, and the cosmos as well. It was for the messianic renewal of the world (*tikkun olam*) that Jesus suffered, died, and was raised. The call now to disciples is to believe and live this gospel that ". . . God has made him Lord and Christ" and to follow Him in that "Way." Paul's construal of the gospel, claims Beker, is that of apocalyptic Judaism. A new order has been inaugurated from the passing away of the old. It involves the triumph of God over the resistance of the world, the messianic consummation of history (where these kingdoms become His kingdom) and the transfiguration of all past and present history and nature into Christ's redeemed "new creation."

Through the entry point of faith-procured righteousness, we gain portal to the Reign of God (*Regnum Christi*) which, though still on the horizon, has already been gained in Christ's atonement. To faith in community, it is already palpable. To Jesus, careful articulation of the features of messianic reign along with Peter's abrupt confession: You are Messiah. Paul weaves a fabric of Hebrew background, prophetic content, living experience of Jesus—an "apocalyptic texture"—that enlarges and intensifies "the gospel."

JAMES' ALLOWANCE

After the death of Jesus, the Twelve established themselves in Jerusalem, the epicenter of the Jewish pilgrimages from out of the Diaspora. James, the brother of the Lord, perhaps an early skeptic about his older brother's received messiah acclamations (his family doubted him and the "without honor at home" phenomenon), now became a "pillar" of the Jerusalem company and the advocate of Paul's Gentile mission. The somewhat concurrent events of Stephen's stoning, Paul's conversion, and Pentecost gave a dramatic context to their daily life of prayers in the temple, house fellowship with Jesus' family, and explaining among the Twelve and a small band of friends and followers. Perhaps 120 strong (Acts 1.15), the Ananias/Sapphira incident, whatever actually happened, showed the close-knit interdependence that bonded the company.

With Paul, an outsider even more than the Galileans, the Jerusalem church began planting subordinate congregations in the near vicinity, and the drama among James, Peter and Paul became an occasion for another great challenge to the mission's accomplishment. The issue had to do with the measure of Jewish law (circumcision, Kosher laws) that was viewed incumbent on a primarily Gentile offspring-church, in this case, Antioch. James, a witness to the resurrection (1 Cor 15.7), was thought by Paul to be "one of the Apostles" (Gal 1.19). It seems that with Peter and John, he directed the mission (witness) to the Jews. In keeping with our thesis on the "staging" of the gospel, James knew that the Jewish mission was prelude to that to the Gentiles. The letter bearing his name reveals that he had formulated a high-order synthesis between Torah duty and mystic salvation, much in accord with the grand moments of Hebrew faith and life. He likely believed, with Paul, that the surprising inclusion and conversion of the Gentiles was indicative of the salvation of Jesus.

In Acts 15.1–29, we have Luke's account of this provocative conference following the setting of context: Paul's plea for openness, objection by the observant, Peter's waffling, James offers a concession "allowance" based on the received joy and self-evident efficacy of the Gentile mission. The Gentiles must adhere to the deep stipulates of Torah (singular belief, confession, etc.). Moral-ethical marks, certainly filial piety, murder, idolatry, chastity, etc., also "food offered to idols," and philanthropy to the poor should continue. The converts are absented from the ceremonial requirement, especially circumcision and food laws.

> But some men came down from Judea and were teaching the brethren, "Unless you are circumcised according to the custom of Moses, you cannot be saved." And when Paul and Barnabas had no small dissension and debate with them, Paul and Barnabas and some of the others were appointed to go up to Jerusalem to the apostles and elders about this question. So, being sent on their way by the church, they passed through both Phoenicia and Samaria, reporting the conversion of the Gentiles, and they gave great joy to all the brethren. When they came to Jerusalem, they were welcomed by the church and the apostles and the elders, and they declared all that God had done with them. But some believers who belonged to the part of the Pharisees rose up, and said, "It is necessary to circumcise them, and to charge them to keep the law of Moses."
>
> The apostles and the elders were gathered together to consider this matter. And after there had been much debate, Peter rose and said to them, "Brethren, you know that in the early days, God made choice among you, that by my mouth, the Gentiles should hear the word of the gospel and believe. And God who knows the heart bore witness to them, giving them the Holy Spirit just as he did to us, and he made no distinction between us and them, but cleansed their hearts by faith. Now, therefore, why do you make trial of God by putting a yoke upon the neck of the disciples, which neither our fathers nor we have been able to bear? But we believe that we shall be saved through the grace of the Lord Jesus, just as they will."
>
> And all the assembly kept silence, and they listened to Barnabas and Paul as they related what signs and wonders God had done through them among the Gentiles. After they finished

speaking, James replied, "Brethren, listen to me. Simeon has related how God first visited the Gentiles, to take out of them a people for his name. And with this, the words of the prophets agree, as it is written:

After this I will return, and I will rebuild the dwelling of David, which has fallen. I will rebuild its ruins, and I will set it up, that the rest of men may seek the Lord, and all the Gentiles who are called by my name, says the Lord, who has made these things known from of old.

Therefore, my judgment is that we should not trouble those of the Gentiles who turn to God, but should write to them to abstain from the pollutions of idols and from unchastity and from what is strangled and from blood. For from early generations, Moses has had in every city those who preach him, for he is read every Sabbath in the synagogues."

Then it seemed good to the apostles and the elders, with the whole church, to choose men from among them and to send them to Antioch with Paul and Barnabas. They sent Judas called Barsabbas, and Silas, leading men among the brethren, with the following letter:

"The brethren, both the apostles and the elders, to the brethren who are of the Gentiles in Antioch and Syria and Cilicia, greetings. Since we have heard that some persons from us have troubled you with words, unsettling your minds, although we gave them no instructions, it has seemed good to us, having come to one accord, to choose men and send them to you with our beloved Barnabas and Paul, men who have risked their lives for the sake of our Lord Jesus Christ. We have, therefore, sent Judas and Silas, who themselves will tell you the same things by word of mouth. For it has seemed good to the Holy Spirit and to us to lay upon you no greater burden than these necessary things, that you abstain from what has been sacrificed to idols and from blood and from what is strangled and from unchastity. If you keep yourselves from these, you will do well. Farewell." (Acts 15.1–29)

What of the confrontation, which focuses on these three persons (Paul, Peter, James) and this showdown in Jerusalem? Obviously, Jesus, Peter, Paul, and James are all calling people to rediscover the "living God" of Abraham, Isaac, and Jacob, of Moses and the prophets, the God and father of Jesus, become Christ. They are calling people to vital faith in the God of Israel who is Lord of the universe. They all plead for repentance, "forgiveness of sins," worthy sacrifice, and lives bearing fruit "worthy of repentance." They all yearn for the dawning of the new age, the messianic age, the year of the Lord's favor—Jubilee—when, with apocalyptic freshness, the old oppressions, sicknesses, impoverishments will pass and the age of knowledge of God and pursuing of "his ways" will ensue.

The question is this: Does this new age, new man, new community, and new Israel mean the repudiation and dismissal of present Israel? Or are two covenants, even three (Islam), being called for by the God of Abraham? Surely the particular is in search of the universal. God rules the whole Earth!

This crisis is only overcome in Pentecost, where Spirit and law (Way) are blended for all time in the historic manifestations of God as they always had coexisted in the being of God. In some ways, the Jamesian "gospel crisis" still endures, as the warring sons of Abraham blow each other up and terrorize the *shalom* of the Earth. I have come to believe that the lingering antagonism of Jews, Christians, and Muslims—Crusades, Holocaust, and terrorism—is the stigma of this unresolved gospel crisis. The grand moments of brotherhood—Andalusia Spain before the Crusades and Inquisition and some seventh- and eighth-century islands of concord and amazing ecumenical work—are foretastes of this final culmination of the gospel in world history.

In *Jew, Christian, Muslim*, I offer the following thesis:

> . . . a filial affinity is to be found among the three Abraham faiths, an affinity which, when nurtured, invigorates the member religions and sustains faith, justice, and peace in the world. When severed and antagonized, the particular faiths are distorted and the world is threatened and terrorized.[16]

Not only gospel viability, but the peace and justice of the world, hang on the Jamesian crisis. The Abrahamic faiths "that receive and envision a God who leads" also seem to "construct life as a test" (persecution).[17] This may be the clue to fathoming the persecutions, which inevitably accompany gospel witness (martyrdom).

As a test or "ordeal"—Exodus, temptation, crucifixion—is overcome in the life of God, a furtherance of the gospel is accomplished. Similarly, in the life of those who follow and attest the gospel of God, such "tribulations" mark proleptic moments of "thrust forward" of the message.

16. Vaux, *Jew, Christian, Muslim*, 8.

17. Ibid., 68.

The final and decisive removal of a roadblock to the travel (and travail) of the gospel occurs in the years before the Jewish revolt against Rome, the destruction of the temple and Masada and the Diaspora, not only of Palestinian Jews but Jewish Christians. At this time, the still relatively small band of Palestinian Christians lived near the Joppa gate—the northwest corner of the Old City.

There is considerable evidence that Essene Jews and the central band (the Twelve, Mary, Jesus' Mother, and his family) lived together, perhaps sharing a common baptismal bath. Jesus' annunciation of his mission, now seen in the light of his passion and rising, was celebrated in the ritual of "passion night"—vigil from Holy Thursday evening to Friday at sunset, when Christians may have fasted in sympathetic celebration of the Jewish Passover, when that sister communion, similarly embattled, reviewed their salvation history, and the Paschal lamb was sacrificed. The Christian commune also held meals in common, perhaps co-worshipped and studied at temple and synagogue, and watched at prayer as a mission message was being formulated and furthered.

The Gentile phase had taken off. Yet Paul's evangel still hinged on the destiny of this small band of Judean followers. Paul believed (Romans) that the success of the Aegean and European (Italy and Spain) witness depended on those in the West "remembering" and aiding those who were tormented and sorely persecuted in the East. The offering to help the poor ethically seemed to be a precondition for the gospel to succeed spiritually at the Western gates of Europe. A synthesis or reciprocity, similar to James' accession in Antioch, seems to have been established as ethical and theological ingredients of the gospel live and thrive in creative synergy.

For this band of twelve, along with a larger circle of perhaps twelve disciples per apostle, and along with an ever wider circle of small house fellowships of perhaps twelve for those twelve, the gospel was now poised to launch out in Mesopotamia, India, East into Armenia and Edesa, North into Egypt and Africa, South into Asia Minor and East as it was further consolidated in the Aegean and Europe. For this endeavor to begin and succeed, the Apostles and disciples had to be ready for martyrdom and have an uncanny confidence to preach the gospel. Three moments stand out in this preparedness and readiness. They all have to do with speech and communication. We highlight the upper room; Pentecost; and the Apostolate (sending/speaking).

THE APOSTLES' PROGRESS

Upper Room. In the upper room (Acts 1.12ff), now believed to be near that Essene compound, the (120) interrupted their fellowship and prayer (James/"camel knees") and listened as Peter rose and proclaimed, "Friends, . . . the Scripture had to be fulfilled—Judas' betrayer was part of the plan . . . let us pray to replace him in "this ministry and apostolate." The community was "lying low," waiting, praying hard, and setting the stage for what was to come. In the book of Acts, Luke chronicles the eastern but mainly the western mission with his companion, Paul. We can surmise that the mother and brothers, especially James, were also "hunted," but they knew their teaching was essential.

We can only conjecture about the inner dynamics of that didache. From Peter's early sermons, we infer a proclamation grounded in the Hebrew Bible or perhaps in Aramaic (*cf.* Mel Gibson's *The Passion of the Christ*). The call was to celebrate the grand, messianic plan of the ages, conveyed through Israel's history, the law and prophets, and now fulfilled in Jesus.

Confronted with Jesus made Savior and Lord, people were called to repentance for the forgiveness of sins and belief. Finally, his preaching held forth the Pentecost promise of the "Holy Spirit." Mary, who must have been a theologian of searching wisdom, "kept all these things and pondered them in her heart," until Luke, then John the Apostle, came to the well. And James, as his letter conveys, sublime wisdom and resurrection grace.

The boldness of belief and confidence in divine companionship presaged the great success of the forthcoming mission.

Pentecost. At Pentecost, an amazing coincidence occurs, as Jews from throughout the Diaspora converge for Shavuot, the festival of the law, and experience an awesome pouring forth of Spirit, just as Moses had experienced with the 70 elders in Numbers 11. The way, Torah, was not conveyed in the light, fire, and wind of the gospel proclamation and impediments to speech, understanding, and progression flew to the winds. Now the four corners of the Earth, the reversal of the tower of Babel with the deaf and dumb world that pretense had yielded, were swept together with one universe of discourse. The sound had gone out unto all the Earth. We all hear the "good news" in our own language and "everyone who calls on the Name of the Lord (commandment 3) will be saved." Speech is profession yielding confession seeking confession. In the third commandment and in the history of Israel and the church, we are commanded to confess, not curse (or disavow) the name ("of the Lord"). Confession with the tongue (remember James' Epistle) conveys belief to the heart. Not only had impediments, stumbling blocks, offenses (Jews and Greeks) been removed, but a smooth, straight highway, a crooked path made straight (Torah) had been laid out. And the travel of the messengers begins.

Apostolate. Finally the sent-forth (*apo-stelon*) move out, and the world awaits its transformation and renewal. Irrepressibility of the messengers' receptivity of heaven marks the concourse of the gospel. The Isaianic text was now fulfilled:

> . . . How shall they know unless they hear, and how shall they hear without a preacher? How beautiful upon the mountains are the feet of the messengers who announce peace, who bring good news, who announce salvation (Isa 52.74).

> And, day by day, as they spent much time together in the temple and broke bread at home, they ate their bread with glad and generous hearts, praising God and having the goodwill of all the people (Acts 2.46, 47).

It was nip and tuck, touch and go, although hindsight sees a grand and goodly providence, a well-paved highway and smooth passage. For the message to travel at that time, it was more like the lad I saw in Paris trying to find his girlfriend at a prearranged rendezvous point on their dueling cell phones—and there she was, right behind a pillar. Yet the message gets through. The gospel proceeded on its way, in part, because of the successful transactions of Jesus and Peter, Paul, James, and the apostolic company. And, today, we continue that concourse in communication and intercommunion throughout all the world.

Paris, March 2004

This interpretive travelogue has offered the reader another window into Ken Vaux's heart and soul and, hopefully, your own. I conclude this diary with a set of theological-political reflections from this topographical journey.

Perhaps the ultimate way to reflect on some *rapprochement* between the evangelical and ethical impulses, or between the sacred and the secular, is to ruminate about religion and society, church and state in some of the places we visited in 1996: Israel and Turkey, Greece and France.

THE HISTORICAL PROPAGATION OF THE GOSPEL OF GOD

Sociologists, especially in the French tradition—Comte, Levi-Strauss, Levy-Bruhl, and Durkheim—have explored the interplay and oft-times solidarity between the religious assembly and the nation. In primitive society, they are one and the same. In ancient Israel, Greece, and Rome, the *q'hal*—the national assembly and the religious communion—are the same. As modern societies have unfolded, in part bearing out Comte's analysis that the positivist would supersede the sacred, then metaphysical phases of history reveals distance between church and state. North America is the most pronounced experiment of this separation. Now, in the early 21st century, we see a return to some facsimile of the organic religious state.

Let me offer some reflections about this development. The structure of my social-political conscience begins with:

- the foundations of creation and law in Judaic Israel;

- the transition through Semitic thought into Islamic Turkey;

- the transition to ecumenical ethics in Orthodox Greece;

- the embodiment of public European ethics in Catholic France; and

- the search for a newer world in the ecumenical United States.

The evolution of a public ethic can be observed as it passes through each of these cultural expressions. As I search in my own work now for a "family-life" ethic that safeguards and wellkeeps "unwed mothers and their children," or an "economic" ethic that facilitates "low- or no-interest loans to the poor," a current look at these several stations of an emerging religious public policy or evangelical ethic may offer illumination.

Israel. At the end of a tumultuous century and millennium, Israel found itself on the verge of near perpetual *intifada*. The world, with the exception of the U.S. and Israel, recognizes the situation as a political calamity and humanitarian disaster. After the terrible bus bombings by *Hamas* terrorists, the assassination of Yithzak Rabin, the election of Benjamin Netanyahu, Ehud Barak, Ariel Sharon, Ehud Olmert, and now Benjamin Netanyahu again—and a fragile coalition of *Likud*, liberal, and Orthodox religious parties—we realize the enormous political mistake of striking spark to kindling by opening an entrance to the old tunnel under the West Wall along the edge of the Islamic holy site, the Dome of the Rock, and of constructing the wall. After the death of President Assad of Syria and the election of Sharon, it became clear that Israel is no exemplar of justice or ethics to the world, nor are the Palestinians. Despite Israel's profound ethical heritage and the religious recrudescence in recent years, it now seems to be retreating from a public policy that insures the rights of all people—Jews, Christians, and Muslims. Confiscations of property and violations of human rights continue. While doing a commendable job looking after the health, welfare, and rights of its own Jewish citizens (who is my neighbor?), the abuse of those same fundamental freedoms for Arabs, Christians, and Muslims is pronounced and grievous. Once 20 percent, Christians in Israel-Palestine now constitute less than one percent of the population. Even if Israel does not acknowledge the rights of these ancient inhabitants, or even if the tribes and communities who have settled here in Palestine in recent centuries are viewed as outsiders, Israel should be moved by its ancient law of hospitality and sanctuary for the stranger in its midst. In this ethical custom, traceable to the patriarchal wanderings of Abraham and his offspring, the requirement to look after the well-being of the "stranger," even the "adversary" within your gates, is binding—an obligation of the Yahweh covenant.

Israel today is enlarging the scope of "rabbinic" law within the public sphere. Family law, marriage, sexuality matters, birth and death law are framed within this realm. In Northwest Jerusalem, the Orthodox community now seeks to reactivate Sabbath law by stopping the flow of traffic on the major north-south artery to Ramallah, Nablus, etc. Major challenges appear on the horizon in the area of business law (*e.g.*, refusing loans to Palestinians and Bedouins in order to confiscate their property); and eco-laws about land ownership and protecting the environment. The Jordan River, for example, is being so grievously exploited by settlements that its banks have severely constricted the expanse of the Dead Sea. Israel's destiny in world history is to custodian divine law. The Holocaust confirms that messianic destiny. Grounding the state of Israel securely in the midst of what was once Jesus' world, then Constantinian Christendom, and now the Islamic *al-ummi* (nation), so that justice and peace might ensue, should be uppermost policy commitment among the world's nations.

The thesis I here offer is that there is integrity, wholeness, and completion in each historical Abrahamic faith. Part of this intrinsic and extrinsic holiness is a historical continuum in which a prelude, interlude, and postlude flow into a unified symphony. Neither the election of Israel, the formation of the church, or the rise of Islam is an accident. Together, they constitute the historic will of the God of Abraham.

Turkey. The biblical history of Turkey (Asia Minor) gives it a unique purpose in the community of nations and in a history of political ethics. In the mythic recesses of history, we read that the primal eco-catastrophe (flood) came to its end as Mount Ararat appeared from the receding waters. Now the human and animal world would have another chance. Abraham's call to lead humanity toward a new vision of faith came in Harran. In Antioch in Anatolia, Jesus disciples were first called Christians. Ararat, Harran, Antioch, eastern, southern, and southwestern Turkey. The prehistory of Asia Minor is intriguing. From here, the departure of the sons of Noah; Shem, Ham, and Japheth (Gen 10) began. However, this corresponds with the pre-historical migrations of the human race after the withdrawal of the last ice age, where we find in ancient Armenia-Turkey a crucible of civilization. One can wonder about the ancient origins of the Lydians, Hittites, Canaanites, Philistines, Arameans, and others. By the time that history dawns in ancient Sumer, we find all of these peoples well established.

Our interest in Turkey is as a mediating civilization between Jewish and Christian beginnings, the Greco-Latin-European phase of world history, and the emergence of Islamic civilization. At Odessa, for example, we have an important early city in the history of Christianity. Here, just north of Abraham's Harran, the Christian community came to understand "the law of the messiah" two centuries before Augustine's *civitas Dei*. Who were the people here? What was their vision of a "just and good society?" We know that they were conquered in turn by the Persians, Greeks, and Romans. But who were the indigenous people, and what was their cultural ethos? Paul's ministry can be said to have taken root in Anatolia. Although his home region included Antioch and Syria, Tarsus was in old Anatolia. The reception of a universal revelation—Judaism into the world—can be said to begin here.

Most Anatolian cities had small Jewish populations. Some, like Paul's father, had become Roman citizens. But cities like Tarsus and Cilicia, Lydia and Phrygia, Pergamum and Ephesus were sophisticated, learned, and highly cultured cities with a religioethical propensity stemming from high pagan traditions, the Judaic influence, the mobility of the Hellenic-Roman law and morality, and the new impulses of the Jesus movement. Whether it was the underground church (as was found in a cave in Antioch in the Orantes) or the blessed persecuted communities throughout Pontus, Phrygia, Galatia, and the rest of the Constantian established church, here is *terra sancta*.

Crises in modern Istanbul and in Eastern Anatolia focus the dilemma of the new Islamic, yet secular, state of Turkey. In Istanbul, controversy raged over the issue of beginning Islamic prayer services in historic Hagia Sophia, the great Santa Sophia cathedral founded by Emperor Constantine, now a museum open to Islamic and Christian pilgrims. The Greek patriarch is based in Istanbul, for old Constantinople was the capital of the Byzantine Empire. In Eastern Anatolia today, Turk police and army carried out a purge of Kurds in the same way that they "cleansed" the region of Armenians at the beginning of the century. The government trembled at the prospect of an independent state of Kurdistan-Iraq. Turkish women scholars wear the *hijab* even when members of parliament, and this incenses the secular authorities.

The Ottoman Muslim state implemented *Sharī'ah* (Islamic law) in a very modest sense. Yet *Sharī'ah* law is comprehensive covering all political, social, domestic, and individual matters, as well as religious. The French Revolution profoundly secularized Turkish culture. The Turk revolution of 1908 sought to combine a Turkish-Muslim state with a parliamentary, democratic constitution. Defeat in the first World War shattered this fragile experiment. Atatürk sought to create a "natural" and "scientific" religion that was profoundly secular and sacred. In abolishing the caliphate, he effectively destroyed the theological foundations of the state. In 1996, Turkey's government sought to join the Islamic Welfare Party with the more conservative True Path in order to reestablish these connections. True Path leaders were responsible for overseeing defense, interior education, health and trade, as well as other departments. It remains to be seen what working policies will come in these departments and how they will reflect the rich reservoirs of *Sharī'ah*.

Turkey seems poised to become a mediating nation in a world increasingly polarized between Christians and Muslims and Jews and Muslims. In the post Kuwait-Iraq age, we might hope that the historic animosity of the U.S. with Iran will soften, as greater justice for Palestinians and poor Arabs generally reduces the call for terrorism—and Turkey, Pakistan, Bosnia, and other great Islamic societies could then mediate understanding and cooperation. The war on terrorism after the events of September 11th, 2001 and the second U.S. war with Iraq (beginning in 2003) put all of this on hold. Some day, perhaps we could study and implement some of the thoughtful and just statutes of Islamic law into world order. In the summer of 2000, the European Union said that Europe (with its falling population) must become an increasingly pluralist commonwealth, accepting some 70 million refugees from the South and East in the next 50 years. In 2006, an Islamic college opened at Oxford. Perhaps a great concourse of justice is being opened.

Greece. Greece has always been a land of dramatic contrasts. Hot and dry inland plains descend to delightful islands and coastal cities. Political parties range from traditional orthodox to revolutionary communists. Today, Greece, along with the new state of Armenia, seeks to implement a political ethos that in some way is shaped by Eastern Orthodox faith.

The religious-philosophical-political history of Greece points in this direction. Ancient Olympian religion firmly undergirded the piety required for the great age of Pericles, Plato, Aristotle, and Alexander. Again, the missionary Christianity of Paul, Timothy, and Silas fashioned an unbroken theocratic state that has endured 2000 years. The severe challenges of eighth-century Islam and the Ottoman Empire, and the challenge today of threatening states in Macedonia, Serbia, Slovenia, and Albania, have only confirmed the ancient commitments of this remarkable nation.

In modern Greece, tensions abound as the country struggles economically, joining Spain and the new Eastern European entrants as the poor outliers of the vital European economic community. The tension with Turkey is stark, especially on Cyprus, where constant eruptions of violence occur as Greek Cyprists and Muslim militants clashed at the United Nations neutral zone. It may be significant that the closest friends of President Bush in West and Central Europe were the palpably religious states: Greece, Spain, Poland, and Turkey. A new ethos may emerge in the European community that is at once spiritual-moral and secular-pluralistic.

Today, Greece is a Christian welfare state with a new social-welfare oriented government. A binding solidarity of the people allows prejudice against the outsider through xenophobia, but also fosters a mutual concern for the welfare of the poor. Although such government policies infuriate the entrepreneurial investors, they reflect a humanity- and social-justice derivative of the great monasteries of the past: Mount Athos and Patmos, for example.

Today, both Turkey and Greece suffer badly from the coercion of the arms race and the striving for military supremacy. Both economies devote far too great a portion of the national budget to defense, security, and armaments. If a truly viable European Union could be established, so that the Greece-Turkey animosity could be defused as both nations disarmed, a new atmosphere of peace and prosperity might ensue.

France. To live in France, Germany, Benelux, or Scandinavia at the beginning of the 21st century is to live in remarkably affluent and governmentally provident states, stretched now to the point of some discomfort by expanding guest-worker immigrant populations. In 1996, Pope John Paul II celebrated mass outside Rheims cathedral and extolled the baptism of Clovis in the fifth century as the founding of "Catholic France." While the Pope's history may have been questionable, he did point to a crucial period of history when the southern Roman Empire was waning in power and northern Europe was becoming the dynamic center of global Christianity. During the days from Clovis until Charlemagne, the Apostles' Creed, we may recall, became doctoral authority on Rome proceeding from the Franks.

France may have the best mother-child well-being system in the world. Every baby and mother is a special religious-political sacred trust to be provided every mode of provident care. While *clochards* exist, you look hard to find the mother with child begging on the streets of France that you find so readily in Chicago, Istanbul, and Jerusalem. Regrettably, in the present day, one does see (mostly foreign) moms with kids begging at the French cathedrals.

Care for elders is also a state priority, so that life retains a dignity and respect to the very end of one's days. Regrettably, France also has an intense militaristic culture, which fortunately is not now unleashed against the Vietnamese or Algerians, but in the service of United Nations peacekeeping and general NATO defense. If France and Europe can deter the U.S. from the further folly of "Star Wars" defense or incursions against "the evil axis," we would be well served.

Pursuing the Pope's provocative suggestion at Rheims, one can ask, "is France a Catholic country?" From my vantage point in Strasbourg, I am reminded of the virulence of the French counter-reformative reaction. Still. the Protestant spirit is strong in Alsace and into French-speaking Switzerland (Geneva and environs). To me, the French and German Catholic bishops, faculties, and congregations are powerful forces for good in this world that could so easily degenerate into selfish materialism and *laissez-faire*, profiteering social policies.

I'm also intrigued by Emmanuel Levinas' notions that Europe—even post-*Shoah* Europe—is the *avant garde* for Hebraic consciousness (justice and the "sacred other") for world history.

The United States. As I return to the U.S. at the end of sabbatical sojourns in Europe and the Bible lands, I am always reminded how our history is steeped in the traditions we have reviewed. Oh yes, we have an aboriginal heritage, and Ecuadorian minstrels play in Place de la Cathédrale, Strasbourg. But we effectively exterminated the aboriginals away, at least in North America (less than one percent of our population is Native American, along with 12 percent African-American and 15 percent Hispanic American). In this remarkable eclectic, pluralistic, and syncretistic place, we seek to implement a historic Protestant ethos, mingling individual freedom with communal responsibility.

In America, which Reinhold Niebuhr thought grew dramatically better and worse, concurrently, at the beginning of this millennium, wealth accrues and also concentrates. Poverty is growing more acute in America. The lower-middle-class is being squeezed out of the possibility for excellent education, any kind of higher education, adequate health-care insurance, and investment potential to offset increasingly threatened public retirement provision and old-age security.

What Weber called "the Protestant ethic" and Tillich "the Protestant principle" needs to reawaken the impulses to justice, mercy, and reconciliation in our country. The Christian "right" needs to join its commendable spirituality and evangelical passion with the ethical commitments of the liberal heritage that can transform the society in the same way that Christ can transform the lives of believers. The "left" that knows so well the imperatives of social justice needs to advocate these in an atmosphere of freedom. Salvation and social justice—the conjunction is crucial.

America is blessed with an exuberant and generous spirit. If we can only find public and private modes of philanthropy, justice, equality, and provision, I'm sure we will draw back from the "grab-all-you-can-get" culture, where rich are walled off from poor with high O.J. Simpson-compound fences. Michael Jordan gives generously to the black poor of Chicago and the nation. We need to see similar philanthropy from all athletes (instead of steroids and dogfights), entertainers, businesses, and private interests. We also need to transform the public-service sector, so that education, housing, employment, and health care are drawn back from the dangerous precipice where they now hang. I believe this will happen, because in my story, which is our story, the evangelical irresistibly seeks out the ethical, thank God.

These writings provide clues to where and how my work of ministry will proceed on the interfaith horizon in years ahead, *Deo volante*.

INTERFAITH REFLECTION AND
REASONING IN THE FUTURE

> There will be no peace in the world without peace between the religions and no peace between the religions without dialogue.
> —Hans Küng

Hezbollah (party of God) rockets from Lebanon scream into a holiday-packed train station in Haifa, killing eight persons from Israel (struggle with God). Israeli jets tear into biblical Tyre and Sidon in Southern Lebanon, killing nine on a civilian bus. Lebanese Prime Minister Fouad Siniora cries, "The gates of hell have been opened in Lebanon," and Israel Prime Minister Ehud Olmert, while seeking to deal severe blows to *Hamas* and *Hezbollah*, wants to avoid the "Lebanon mud" and muddles along, inflicting severe destruction on a sovereign nation as he seeks an evasive peace with security for his young nation.

Meanwhile, at the G-8 Summit in St. Petersburg, leaders of dominantly Christian nations Bush and Blair, Putin and Prodi, Merkel and Chirac, counsel caution, afraid of stepping on Israel's toes or offending the Muslim world. Our global theological ignorance and ethical impoverishment again becomes painfully evident.

As the human carnage and infrastructure destruction goes on unabated, the world watches in fear and trembling. The vestiges of "Christian society" in the world ponder its destructive violence toward Jews across the centuries, *Anno Domini*, which culminated in the European *Shoah*. It was that chronic persecution that made necessary the creation of the state of Israel. If we are honest, we Christians also reflect on our fear and hatred of Islam, subliminal and sometimes overt, from the Crusades to the present "clash of civilizations" and war on terrorism. On its part, the Muslim world wonders if and how its freedom-fighting *Mujahadin* have become the blood-stained terrorists of 1000 suicide bombers, and whether her irenic mission in world history—*dar al-Islam*—has become a bellic, permanent *dar al-Harb*. And people Israel, commissioned to bring the freedom, justice, truth and *shalom* of the One God—*Shemah/Hashem*—to the world, asks plaintively: "What on Earth have we become?"

Such world crises, with their religious undercurrents and overtones, cry out for justice, reconciliation, and peace. And although they require delicate diplomacy and sensitive geo-politics, much more do they require the undergirding of foundational faith, hope, and love from these involved religions and the wisdom of their respective sacred texts.

PROJECT INTERFAITH

A new five-year initiative, Project Interfaith, proposes to bring the experiences of interfaith reasoning ("Come let us reason together, says the Lord," Isa 1.18), where Jews, Christians, and Muslims explore their scriptures in order to find pathways of understanding and peace to bear on these cultural and global issues. Over the last 20 years of my profession as a Christian pastor and professor of biblical theology and ethics, my work has focused on the discourse between faith and ethics. I have written about the wars in the Middle East, the war on terrorism, and the broad interactions among Jews, Christians, and Muslims. This decades-long endeavor recently has been honored by my being named Visiting Fellow at CARTS in Cambridge, England (Centre for Advanced Religious and Theological Studies).

Spiritual and ethical leaders need to be trained for justice-seeking and peace-making activities. Comparative scripture study in sanctuaries, homes, and workplaces is the best means to this end. Project Interfaith will prepare training materials and conduct workshops for this leadership in three settings: First, religious leaders will be brought together for rigorous training in order to return to their congregations and conduct dialogue events in their own houses of worship. Second, laypersons will be trained for cross-faith events in homes and work-places in the community. Finally, "street preachers," fundamentalist and evangelical grass-roots leaders and community organizers—those who often have the greatest influence on believers' sympathies and activities—will be convened to deepen convictions, commitments, and understandings in order to challenge and empower their ministries.

Such dialogue offers a valuable instrument, not only for personal and religious growth, but also for identifying normative directions for social and public-policy decisions. Such ethical and value sharing is essential for the vitality of the spiritual/ethical commitments and institutions that undergird those political processes.

The project will consist of two program activities: research and conferences.

Research. Colleagues at Northwestern University and the other universities in Chicago in Judaic, Christian, and Islamic Studies, along with other scholars in Chicago's unique and unparalleled theological consortium and throughout the world, will be enlisted in the conceptual (manuals and conferences) and practical (field-testing) aspects of the project. My own research will focus for several years on the themes of Abrahamic dialogue and world crisis. I will publish essays, articles, teaching materials, and other items (*e.g.*, congregational aids) from this research. Several handbooks will be prepared from this research. One will examine several dozen chains of scriptural readings, where a Christian text is juxtaposed between a Hebrew Bible text from which it derives and a sequel text from the Qu'ran or *hadith*. The other handbook will summarize, document, and offer commentary on the teachings of the three Abrahamic faiths on matters of war and peace, justice, and reconciliation.

Conferences. Once each year a conference will be held—in Chicago, Cambridge, or Antwerp—bringing together American, British, and European colleagues. Participants from Asia, the Middle-East, and Africa also will be prominent in the conferences and in all aspects of the project. Groups of religious leaders will be brought together in cities around the world to engage in Scriptural Reasoning and to test the materials. After the handbooks and other materials have been tested in various settings where the three faith populations are represented and strong (*e.g.*, Jerusalem, Cairo, Marrakesh, London, Paris, Chicago, New York, Los Angeles, Madrid, Antwerp, Amsterdam, etc.), they will be employed by action groups around the world.

LINGERING QUESTIONS

The following two theological essays done during my present fellowship at CARTS (Centre for Advanced Religious and Theological Studies) fill in the theological substance of "interfaith reflection," which I have learned from people like David Burrell and Kenneth Cragg. I would like to fashion a new mode of essay writing (preaching), which is scripture-laden from the three Abrahamic "Peoples of the Book," yet troublesomely contemporary.

Do Jews, Christians, and Muslims Worship the Same God?

It may take an historical calamity to ask an old question in a new way. Many around the world, because of religious undertones and overtones (particularly Jews, Christians, and Muslims) have been forced by the events of September 11th to examine the interstitial theologies and ethics between the faiths of Abraham. This introspection about whether we love, hate, or just respect and avoid each other is even more the case as a result of the profound concomitant tragedies of Iraq and Israel/Palestine that have come to define contemporary theological history. If Holocaust is an event of biblical moment for Jews, then what of the cleansing and genocide now proceeding in Iraq under the tutelage of Christian Anglo-America? And as military surge ensues in defiance of the American electorate, we ask if we are witnessing again events of religious significance, now with Muslims, Christians, and even Jews stirring the furies of Holy War.

The global religio-political crisis is further exacerbated as Pope Benedict lets slip in Regensburg, then Istanbul, a frightful Islamophobia and theological disdain for our sister Abrahamic faiths. Rather than shock the world, we shake off his gaffs to the resurgent orthodoxy and enmity found rising today in all three faith traditions. All this prompts me to ask again an ancient theological question: Do Jews, Christians and Muslims worship and serve the same God? If we do, is the present violence fratricidal, even blasphemous? In the *jus post bellum* we hope now draws near as the war on terrorism shudders from acute conflict into a chronic permanence, should there be charges of religious murder as well as war crimes? If we decide that we are not accountable to the same God, then what are the implications for religious and public policy, local and global?

These pragmatic issues hinge on the ultimate question: Is the God of Abraham and Israel, the God and Father of the Lord Jesus Christ, and Allah of Muhammad and Islam—one and the same? Though each faith asserts shared origins, historic continuities, and affinities, the strong aniconic (anti-idol)—even fratricidal—impulse within each becomes fervent, especially in such times of trouble as today.

Despite the current drift, I contend that one God is the focal power of the three faiths. Calling on motifs central to the logic and substance of these great faith tradition, I present four lines of evidence to establish the case:

- the Name of God;
- the singularity and unity of God;
- historical derivation and continuity; and
- the experience of interfaith dialogue.

The Name of God

As we have noted with our consideration of Pseudo-Dionysius and Soskice, the Name of God goes to the heart of the matter of the reality of God. "One God" is at the essence of the being, speaking, and hearing of the *Memra*, the Word, and Name in the faiths of Abraham. Starting with *Shema*—"Hear Israel, the Lord is our God, the Lord is One"—we are commanded to have no other gods. The *Hashem* reminds us that the Name is not to be taken lightly or manhandled. The third facet of the first Word of the three faiths is "You shall *not take the name of the Lord your God in vain" (Exod* 20.7). These are the true faith commandments.

Names are potent, especially the Name of God. To be given the Name, or to use the Name, is fraught with privilege and danger. A human name bestows meaning and possession. In ancient Rome, children were not named until they were claimed. To place a name on God is highly dangerous. It is to locate, define, and control. Jews will not utter or spell the Name—a refreshing silence in the blathering, babbling age of God-talk in which we live. Many religions believe that God, the ineffable, indefinable, and un-namable One, gives over his Name—as password—to his beloved, a holy and righteous people. God now presumably goes on call by that Name to that people. As Harold Bloom has shown in *Jesus and Yahweh: The Names Divine* that Yahweh, Jesus, and Allah are interweaving, inter-illuminating designations.[18] To belong to this Name is to belong to each other. An invet-erate Shakespearean, Bloom cites the Anglo-literary epitome of this name-calling as William Tyndale's New Testament of 1526, smuggled over from Antwerp to sustain his beloved, nascent English church with its epicenters in Cambridge and London.

To take a name or to become known by a name was something like the outgiving of God's self by which the creation came into being. As Ivan Illich has shown in his studies of Medieval friars munching on the Word,[19] naming imparts *exousia* or bread—the very substance and sustenance of the giver. *Kabbalah*, and its precursor archaic cosmogonies, according to Mircea Eliade, affirms that a primal fullness (*pleroma*) is emptied in order to make room and give freedom for responsive creation and humanity.

In Christianity, Philippians 2 develops this *kenosis*, the voiding of namesake in the name of love: ". . . though he was in the form of God, did not regard equality with God . . . but emptied himself . . . therefore God also highly exalted him and gave him the name that is above every name . . ." (Phil 2.5–9) You know the parallel texts in Judaism and Islam.

There is something glorious yet tragic in *kenosis*—in Name-giving. In Kitamori's language, it involves the theology of the pain of God. It is pain to God, that rather than being met by outflow and generosity to mimic the Divine self-giving, all human religions, including those of Abraham, tend to clam up, shut in, and exclude—the bright world goes dark. Separatism or supercessionism then leads one and all of our three faiths to part ways with the others by saying "we worship another God."

Here we must confront the human tragedy or the divine mystery of Judaism and Christianity excommunicating and un-naming each other from the first century until the final venom of the *Shoah*. We must also ponder the enigma of Islam rejecting and being rejected by its heritage in Crusade and Inquisition, ancient and modern. Our political and religious leaders today look as foolish as the administrators of Trinity College excori-ating Jewish student Abrams in the film *Chariots of Fire*: "another mountain,

---

18. See Bloom, *Jesus and Yahweh*.

19. See Illich, *In the Vineyard of the Text*.

another God," they snidely observe at his impieties. Much more commend-able is Clint Eastwood's pair of films on *Iwo Jima*, in which inter-perspective empathy is sought.

Although affirming an affinity with Israel, evangelical Christians today have great difficulty acknowledging that Jews worship and serve the same God. And Muslims are not even on the radar. This, even though Jesus likely addressed God with the Aramaic *El Lah*—the name Muslims invoke today.

Although the Divine Name is always defamed by those called by that Name, the Name remains sovereign. In his metaphysical historical theology, Wolfhart Pannenberg argues that humans do not project soul, name, goodness, or justice onto transcendence as the Enlightenment, Feuerbach, Marx, and Freud held. Rather, the Divine Name creates soul and contains body and creation. In this holistic view, Spirit initiates and contains body. This more biblical view overturns the Greek ontology in which body contains and confines soul. An Abrahamic ontology—one in accord with Ibn Sina (Avicenna), Maimonides, and Aquinas, where the divine Name shines within world, body, and community—is the first evidence that we worship the same God.

I will go farther and offer an even more radical thesis for which I may be the only proponent even among the broad spectrum of theology found here at Cambridge. I believe that Christianity does and should resonate the inner meaning of Judaism and Islam. In the same way Judaism resonates the inner meaning of Christianity and Islam, and Islam bears out the inner meaning of Judaism and Christianity. The thesis of my book *Jew, Christian, Muslim* is that we will either rediscover or discover for the first time a vital and reciprocally illuminating tri-unity or we will perish in fateful trifurcation. More on this inter-religious eschatology in a moment.

For now, painfully, we live in a world crisis where anti-Semitism, anti-Christianism, and anti-Islamism abound. Holy Warrior Jews kill innocent Muslims in a housing block in Gaza or at prayer in a Hebron *masjid*. Christian crusaders kill Jews in skinhead attacks in Europe or Muslims in Afghanistan, Iraq, or Somalia; Muslim suicide-bombers kill themselves and innocent Jews and Christians at a Tel Aviv bus station and London or Christian children at a Beslan school in Russia. In Iraq now, we witness the final apocalyptic violence as Muslims devour their own children and betray and kill their own.

Against this fratricidal impulse, the Name of the One God insists that God visits and is adored and served by all of his flocks. The Name of God signals proleptically, if not actually, the inner coherence and unity of those bound in faith and service.

THE SINGULARITY AND UNITY OF GOD

The second argument for the same-God thesis is the singularity and unity of God. Beyond the obvious insight that we live in a manifest *universe*, not *pluri-verse*—where we all see, hear, and comprehend the same objects and phenomenon and that these sensations are commonly knowable and explicable by reason, mathematics, causality and science—we also live in a religious salience that allows us to apprehend, as Whitehead has shown, that unified realm of space and time, eternity and infinity. Voting for Polkinghorne instead of Dawkins, I contend that God is One and is behind all knowledge and faith, all science and theology.

Hebrew Faith Constructed on Shema. "*Sh'ma Yis'ra'eil Adonai Eloheinu Adonai echad*"—"Hear, Israel, the Lord is our God, the Lord is One . . ." (Deut 6.4–9)

Like Name, this is the most disturbing and transforming Word ever sent out to this world and its people. It writes the world's history. It sets off tumult in space and time. It creates the history of Israel, the rise of Christianity, the emergence of Islam and recently the rise of a planetary, cosmopolitan, scientific, and economic world and a universal history. The One God of all life signals the Apostle Paul in Romans 8, sets off a redemptive labor in the cosmos whose birth pangs and delivery, though yet to be received, are inevitably coming into being.

Even though this new world arises from polytheism and pluralism, in God-induced- apperception, Abraham senses a singular and ethical God. *Gott* (God) and *gut* (good), in etymology, are interchangeable words—a unified neuro-linguistic heritage.

How do singularity and unity arise? The influences of Egypt, Sumeria, Persia, and India, Julius Lipner would show us, are unmistakable. The idea of the high and Holy, mighty and good One—out there and in here, One who is Lord of all, One who demands awe, association and allegiance—is manifestly evident. And, as Brahms meditated on the North Sea rocks one day in his *Schicksaalied*, the human heart perennially longs for such singular strength and purpose, despite the crashing waves of seemingly blind destiny all around.

Like the *kenotic* element found in the phenomenon of Name, the God who finally acts on Abraham in Genesis 12–25 condescends into history and nature. Abraham's father Terah had felt some beckoning and moved from Chaldea to Haran. His sons were now poised toward Canaan. High God is becoming Earth-God with the purification of each pagan preparation. This new God not only succors and provokes obeisance, He companions and guides. He befriends and chides. He is *Akbar* and full of *Hesed*. He is *Ramah*, great and good in demand, love, and mercy.

Tikkun olam has begun—mending the unraveling state of affairs. Recreation is undertaken to restore the disturbed creation. Some primal remembrance as echoed in Gilgamesh or Hammurabi, memory that will be recollected in the exile, is at work: creation/fall, Adam/Eve, Cain/Abel, Noah and sons—all mythic story is libidinally present. Partnership was now needed if there was any chance left to make good the world. In Abraham, then Moses, this God and good would be constituted. Unification and reconciliation of God and the world had begun.

What Hinduism and Hellenism would one day understand as "the One and the many" were now made synergetic in purpose. The dialectic that Pythagoras and Plato would understand as the interplay of matter and spirit would now begin to collapse into integrated dynamic tension and movement known as the Spirit of God in the world. The eternal and earthly breach, symbolically affected by fallen angels, would now begin to be healed as redemptive, repairing process began within earthly process. The world had turned the corner. As filmmaker Krzysztof Kieslowski would show with his planes and angles, singularity now began to yield meaning and unity. God was the One for the world. Leviathan of sea and land was given notice.

Oneness with the Fellowship. As in Judaism, the declaration of faith in Christianity also focuses on the Oneness of God and Christ with the fellowship. John remembers Jesus saying:

> "There will be one flock, one shepherd." (John 10.16)

> "The Father and I are One." (10.30)

> "Holy Father, protect them in your name that you have given me . . ." (17.11b)

> ". . . so that they may be one, as we are one . . ." (17.11b)

> "that they may all be one . . . so that the world may believe you have sent me." (17.21)

Again Paul writes to the congregation in Corinth:

> . . . there is one God, the Father . . . and one Lord, Jesus Christ . . . (1 Cor 8.4–6)

> there is one bread . . . one body, for we all partake of the one bread.
> (10.17)

> . . . all the members of the body, though many, are one body . . . (12.12)

The Christian tradition summarizes: . . . One Lord, one faith, one baptism, one God and Father of all . . . (Eph 4.5–6). In Romans 3, Paul further focuses this Oneness motif:

> Is God for Jews alone?
>
> Is he not for the Gentiles too?
>
> Most certainly for Gentiles too!
>
> If, indeed God is "One," who will set right the circumcision from faith?
>
> and the uncircumcision by the faith? (Rom 3.29–30)[20]

In its three movements, the Abrahamic faiths perform the symphony of divine singularity and unity. In symphony, particular instruments are meant to play together in timed entrance, occasionally in solo, other times in concert—often in dissonance then resonance, B minor then C major, Shostakovich then Brahms. God's unity both composes and evokes reciprocity among the three movements and instruments. Therefore all boasting and blasting must cease so that each voice may be heard in its solitary and solidarity beauty. Here we can entertain the suggestion of Peter Ochs that trinity may not only be a cacophony and stumbling block in the "bosom of Abraham," but in some mysterious sense a *munus triplex*—a binding and releasing of all of the faiths into a higher sublimity.

Such concord or harmony is seen to be essential if the world is to believe. That divine oneness demands human unity is found when Christianity rebukes Israel's exclusivism and affirms Abrahamic universalism: "I will multiply thy seed as the stars of the heaven and as the sand which is upon the seashore." (Gen 22.17) When Christianity is tempted to exclusivism, both Judaism and Islam serve as monotheistic checks. The end and purpose of Torah is the world, not Israel alone. But what if the world remains committed to eliminate Israel? Here arises the controversy of Jimmy Carter's book on Palestine and the outrage it provokes. One God as a force in history means to make right—circumcision, uncircumcision, then circumcision again—what's going on? Somehow these three faith/works, working/faiths are involved, but how?

This One God (*eis theos*) formula—which, we remember, is divine and worldly reality to the Jewish-Christian Paul—points back to the Egyptian

---

20. Jewett et al., *Romans: A Commentary*.

amulet's formula, "There is One God who heals every illness" (15th-century B.C.E.), and was already deeply imbedded in Pythagoras, Plato, and Aristotle. Oneness was connected with righteousness through mediation of Word and Wisdom. Messiah, *Mediato*, and *Mahdi* are representations woven into the fabric of this Oneness. These manifestations, at root, are also one.

The unity of God elicits the focal unity of faith and the derived unity of humanity. As Augustine sharply advocates in *The City of God*, only one God, one faith, and one body can guarantee one world. Though Augustine, like the Fathers, seems to feel that the Jewish *ecclesia* will eventually dissolve into *corpus Christianum*, Aquinas—if only because his Napoleatan origins were in *dar al-Islam* and the theological seriousness with which he takes thinkers like Maimonides and Averroës—takes Judaism and Islam into account in his thinking about One Body. In my view, the communal spiritual body of the three monotheistic Abrahamic faiths weaves interpenetrably into the one world body.

Affirmation of Divine and Human Unity. Islam, as well as Judaism and Christianity, affirms this divine and human unity. *Al'Islam* (surrender) is submission to this singular loyalty. The sacred Qur'an is, in the words of Sura 2 (136), a rendition of the communicative Word of God through "Abraham, Ishmael, Isaac, Jacob, the tribes and Jesus." The creed, "there is no God but Allah" codifies a universe of God, humanity, and the world that will decisively shape theology, human history, and science—not only for *dar al-Islam*, the Muslim realm and reality, but for the entire world. Philosophy and science come to modern Europe and then the whole world from the Muslims. The lasting truth of this medieval revolution is found in its convictions of unity and universality. In my recent study, *An Abrahamic Theology for Science*, I show that such theology is woven into the very conceptual and ethical substance of modern science itself.[21]

A Qur'anic text that reflects this monotheistic synthesis and synergy is Sura 17:

> Do not set other gods alongside Allah;
>
> Honor the parents and family as God's gift;
>
> Have mercy on the weak and poor;
>
> Wounding or killing others imposes bloodguilt;
>
> Respect the Earth; and
>
> God knows all and holds all responsible for their acts.

21. Vaux, *An Abrahamic Theology for Science*.

This text is suffused with the Spirit of Israel's *Shema* and Decalogue and Jesus' Sermon on the Mount and high priestly prayer. It is an ascription to the same God.

Human action in the world is extrapolated from the nature of God. God is holy, just, good, and merciful. To maintain communion in righteousness with and before God, we must be similarly holy and just. Many passages from *hadith* and the great commentaries from the eighth century onward focus on the unbrokenness and unity of God, and of the association of God with humanity and the world. These teachings document our first assertion that there is only one God—the same for all the faiths of Abraham.

HISTORICAL DERIVATION AND CONTINUITY

Judaism appeared among the family of Semitic tribes and nations in the ancient Near East when the great peoples and empires of the region—the far East (China and India) and West (Greece)—were far more impressive. Amid the great empires of Egypt, Assyria, and Persia, Israel was a small player on the stage of history. It was into the empires of Greece and Rome that Christianity appeared within the bosom of Judaism. Together, rabbinic Judaism and nascent Christianity began a process of robust universalist and unitary monotheism. Cosmopolitan and comfortable Rome, tolerant of the plethora of diverse cults and religions, was shocked by this bold new reality when the Apostle Paul proclaimed that One God and Father—the Lord of history—now reigned over the *oikumene*, the whole inhabited Earth. The preceding deities and cults had offered their indispensable preparation, now the whole world—(*olam*, Hebrew, *ulam*, Aramaic/ Arabic) was the realm of the One God and Savior—the Lord of Nations.

Israel's God, theology, and way of life would assume a dominant influence in the world through its irascible offspring: Christianity and Islam. While Judaism claims fewer than 20 million adherents worldwide, it exerts a vast influence on the stage of history and culture. Judaism's law is universally codified, its ethics globally emulated, and its God worshipped to the distant coasts. At nearly 2 billion constituents each, Christianity and Islam together constitute more than half of the world's population.

How did Christianity convey and perpetrate the Name (presence and power) of the God of Israel? Simultaneous to the Roman destruction of the Jerusalem temple (c. 66 C.E.), Paul announced that the cross and resurrection of Jesus Christ proceeded into the world as the home and temple of God. Israel now clung to a synagogic Diaspora with an episodic yearning for return to Zion. Israel's future became interwoven with Christianity for good and for great evil (Crusades, Inquisition, and Holocaust). In both of these traditions, synagogue and scripture, the worshipping community, and the Bible became the Lord's conveyance.

In a most vital form of Christianity—Jewish Christianity—the faith conferred on people the theology, ethic, way, wisdom, and worship of Israel. This convergence was not supercessionism, but the respectful conveyance of the salient, generative power of Judaism. The Kingship, Lordship, and *Logos* wisdom of Jesus in world history, however, remained enigmatic. It may well be further clarified by the mystery of messianic history embodied in ongoing Judaism and global Islam. As John Howard Yoder and Jack Miles show, Jesus' kingship—much to the dismay of the insurgent onward Christian soldiers—was that of the Lamb (Rev 22.1), as the nations became "the kingdoms of our Lord and of His Christ." This displacement, even in the seemingly endless age of empires, was to be eschatological and ethical, not political. Purveying the silent and salient Name and Wisdom of the God of Abraham and the saving, righteous inheritance embedded in the "seed of Abraham" surely involved the religious history of Israel, Christianity, and Islam.

THE LEGACY OF JUDAISM

The theological connections of Judaism and Christianity were much discussed in first-century scholarship. Some of the elements of Hebraic faith that Christianity entirely adopted or adapted are:

- the creation of the world *ex nihilo*;
- the construal of history as salvation history;
- the advent and destiny of the Messiah;
- the *Akedic* structure of redemption; and
- Yahweh's "Day of the Lord" as the consummation of nature and history.

Creation. Greek philosophy and Hindu cosmogony conceived the world as an eternal, Parmidean process with patterns recurring and fluctuations flowing cyclically and rhythmically. Judaism, through Christianity and Islam, introduced the dimensions of space and time, nature and history now marked by concrete and linear reality as divine allocation and allotment. That the creation proceeded from *nihil* point through purposive expansion, elaboration, and eventual expiration became a secular, scientific datum—derived from faith.

That there is a creator and consummator of this world and all worlds is a common belief of Jews, Christians, and Muslims—proof of their fraternal theology.

Salvation History. Cosmic history may be ameliorative, *tikkun olam,* and restorative of paradise. It also may be entropic and apocalyptic—a kind of stage for the pilgrimage of creation, as Augustine and Bunyan conceive, ending in the view of most cosmologists today, in cosmic conflagration or deep freeze. Modest good sense keeps open the question of John Polkinghorne's *The End of the World and the Ends of God.*[22] Abrahamic peoples all proclaimed a pathway of meaning in nature and history wherein "God is working his purpose out as year proceeds to year." Providence verging toward predestination is a conviction of fundamentalist, Orthodox, and liberal faith. A deep and abiding faith that "God watches out over his own," ever troubling to unionists and co-federalists in their opposing trenches, is deep-seated in the three faiths.

Messiah. The concept of messiah, the anointed One—agent of divine purpose, sent messenger and prophet—pervades the three faiths, both uniting and dividing. The King resides in the Adamic, Abrahamic, Mosaic, and Davidic line. Son of God and Son of Man[23] are promising, yet deeply problematic notions. Demi-god and demi-man are offensive to all. True God and true human ring with authenticity in each facet of the heritage.

While writers like Peter Ochs and Khalil Gibran explore *perichoretic* Godhead within Jewish and Muslim parameters, most in those traditions find the Trinity at best perplexing and at worst polytheistic. Two responses seem relevant: While Jesus himself seems reticent to invoke divinity ("Why do you call me good?"), scholarship today (such as that of Larry W. Hurtado, head of the Divinity School at the University of Edinburgh) sees a sublimely high Christology—King and Lord—fully in keeping with the enveloping Judaic thought world. It now appears that Judaism had a full concept of Messiah, *Logos,* Word, Son, and Wisdom until the final mutual excommunication in the fourth century.[24]

22. See Polkinghorne and Welker, *The End of the World and the Ends of God.*

23. The word *anthropos*—often translated as "mankind"—means "human being" or "person" (as opposed to "*andros,*" the Greek word for "man"). The phrase "Son of Man" is more accurately translated as "Son of the Human Being."

24. See Boyarin, *Border Lines.*

From the Christian side, we realize that Trinitarianism is highly colored by a Greek metaphysics somewhat at variance with Semitic thought. Modern theology from Moltmann and Ford, Derrida and Levinas, Soskice and Pickstock to Ruether and Webster, show that biblically and Hebraically-tenored Christology is safely and solidly monotheistic and intellectually coherent. Somehow, sometime, in some way, I believe Messiah, Divine Wisdom—*hikmah* and *Sophia*—will complete Israel, fulfill Christianity, and consummate Islam. Such embrace will finally realize the whole family of God.

The Akedah. My recent research[25] convinces me of the central theological substance of the three faiths in the *Akedah*—Abraham's sacrifice of the beloved son. Here is the matrix of the redemption/resurrection motif fundamental to each tradition. In Judaism, it informs Passover, exodus, *Rosh Hashanah*, even tribulation.[26] When Jon Levenson lived in Skokie and taught at the University of Chicago, he wrote, in our library in Evanston, the masterwork of this literature, *The Death and Resurrection of the Beloved Son*. Paul Matthews Van Buren (the great scholar of Jewish-Christian relations) and Donald Juul (New Testament professor) further illumine this motif in the Christian faith.[27] Think of Romans 8.32—"who did not withhold His only Son, but gave him up for us all, will not he freely give us all things in him." Think of John 3.16—"God loved the world so that he gave His only Son" (*monogenos/agapetos*). The temptation, baptism, and transfiguration of Jesus, as well, are thoroughly *Akedic* texts.

The theme is felt perhaps most profoundly in Islam. In the *Eid al-Adha*, we find the travail of the two mothers and two sons, the crisis of historical tribulation, the matrix of temptation, the anguish of Islam's elymosenary mission to the poor, whose wretched residence sweeps the central swath around the Earth. All the while, as Max Weber foresaw, Judaism and Christianity prefer comfortable, prosperous, middle-class existence.

Akedah is to me the irrefutable evidence that we are brothers and sisters at the very essence of faith and value. We are therefore to put on the new humanity—where there is neither Jew nor Greek, slave or free, but God who is One is all in all.

---

25. See Vaux, *Jew, Christian, Muslim* and *An Abrahamic Theology for Science*.

26. See Spiegel, *The Last Trial*.

27. See Levenson, *The Death and Resurrection of the Beloved Son*; Van Buren, *According to the Scriptures*; Juul, *Messianic Exegesis*.

At the root of Christian scripture is the Bible of the Jews. When Philip Yancey writes of the Bible Jesus read and Paul the Apostle alludes to sacred writ, they speak of Hebrew scripture.[28] Both Jews and Paul likely knew of sacred writings (scrolls or parchment folios) that included texts in Hebrew, the Septuagint (an entire Hebrew Bible in Greek) and certain sacred writings in Aramaic—the vernacular Hebrew of the Greco-Roman world—what could be seen as a cognate language of Arabic.

As the Christian era dawned and the two news faiths emerged, rabbinic Judaism and early Christianity, Jewish scripture existed in an entire Hebrew text—the *Tanakh*—which we know from the Qumran community evidence in the Dead Sea Scrolls. Jesus read the *Tanakh* scroll in the Capernaum Synagogue (Luke 4.16–30), and Paul studied the same, we may believe, with Gamaliel (Acts 5.34). Both, we may conjecture, read (heard) LXX (Septuagint), which was widely known in the great Greco-Roman *metropoliti* of Nazareth (Sepphoris) and Antioch.

Yahweh's Day of the Lord. Eschatology is a common culminating scriptural motif. The climax of world history will be a cataclysm (paroxysm) of judgment and grace, when all humanity and creation will be called to account for its use of life and freedom. Here the prevalent mistakes of life on Earth will be rectified: the poor will be vindicated and blessed and, in surprising, topsy-turvy disclosure (quite unlike the "left-behind" fantasies), the tables will be turned, and God's good way for this world and eternity will become clear.

CHRISTIAN SCRIPTURE

Christian scriptural canon was not settled for centuries. The Marcion, Manichean, and other Gnostic challenges sought to excise the Hebrew Bible and much gospel material in favor of dualistic, spiritualistic, and unbiblical perspectives and these nearly prevailed. Hundreds of gospels, psalms, acts, and apocalypses abounded. In my own view, corroboration of Torah-focused, Decalogic, prophetic, and Abrahamic (*Akedic*) horizons is useful in determining what is authentically spiritual. For Christians, *midrashic* corroboration back to Judaism and forward into Islam is helpful and supportive to understanding. Jewish Christianity (James, Thomas, pseudo-Clementine, etc. materials) counterbalance Gnostic, spiritualistic, and hyper-apocalyptic approaches, grounding Christian scripture in Semitic

28. See Yancey, *The Bible Jesus Read.*

prequel and sequel literature with more thoroughgoing worldly and ethical substance.

Christian scripture, through a rich tapestry of Hebrew texts—from Daniel to Proverbs to 4 Maccabees and new covenant materials from John to James—is grounded in an Abrahamic and Mosaic prophetic and Christic (messianic/*Logos*) ethos. Though first-hand apostolic witness became the criterion of the canon, interfaith scriptural study best fathoms the *midrashic* chain. "Thus saith the Lord" becomes the overriding authority.

I learned this when I first read Jaroslav Pelikan's *Mary Through the Centuries*, in which his textual foundations ran from the Samuel stories through the gospels (Annunciation and *Magnificat*) through to the Qur'an (*e.g.*, Sura 19).[29]

MUSLIM SCRIPTURE

Touching on the *Eid al-Adha* (the Feast of Sacrifice) and the *Akedah* (perhaps the pivotal theological axis of Islam with its Isaac/Ishmael fulcrum) reminds me of the relative ignorance of Islam portrayed thus far in this essay.

Stanley Fish has bitingly attacked my oversight in a 2007 essay in the *New York Times*. Addressing the irony of ignored truth claims in our world of profuse religiosity (yet absent theology), he reflects that this mischievous yet essential "one true God" stuff is being obfuscated by silly debates of whether America is a Christian, Judeo-Christian, or a none-of-the-above culture. Governor Fordice (who prefers the "Christian" to the "Judeo-Christian" designation) will not join the "multiculturalist appreciators of everything." Fish demurs: "Once it's Judeo-Christian, it will soon be Judeo-Islamic Christian and then Judeo-Islamic-Native American Christian and then . . ."[30]

Not enamored with Alasdair MacIntyre's provincialism as is fellow post-modernist Fish, I prefer to struggle on into the difficult twilight of the theological horizon of "One God," inter-Abrahamic Scriptural Reasoning. Not only truth and goodness, but survival itself, I believe, may hang on this quest.

This by way of prefacing my admittedly novice treatment of Islam's relationship to its forerunners Judaism and Christianity. The three Abrahamic faiths, I propose, consummately see the One and unified God as the finisher of faith (perhaps through faith-tradition pathways), the One who, at the end of all things, will be "All in All." In that *pleroma* (fullness) or *Parousia* (para-

---

29. See Pelikan, *Mary Through the Centuries*.

30. Fish, "Religion Without Truth."

dise in Aramaic/Arabic), what we saw only dimly will be seen in clarity, what we have known in part will then be fully known. (1 Cor 13.12).

The pathway and connectivity between Judaism, Christianity, and Islam is complicated, but essential to the establishment of my thesis. I first note the historical continuity.

HISTORICAL LINKS

Many see the origins of Islam in the Jewish/Christian community identified with James, Jesus' brother, his mother and family, and the community called *Ebionim* (the poor ones). After the flight to Pella amid the Roman-Jewish wars, most of the poor faithful were killed in the first Jewish holocaust at the hands of Rome, where "blood flowed down the temple steps like water" (Josephus). Just as the original Semites emigrated from Arabia to Mesopotamia, now from the Mesopotamian cities of Edessa, Antioch, and Pella, a Judeo-Christian remnant may have gravitated south where they would lay the foundations of Islam.

By the seventh century, a form of Christianity was found in Arabia, in Jaba—now modern Yemen. In Muhammad's lifetime, the influence of Syria, Mesopotamia, and Persia was felt in Arabia. Christianity in Abyssinia and Diaspora Judaism in the same region would prepare the soil for the growth of Islam.

The link seems to be Jewish Christianity east and south of Jordan, the Monophysite church of Syria, the Agoa tribe of the mountain peoples of Syria (who still spoke Aramaic), and the Christianized kingdom of Axum, Abyssinia, now Eretria and Ethiopia. Here Muhammad sought refuge in the fifth year of his call, 615 C.E. In this sanctuary and in the revealing pre-Islamic poetry of the region, most Arabists feel, lie the origins of Islam.[31]

Theologically and ethically, Islam seemed, at its outset, to be a reform movement within Christianity. "Why did you wander from your Christian and Jewish origins?" these proto-Muslims were asked by their protector king in Abyssinia:

> 'We were a barbarous nation,' they admitted, 'worshipping idols, killing our own people, devouring the weak. Then God sent us an apostle, one of our own.' He summoned us to God, to believe in his unity, to worship him and abandon stones and idols. He commanded us to speak the truth, to be faithful to our trusts, to observe our duties to kinsfolk and neighbors, to refrain from forbidden

---

31. See Trimingham, *Islam in Ethiopia*.

things and bloodshed, from consuming the property of orphans and widows.'[32]

The Decalogical form of this confession shows that the thread of connection, a virtual life-giving ligature between (Judeo) Christianity and Islam, can be found in the conveyance of Word, Will, and Wisdom of God epitomized in Torah, Decalogue, and *Akedah*—the cardinal Abrahamic, Mosaic, Prophetic, and Christic substance. If this and the former convergence with Judaism are correct, then Christians will want to abandon their supercessionist posture toward Judaism, seeing the only "good Jew" as a "Jew for Jesus." We also can put aside the view that Islam is a Godless, violent, pagan religion whose people are the proper objects of conversion. Muslims are already "for Jesus," I have discovered. We may even wish to view the prophet Muhammad as one in the succession of Amos or Paul—prophets called in the history of God to restore faith and righteousness—the meaning of Torah, Decalogue, and *Akedah* (*Logos*).

To begin to land this plane, which I hope has left you a bit anxious and out of breath but in the end hopeful and ready to go to work, let me say that each faith must continue to fill out its particular evangelizing and proselytizing vocation. My friend, Tariq Ramadan, at the university at the other end of the long rowing course (Oxford), once told me "listen to my story, and I'll ask you to tell me about Jesus." Jews ought to advocate and share with the world Yahweh's way, Torah, Decalogue, prophetic justice, and shalom. Don't give up, we need you. Without you, we Christians and Muslims will lose our way. As Stanley Hauerwas said in his customarily raucous way, Jews should give Christians reasons to become Jews, and Christians give Jews reasons to receive Christ. Christians and Muslims need to be continually renewed and refreshed by the Law and the Prophets—*Tanakh*.

Christians need to share Jesus Christ with the world. He sustains the way of Israel bringing salvation and peace. He is Savior and Lord for the people of the world.

Muslims need to share their distinctive inheritance and mission—the rigor and intensity of synthetic faith and life, the heart for the poor, which is the heart of God.

THE NEED FOR INTER-FAITH SCRIPTURAL REASONING

Muslim tradition speaks of "peoples of the Book" (*Ahl al-Kit b*), Jewish and Christian scriptures: *Taurut* (Torah), *Zabur* (Psalms), and *Injil* (four Gospels).

---

32. Van Leeuwen, *Christianity in World History*, 217.

Jews also use this phrase (*Am Hasefer*) as self-referential—embracing their sacred corpus of Torah, *Tanakh*, as well as *Mishnah* and *Talmud*. Muslims use a similar primary and secondary canonical standard when they combine Qur'an, the direct divine revelation to Muhammad from the angel Gabriel in the Medina and Mecca recitations, and the *hadith*, a more interpretative sequel. Qur'an is direct, literal word of God (*verbum Dei*), perhaps similar to the Decalogue in strictest Judaism and in Christianity where God actually spoke and inscribed (in stone) *vox Dei*.

Some of Christian tradition is typical of the Puritan John Wesley, who in the 18th century studied at Oxford, learning Hebrew and Old Testament, Greek and New Testament and Arabic and Qur'an. This is an exception. In the broader tradition, suspicion and mutual rejection prevails. Jews have repudiated Christian sacred text as idolatrous and polytheistic until very recently when, for example, Jesus' Sermon on the Mount was included in the sacred body of Jewish literature (Reform Judaism). Christians (from Marcion on) have often rejected Jewish texts as crude and violent. Both of these bodies most generally have repudiated the Qur'an as pagan and blasphemous.

Only today—in a world of Christianity repentant of its complicity in the Holocaust and in the post-September-11th Israeli-Palestine-anti-terrorist atmosphere—has an interfaith fascination and interaction developed. Today, interfaith Scriptural Reasoning is cautiously being explored in Americo-Israel and Eurabia in particular—the dominant Judeo-Christian strongholds and cleansed de-Judaized Europe where Islam flourishes—but also throughout the Muslim, African, and Asian worlds. When Muslim-Christian encounters begin in earnest in Pakistan and India, Nigeria and Kenya, Indonesia and Beijing, we will know we have seen the dawn of a new day in a new world.

EXPERIENCE OF INTERFAITH DIALOGUE

A final corroboration of the same-God thesis comes from the experience of interfaith dialogue. Theologians, pastors, and laypersons of all persuasions—Jew, Christian, Muslim—must now make this experience, as you do so well in this university, a norm of your learning, study, service in the world, and prayer. This experience has yet to seep into the tissues of the provincial parish—urban or rural. You must make that happen.

David Ford has written in the highly informative issue of *The Promise of Scriptural Reasoning* that Scriptural Reasoning may be the clue in our time to wisdom-seeking and wisdom-making.[33]

---

33. Ford, "An Interfaith Wisdom: Scriptural Reasoning Between Jews, Christians, and Muslims."

I have offered an argument that the three faiths of Abraham do, in fact, worship and serve the same God. It is a conclusion at once so obvious and so unlikely. The recovery of that common bond alone, I've argued, can heal the current fratricidal tribulation we witness from London to Lebanon, Iraq, Bosnia, Chechnya, Philippines, Sudan, Somalia, Kashmir, Afghanistan, and Pakistan. Only a spiritual unity and concord anchored in our One God and Lord can transmute current strife into justice on the ground, on the streets, and in the sanctuaries. Only such hard fought-for-struggle and care can mute the strident voices of fanatic and violent rabbis, priests, mullahs and, worst of all, politicians, those today at the beck and call of such unworthy court jesters.

> Should this dawning arise, then will come to pass the prophetic dream:

> "But this is the covenant that I will make with the house of Israel after those days," saith the Lord, "I will put My law in their inward parts, and in their heart will I write it . . . and they shall teach no more every man his neighbor, saying, 'Know the Lord' for they shall all know Me from the least of them to the greatest of them. . . "
> (Jer 31.32–33)

And again as the sacred scripture of one tradition ends, another begins with the same words: In that wonderful and dreadful day, "I will turn the hearts of the parents to the children and the children to the parents, Lest I come and smite the Earth with a curse." (Jer 31.33, Mal 4:5–6, Luke 1:17).

Conversion and Religious Freedom

In an earlier essay presented at the Divinity faculty in Cambridge in early 2007, we walked through the rudimentary interfaith question: Do we worship and serve the same God? As I now field-test that study guide, persons offer a recurring response: Though the arguments that Jews, Christians, and Muslims have the same God are convincing, we have been told, people cannot bring themselves at a gut level, to assent to this premise. Attributing the same God to Jews and Muslims would seem to invalidate their own Christian faith. I often ask in response to this reticence what they think it would imply if these three sibling communities, indeed, were not the children of the One God of Abraham. After the initial shock, a terror sets in at the thought that we then might be perpetually condemned to spiritual incompatibility, irreconcilable apartheid, unending strife, perhaps even mutual destruction. So the matters become urgent and of supreme moment. This essay therefore begs the question of intramural conversion and proselytism (voluntary, not coercive) between these three sibling- or stranger-faiths, as the case may be. Three cases illustrate the issues.

- In 1998, 30 Filipino Christians were arrested for distributing Bibles in the closed Islamic state of Saudi Arabia. Only a concerted effort by the U.S., the Philippines, and other European embassies was able to secure their release later that summer. Under Saudi law, you can bring in one Bible in your suitcase, but smuggling 20,000 presented a challenge to the theocratic state. The Western value of free religious expression was at loggerheads with the Islamic value that conversion amounted to apostasy—a sin and crime—meriting severe, even capital, punishment.

- This sanction became clear in the second case. In 2005, the case of Afghan Abduhl Rahman, who had served for years in a Christian relief agency, came to public light. He had converted and become a Christian 15 years earlier, a quite common experience in the heyday of Christian missions in Afghanistan in the early decades of the 20th-century, before American, British, and Russian political machinations led to the Taliban state and the endless strife that endures to this day.

  Five years earlier, Rahman had appealed for custody of his children from their Muslim mom. He was accused of apostasy, disowned, and turned into civil authorities who accused him of breach of the first commandment (no other gods), was therefore a heretic and was given the death penalty. Again, only frantic diplomatic efforts and bald Euro-American economic threats (let's get down to the real gods of our time) saved his skin. Like the celebrated Nigerian woman who also was condemned to death by stoning, in this case for adultery, the simple Rahman was exonerated, exiled, forever removed from his family, and the case was dropped.

- Some Muslims and Christians considered them infidels. The Yazidis are a small, unorthodox sect in northwestern Iraq near the Syrian border. An Indo-European culture of one-third million, influenced by Persian faiths and Islam, they are thought to be infidels because of their venerating of the "blue peacock," which is associated with the devil. Yazidi leaders say they do not believe in evil or the devil (a distinctive Persian belief). The conflict began when a small radical group of Yazidis stoned an 18-year-old girl for forsaking her family, "converting to (Sunni) Islam," and running away with her "Muslim boyfriend." The gruesome killing was shown on television and the Internet and was the precipitating cause of the worst suicide attacks since the coalition attack on Iraq.

Five-hundred Yazidis were killed, supposedly by *al-Qaeda*-linked Sunni insurgents in Ninevah province on the Turkish border. While most insurgent (Sunni) suicide bombers have targeted Americans and Shiahs, this particular "religious revenge" bombing of a fellow Kurdish sect cast new light on the bewildering range of targets in the agonizing war in Iraq. The bizarre event shows the lingering loathing of Kurd and Baathists, but also the religious fervor and fanaticism that inflame evangelism activities via issues of infidelity, blasphemy, and righteous cleansing—especially in times of social disruption.

These cases, admittedly dramatic and quite atypical, raise a specter of issues for pan-Abrahamic interfaith study, including: conversion and proselytizing; ecclesial and civil suppression or assertion of evangelism; public policy issues of religious freedom and expression; the sociopolitical endorsement of particular faith traditions; and, perhaps behind all these quandaries, the inner biblical-theological meanings of the phenomenon of witness and martyrdom. This essay explores the set of questions that must be raised to carefully broach these matters.

I first explicate some of the meanings and parameters of evangelism. Secondly, I look at several interpretations of the expansion and contraction of the particular faiths of Judaism, Christianity, and Islam. Thirdly, I consider what seem to be the possible postures of the state toward the issues of evangelism and how these might bear on ecclesiological policies of synagogue, church, and *masjid* and their broader judicatories. Finally, I offer what I hope will be received as scriptural-theological-political imperatives to live together in this troubled world in truth and righteousness.

Meanings of Evangelism. I begin with the world I know best as a trainer of Christian leaders in a theological seminary. The "evangelistic cosmos" of Christianity sees the whole inhabited world as a realm to be won to Christ.

I interpret this Abrahamic mission, "a light to the Gentiles," as mysteriously integral to the destiny of Israel and Islam in the world as well as to the Jesus movement. World history, I believe, is the concourse of messianic *Logos* into the world through Abrahamic witness. The faiths we call Christianity and the broader family of fraternal faiths of Abraham now constitute nearly three quarters of the peoples of the world. Buddhism, Hinduism, Confucianism, indigenous movements, and secular humanism as spiritual philosophies and ethical schools of conduct complete the roundtable of faith and life commitments we can survey.

Consider with me the concentric circles of Christian evangelistic witness around the core community we will call the "born-again Protestant evangelical faith." Fifty to 80 million Americans and countless millions abroad (*e.g.*, Holiness believers) say this movement defines their spiritual identity. Circles of concentric constituencies that constitute the objects of spiritual "otherness," and therefore evangelistic witness, might be:

- non-believers and nominal (non born-again) members in those particular faith communities, along with the children rising within their own communities;

- Roman Catholics;

- Eastern Orthodox;

- Jews;

- Muslims;

- sects: Mormons, Christian Science, Jehovah Witnesses, Adventists, Baha'i, etc.;

- world religions: indigenous-religious, Buddhist, Hindu, Chinese Confucians, etc.; and

- secularists, non-believers, and all others.

We might imagine a chart with these concentric circles of "groups to be evangelized." Similar charts could be constructed from the epicenter of a Roman Catholic, Lutheran, liberal mainline believer, Muslim, or any other perspective. Different concentric rings of targets of proselytizing might then be displayed. Vast other communities of believers do not subscribe to or emphasize conversion and would opt out of such configurations.

My view is that evangelism or proselytizing is inherent in each of the Abrahamic faiths, so much so that it would violate the very substance of each movement to become non-converting. This leads me to propose the concept of intramural evangelism as a process of mutual enrichment and edification. The only alternative to this, it would seem, is the ever-increasing tendency to draw caricatures and to demonize each other's faith. For example, the sadly and stupidly discriminatory inclinations of the U.S. at present lead us to see the Islamic world as a seedbed of hatred toward our country, places where terrorism festers so that we are more and more inclined to preemptively strike Muslim countries—Afghanistan, Iraq, Iran, Syria and Palestine—thinking that such belligerence or show of force will discourage the enemy. We now even have a military acronym for this "realm of the enemy"—MOPAK—the lands from Morocco to Pakistan, with Iran and Syria in between. This designation, as insidious as AIPEK, an association of Anti-Palestinian Pro Israel organizations, sadly compromises the springs of human rights and democracy in today's troubled world. The dream of *Shema*, Jesus' high priestly prayer, and Mohammed's plea for peace among the Peoples of the Book continues to recede.

My ideal political backdrop to provide the salience for peaceful and just interaction among these several faiths would be the Western Protestant, religiously tolerant and democratic state, assuring all the freedom of religious expression and allowing vital dialogue and lively cross-fertilization such as that which existed in the first centuries of the Christian era, in Medieval *Al-Andalus* in Spain and in present-day Canada, Western Europe, India, and Singapore. This would seem to be the best governmental format to ensure religious vitality and the common good.

Missiologists have sketched various rationales and strategies for these grand designs of faith interactions. Four examples would be Arnold Toynbee, Kenneth Cragg, Vinoth Ramachandra, and J.Z. Smith.

Arnold Toynbee. Arnold Toynbee has ventured a theology of history that sees religions as transcending realities overarching the rise and decline of empires. The quadrilateral of Hinduism and Greek Idealism on the one hand, and Judaism/Christianity and Islam on the other, arise as antidotes to destructive empire, forming an "anti-imperialist matrix of spiritual and ethical truth."[34] Faiths in dialogue offer the best hope for deliverance from mutual destruction. Faiths are the transcendent gifts of God to the transience of world history, allowing the leavening of the eternal kingdom of God to the fleeting empires of this world. Of the 22 empires that have risen and fallen in world history, 19 were less advanced in decadence than the U.S. is at present. Most empires, ironically, are not defeated militarily, but spend themselves into oblivion. Christianity and Islam, and, of course,

---

34. Toynbee, *A Study of History*.

sister Judaism in particular, share a common heritage and destiny having been pilgrim peoples, living in catacombs and tents, in a world they had not created and in which they could never be at home. Even the invasions and conquests, crusades and holy wars, could not, for Toynbee, mute the salutary effect of "High Religion" in world history. These cultures become citadels of truthful and righteous energy, in a world destruction bound by imperial fury fueled by affluence.

Kenneth Cragg. In a massive and monumental work, Bishop Kenneth Cragg, perhaps the most insightful contemporary theological commentator on Islam, professor at Oxford and long-time resident in the Middle East, offers another missiological thesis—not as sweeping and triumphalist as Toynbee—but equally thoughtful and provocative. He spoke of his overarching conviction at a meeting of the Middle East Council of Churches (MECC) in 1999 on the subject of "Judaism, Christianity, and Islam: Divinity in a Political World."

In this address, Cragg reflected on the future of Christian missions in the Muslim world. He noted that missions had evolved through three stages: 1) the era of evangelistic conversion; 2) the period accenting social services, hospitals, and schools; and 3) programs with an emphasis on pastoral and liturgical issues.

Today, as the need for social services has been assumed by indigenous governments, the focus has returned to evangelism—now defined as faith-tradition formulation and formation enriched by intense and profound interfaith dialogue. The emphasis is no longer the conversion of Muslims, which remains intractable and frustrating, but the formation of discipleship and inculcating communities—in the sociopolitical context of religious freedom. When asked about individual conversion in the American voluntaristic mode, Cragg hesitated, suggesting that we work with "educated villagers," accenting concerted interfaith community development. His main emphasis is on the upbuilding of various Christian communities, all the while calling on the public order for the human right of "free religious expression and the freedom to move among religions." An eclectic tri-faith, even amalgam dual faiths (Jew Christians, Christian Muslims), just does not happen. Each faith would seem to have an integrity and richness that enriches the whole.

Vinoth Ramachandra. Vinoth Ramachandra resonates with Cragg's theme from an "evangelical" purview and J.Z. Smith from an "ecumenical" perspective.

Ramachandra's thesis is that a lively companionship of Word and work is the only viable witness in the world today. Verbal proclamation and social action go hand in hand. His charter is that Christian witness is "about what God has done, is doing, and will do for the world He created and loves."[35] With Cragg, he sees vital mission in the making and nurturing of disciples. Social witness comprises in not perpetuating our cultural norms (*e.g.*, Americanism), but in honoring, attending and loving the poor, oppressed and "least of these." The terrible liability of trying to do this as Westerners and Americans nowadays shifts major responsibility for Christian evangelism in the hands of non-Westerners. With Bishop Cragg, Ramachandra feels strongly that indigenous churches must assume the mantle of leadership in building viable and vital faith communities—engaging in dialogue and concerted social action with other faith communities in order to redeem and transform society.

J.Z. Smith. An "ecumenical" version of Cragg's conviction can be found in J.Z. Smith, the landmark religion scholar of the University of Chicago. In *Relating Religion*, Smith explores, in the mode of his mentor, Mircea Eliade, the descriptive phenomenon of religion, along with a more normative quest to examine the new interfaith dialogue between Jews, Christians, and Muslims—seeing what this adds to the contemporary phenomenology of religious experience.[36] Smith's own normative thesis contends that the search towards faith (religion) must be *exempli gratia*—an exercise in the thankful participation in the recognition of "new being" (Tillich) in this new world. This renewal can only come from a comparative exploration in which all parties are open to transformation.

Following his master, Eliade, in his eclectic enamorments, yet with an intrigue for the ascending monotheisms and their compelling urgency for new transformative religious conviction, Smith shakes the dust from his abandoned New York City Jewish roots and examines freshly the Abrahamic faiths in their reciprocal complementarity as well as the salutary condemnation and commendation they offer each other for mutual purification. Smith's analysis provides fresh ground for vital religious witness. In several essays, he lays the foundation for a more wholesome mode of intramural witness among the Abrahamic faiths, especially vis-à-vis Israel, replacing the more insidious anti-Semitic and supercessionist view of Judaism implied in the traditional "Israel-as-sign" eschatology of evangelism.

35. Ramachandra, "What is Integral Mission?"

36. See Smith, *Relating Religion*.

In this view, widespread in Christian theology and dominant throughout Christian history, and now present in a new, virulent form which may be the prevalent Darbyesque heresy of our time, the conversion of the Jews becomes the signal for the inception or culmination of the evangelical "end times" of world history. As antidote to this pernicious understanding, Smith's view, along with recent repentance confessionals by Roman Catholics and other Christian bodies on our anti-Semitic, even genocidal past, put the Jewish and Christian bodies, at long last, on a sound dialogical footing. The challenge of coming centuries will be to extend this rapprochement to Islam.

My own view, developed in *Jew, Christian, Muslim*, finds hope, indeed mutual correction and fulfillment, in what I call "faithful unification" of the three traditions and by contrast, global war and calamity in continuation of the present "fateful trifurcation." For now, the antagonist theorists like Huntington prevail. Scriptural Reasoners, alternatively, provide the best antidote.

Political Formats. Finally, some comments on the conversion-seeking witnessing and evangelism of religious bodies within various sociopolitical formats. The laws of individual nations can enhance or stifle the evangelistic witness activities of religious bodies. The political ethos also influences the freedom of persons to convert or change faiths, a position all faiths embrace by affirming that conversion can never be compulsory. The societal format also influences the maintenance or sustenance of a particular spiritual/ethical salience in the society. The hard rub comes when each intense monotheism sees perdition in disbelief and apostasy in conversion.

Different political formats include: 1) the model of Roman Catholicism and historic European Christendom; 2) the model of *Al-sharī'ah* states and (*dar al-Islam*) regions; and 3) the model of religious freedom, pluralism, and separation of church and state in modern Protestant and Jewish communities. Each of these political theories has advantages and disadvantages according to differing views of the virtue of liberty and uniformity.

A Policy Proposal. I have surveyed the contemporary crisis in religious unity and witness, noting that our splintered and often irrelevant religious organizations often fail to command attention and loyalty in our time. Such formal organizational structures therefore provoke and persistently spin off fundamentalist reactions such as Muslim *madrassas*, which purvey fanatic certainties and prejudices that cannot stand the light of day of intellectual examination, and sectarian Jewish organizations, which forsake the noble

theological and ethical substance of the faith while turning to political ma-
neuverings, both defensive and offensive, and create strife in the world. And
what can one say about Christianity? Perhaps the five-minute impassioned
monologue on "smiling" in a recent tele-evangelistic performance by Joel
Osteen in the converted Houston, Texas basketball arena—now his megachurch—says it all. Inane sermons, banal praise songs, while Bach, Mozart,
Schubert, and the great hymns of the church sit discarded on the shelf, no
longer accessible to our consciousness, fulfill C.S. Lewis' pronouncement
of "fifth-rate texts set to sixth-rate tunes." Now, we face a world of unbeliev-
ers and *ersatz* believers, together setting fire upon the Earth. As a trainer of
Christian ministers, I can only offer a mournful "I'm sorry."

Defensive and simplistic religion is the *soup du jour* of Jews, Christians,
and Muslims, but, surprisingly and shockingly, the faithful clamor for more.
Meanwhile the moderate (should we say lukewarm?) and those who seek
aesthetic and intellectual excellence sit in empty pews. But we yearn for
truth, conviction, and righteousness and someday soon, I believe, we will
cease slaking our thirst at these "broken cisterns that can hold no water."
(Jer 2:13) It is my conviction that these prophetic "days that are coming"
(Malachi) will occur when the better impulses of our faith traditions encounter authentically and creatively the spiritual phenomenology of our
times.

Today, parochialism and xenophobia seem to have won the contest
over conviviality and mutual encouragement. As Christianity further splinters into agonizing schisms and antagonisms, and as alienation from our
parental faith, Judaism, and our offspring faith, Islam, intensifies after the
Holocaust and into the "war on terrorism," a careful reading of the "signs of
the times" and the theological meanings of our history will be an imperative for survival. While Americo-Israeli hegemony seems to command the
support of Judaism and Catholic, Protestant, and Orthodox Christendom,
at the same time, suicidal and terroristic resistance and martyrdom defending homelands from invasion and occupation appears to have achieved
the authority of *mitzvot* and *fatwa* within Islam. All the while beneath the
chaos, the epidemiology of faith and the phenomenology of world religious
history and hope seem to point in more irenic directions.

Despite the events of September 11th, the ethos today seems to be ir-
repressibly interreligious. If this is the global spiritual and ethical salience
within which our witness must occur in the interfaith context, we will need
to recover the brilliant cultural sensitivity of the 14th-century Andalusians,
16th-century Jesuits, or the 19th-century Dutch who understood the great

river of Abrahamic faith—now departing into tributaries, now joining in mighty confluence.

Today, as *madrassas* near the Red Mosque in Islamabad, Pakistan in-filtrate the sanctuary with truckloads of weapons, as the Roman Catholic Archdiocese of Los Angeles settles for $660,000,000 in victim awards and le-gal fees for 70 years of priest abuse of 500 children, and as Jewish rabbis con-tinue to foment righteous disdain by using the title of "terrorist" for *Hamas* and *Fatah*—the rightful and duly-elected government and elymosenary arm of the Palestinian people—we verge on self-induced, not God-induced, apocalyptic fury.

The essay therefore can conclude by offering an appropriate rationale and practical program for evangelism today in light of what we have pro-posed to be the intrinsic logic of theology and the extrinsic epidemiology of religion in the world today. To illustrate our point, we first consider the July 6, 2007 announcement of the Vatican on the subject of "the true faith"—a doc-ument revisiting and clarifying the pre-September 11th document, "*Dominus Jesus*: A Declaration on the Unicity and Salvific Universality of Jesus Christ and the Church." Alongside this, we will comment on the response of the World Alliance of Reformed Churches (July, 2007) and a concurrent docu-ment of "*Dominus Jesus*"—"*Dabru Emet*" of September, 2000.[37] This latter piece, offered by Jewish leaders around the world, including Peter Ochs of our interfaith program, again affirms our position that religious witness today (conversion and religious speech policy) is best formulated with re-spect to our sister Abrahamic faiths and in light of the global crisis to which animosity these faiths have contributed. As Karl Barth taught, as believers, we must read the world with the Bible in one hand and the newspaper in the other.

Pope Benedict's 2007 announcement was meant to allay perplex-ing uncertainties that have been vexing the beliefs and life patterns of the faithful in recent years. The times, as we have noted, seem to be demand-ing greater clarity and conviction while the ecclesial and civil environment has thrown up greater doubts. An assault is felt by the rampant disin-volvement in church caused by an underlying cultural secularism both in America and Europe. Like Protestants, Catholics simply are not observant in Europe. Benedict, however futilely, seems intent on calling Europe back to its Catholic heritage, arguing that neither society nor church can long endure without some renewal of the medieval synthesis. His confrontation

---

37. "*Dabru Emet*" is a Jewish statement that articulates eight principles to guide Jewish-Christian relations/ for more information, see the Jewish-Christian Relations Web site, http://www.jcrelations.net/en?item=1014.

with insurgent Islam—which seems to transit throughout Europe into the so-called "clash of civilizations" and the surge of conversions away from mother church into evangelical and Pentecostal communities, especially in Asia, South America, and Africa—constitute a further erosion. Though Catholic faith remains vital in China, it is being outstripped by neo-evangelical house churches always suspect of being less than loyal to the "sacred state."

When "*Dominus Jesus*" appears either in origin (2000) or update (2007), this tableau reflects on the Catholic mind as it is challenged by the inescapable interfaith reality. The World Alliance of Reformed Churches, an affiliation of some 100 million Calvinists and Baptists, registers its own dismay to the document. General Secretary Dr. Setri Nyomi comments on the 10 July, 2007 statement of the Congregation of the Doctrine of the Faith that it "seems puzzling at this time in the history of the church and society" and that the "signs of the times" would rather encourage "common witness in our oneness in Christ" and our "commitment to the unity and peace of the world."[38] Though ecclesiastical structures are far less prominent in Protestantism than in the Roman Communion, Reformed Christians—in my view, as a theologian in that heritage—would ask whether in any land and any time the "Word of God" is "rightly preached" and the sacraments are "rightly administered." Only under such conditions is "truth" and "civil righteousness" possible. Amid the plethora of evangelistic efforts and power moves effecting free expression of religion, the Reformed faith seeks to preserve in history free range for biblical-evangelical faith. As index of the seriousness of this matter, it has often gone to the wall of martyrdom to preserve this freedom of testimony.

At the very least, evangelical Protestantism will insist that absolutist ecclesial/civil forms such as Islam and Roman Catholicism guarantee the rights of religious freedom, expression, and toleration for all citizens. The deal struck between the Afghan Taliban and the government of South Korea (binding on its Presbyterian missionaries)—to desist from evangelism activities in that land after the kidnapping of some 20 and the killing of two—becomes problematic in the light of this principle.

"*Dabru Emet*" furthers this understanding in its first principle:

> Jews and Christians worship the same God. Before the rise of Christianity, Jews were the only worshippers of the God of Israel. But Christians also worship the God of Abraham, Isaac, and Jacob; creator of heaven and Earth. While Christian worship is not a vi-

---

38. World Alliance of Reformed Churches document of July 7, 2007.

able religious choice for Jews, as Jewish theologians we rejoice that, through Christianity, hundreds of millions of people have entered into relationship with the God of Israel.[39]

My view within the project of interfaith exploration is that the church, Abrahamic Faith and certainly the state, have not yet reached ultimate truth about who is included and excluded from the kingdom of God and that therefore political programs should remain open. Further proliferation and elaboration of movements within the three Abrahamic families of faith are to be expected. Indeed this openness to the spirit (*semper reformanda*) is the inherent original ethos of each faith tradition at its best. Scriptural Reasoning stands ready to further this process.

A recent sermon—preached at Garrett-Evangelical Theological Seminary during Advent season—points to the common threads of divine guidance and human obedience found in Torah, law of Christ, and *Taurut*.

Johnny's Simple Song

Garrett-Evangelical Theological Seminary,
December 8, 2009 (Advent)

Luke 11.16–12.6, Luke 3.3–14

(Prayer/Chant: L Bernstein's "Simple Song")

Well, here we go again.

Christmas bells are ringing.

Children are merrily singing.

The zhu zhu hamster tops the hit parade of toys, as mad-dog parents stampede Wal-Marts . . . and on those city sidewalks, black Friday and cyber-Monday turn to white Christmas.

But wait, what's that aroma wafting through the air?

Are those chestnuts roasting on an open fire?

No way! . . . it's something even more savory.

Locusts and (whiff) wild honey, for sure. Pooh-Bah, where are you?

39. "*Dabru Emet*," 1.

And barren branches on the brush fire . . .

and then . . . suddenly and scarily,

the ghastly gaze through the hedge. . .

the glistening teeth and wild hair . . . those gleaming, *shining* teeth
. . . is it an L.A. Laker's game? Do I see Kobe Bryant?

No, it's . . . heeeeeere's Johnny. This guy's all over Advent . . . shall we
call him Jack?

Obsequious? Deferential? Courteous? Fawning? Forget it. He's like the
bad uncle Jim, who you keep in his room, or the student who turns your
every statement on its ear and, even worse, she's always right.

And he's a regular party-pooper . . . or is he? He shouts about knives and
axes, vermin and vipers, repent and believe, be and do right for a change.
He's like that nasty preacher Jonathan Edwards . . . again that name . . . re-
viled in high-school textbooks. With his sermon on "sinners in the hands of
an angry God," dangling sinners over the fires of hell. Actually, Jonathan is
widely recognized as "the finest of American philosophers," and John . . . a
composed rabbinic Nabi/prophet/ is the one of whom another rabbi said
"the greatest ever born among men."

If truth be known, he is a learned Torah instructor. We know from
Luke (1.5ff.) that he is born into the pious, priestly family of Zacharias and
Elisabeth.

Whatever, we can't bear him, nor could Herod, although he trembled
knowing the man was just. So, the day and night was won by Herodius, the
conniving wife and the belly-dancing, teenie-bopper daughter—Josephus
says her name was Salome—a real peacenik . . . *riiight*!

Or so it seemed . . .

Actually, John is proclaiming the heart of theology; being made right
with God and the neighbor is the essence of salvation, redemption, and all
righteousness.

And John tells this simple story sure and strong. The highway is made
straight through the gnarled and crooked wilderness of human chicanery.
Lowly valleys are lifted up; the mighty mountains are brought low. Moral
metaphors. Remember the Magnificat?—the lowly will be exalted and the
powerful brought low. Rough places become plain: advent, Emmanuel.
When God draws near, lie turns toward truth, killing toward life-giving, promiscuity toward fidelity, hoarding toward giving. Only holiness can stand.
Awareness evokes confession and forgiveness and new life, which we celebrate in Eucharist.

This is Amos' plumb line amid all the crooked edges and planes of human chicanery. We recognize here images of Torah. Your way is straight and perfect, guiding our meandering and missing-the-mark. Your commandments safeguard our pathways. God is simple—a word on your forehead and doorpost.

Torah, law of Christ, *Taurut*, yoke, rule, light, path, *pedagogos* . . . it's all the same. The Baptist has one simple message—divine guidance and human obedience. Our text is GPS stellar guidance for our narrative journey and for the night journey.

NARRATIVE JOURNEY

As our liturgical year begins, as Holy History measures time, we meditate again on the Way and pathway of God. Our Luke text capsules what must have been a *midrash* on Decalogue. Like Jesus' Sermon on the Mount or Plain, the harangue at Herod's compound was likely about the 50 substipulates of the marriage/adultery commandment, and it was right in Herod's face. This mode of theological and ethical discourse is best known to our brothers and sisters in Judaism and Islam—in Yeshiva and *madrassas*—fine-grained situational instruction.

Our narrative journey of faith begins with Abraham. It flows from the covenant that God works out with Abraham and his following. Abraham was the protohuman, buried at Hebron and Machpelah, the mythical death-abode of Adam and Eve—at Hebron on the Jerusalem-Bethlehem road. The Father of the Way leads all the train of Earth's people of spirit and justice.

Abraham had heard the promise: "Your progeny will be as the sands of the seashore and the stars of the sky." And then along that great faith trail comes mighty Yahweh—God of Israel. And Moses— *Ehyeh asher ehyeh*—I am that am, I will be whom I will be. Are you coming along?

And the Son of Man—and John's proclaimed "Lamb of God" (Ezek 1 and Gen 22) both God understandings honed in the Exile. The glory which shone in the face of John's rabbi. I baptize you with water, He with the Holy Spirit and fire. Advent is the reprise of the history of God and the background of our text.

The interrogators of John, we may infer, had posed questions. They were those deep and perennial questions:

- Moses' "How can I speak?"

- Isaiah's "Who will go?"

- Socrates and Jesus' "What is truth?"

- That certain lawyer's "What must I do to gain eternal life?"

- And Kant and all the philosophers and sages of the ages: "What can I know? What must I do?

- What can I believe and hope? In sum, Who am I, if God is God?"

The capsules are a simple refrain. To the common folk: Share that extra coat, your food, your very substance. To lawyers, CEOs, and publicans: Take only enough, don't put out contracts on your fellow human-beings. Don't treat persons as objects, consumers, customers to be had. Don't reduce folk to debt slavery, shady mortgages, credit-card usury, and student loans. To soldiers: Make war only for justice and peace keeping. No violence, no lying, no propaganda. Make do with your wages.

It sounds like Paul's behavioral code in Romans. Give to each his due: honor, custom, fear, tribute. Owe no one anything—but to love one another. Loving each other fulfills the law. As with the desperate straights of the French Revolution, we hear the simple song in Victor Hugo's "Les Misérables," and we learn that "who loves another sees the face of God."

So Paul concludes: Sleepers awake, shake off the works of darkness, put on the armor of light. John is calling us finally on a night journey, what the Germans call *Winterreise*, the ultimal and decisive journey.

Night Journey

This is Passover, Pilgrimage, *hajj*, Advent . . .

Think of the night flight of Habiru from Egypt, of Jacob's dream at Bethel, of holy family arriving by night in Bethlehem—then flight into Egypt, of Muhammad's night journey to Jerusalem in Sura 17. Advent chronicles the sublime event-history that would grow out of biblical Judaism, as the Jesus people were grafted into the vine and stock of Israel. When the night was far spent, God sent his *agapetos*, the beloved Son, into the world. It's the old story—a simple song.

Augustine, in *De Trinitate*, writes that God is identical with his greatness, which is his goodness, which is his wisdom and truth. The simplicity of God, which basically means that God's being is God's action, is defined by Thomas Aquinas in this way:

> In every simple thing God's being is its manifestation.
>
> From One only One can come.
>
> The glorious multiplicity of creation rises immediately from the sublime simplicity of God.

If God is a verb (Buber) or adverb (Levinas), and God is as God does, then our comings and goings are embraced by God's Advent. "If I flee to the edge of the world—even there you are with me-your hand holds me and leads me."

A little child was the GPS leading Scrooge home from his night journey. It leads to his reawakening and redemption. It happens in the second nightmare and in the blessed wound of Tiny Tim. The spirit-vision leads Ebenezer on a nocturnal journey into his misguided youth, where he chose money over love.

Then he was shown the starving child under the skirts of the ghost of Christmas yet to come. Only then could he see for the first time, in the spectre of the sick and dying, the poor and wretched of the Earth—and this in God's good world, that his greed was intricated with the misery of the wretched of the Earth. Their plight was brought on not by economic cycles or "the poor we will always have with us," but by ignorance and want, from human carelessness in this provident world of a provident Lord. As Amartya Sen claimed, famine and crash is not an act of God, but a failure of human prevention and intervention. Even today, as Noah's deluge sweeps over Bangladesh, beginning the ecological migration that are the inevitable consequence of global warming, the two chief culprits—America and China—twiddle their thumbs as the world cries out at Copenhagen.

Though we may not, through sheer grace, Scrooge changes. Conviction of sin ensues, repentance of spirit, change of heart, and amended ways—all within the heart of God who is love. Scrooge, the problem, at last becomes part of the solution.

At the G-20 Summit in Pittsburgh, it was Nobel economists Joe Siglitz and Amartya Sen who saw the same vision, and argued that economics was not about GDP and growth rates, but about human well-being. The question lingers of whether corporations and national economies can follow Scrooge and turn from money-counting to caring for the poor.

So we are left with the Baptist's triptych. It is Lazarus in the bosom of Abraham . . . and the rich man and the tortured cry back from beyond, "Send Lazarus to cool my tongue." Father Abraham's words are "remember in your life time you received good things" . . . here and now is your life . . . so get life!

On this side of the great divide, we crave security, prosperity, and end in greed and neglect of others, but grace in Abraham—now as then with Christ *Logos* as King of creation—proffers justice, *koinonia*, and peace.

As dawn breaks, this grace/*Logos* shines as the sunrise across the membrane of time and eternity. Scrooge parts the velvet curtains on the window of his apartment. Christmas bells are ringing, and the children are still singing. The goose hangs in the butcher shop, and Tiny Tim has risen to a new day.

Yes, the world is still at sixes and sevens, and God's way is topsy-turvy with ours. Some few have almost everything, and most have barely enough. Nearly one billion have slid into hunger and starvation just this past year. Fevered brows cry out for the cup of water, and for health care and jobs and the return of their ancestral lands already in the vaults of banks, brokers, developers, and tyrants as Torah abrogation—idolatry, injustice, and immorality—remain all around. So John's fierce jeremiad still holds, as does his startling assertion that kingdom is here and now, ready for the receiving and doing. It happened in that one group baptism, when his own rabbi waded in and the heavens opened and the voice—*beneyedee, agapetos*—you are my beloved child . . . I am well pleased.

It is this only-begotten One, the beloved One, *agapetos*, who was given that the world might be saved. He is Torah. He is Way, truth, and life. He embodies and shows and is the Way. Taking our sins on his own body on the cross—*pecatta mundi*—he makes us his "workmanship for good works" (Eph 2.10)

Friends, the way of Torah/*Logos* claims that God has made the world perfectly provident. In Calvin's words, it is made so that "none need have too little, and none too much." Only if we offset its course by greed and injustice, will creation and incarnation be contradicted. Every human is meant for a job, shelter, ancestral land, health care, education, and supportive love. So let's get back on track and go there.

At the end of the day and the night, the giveaway of our passage is a few chapters ahead in Luke 7. Remember the dispatch John sent and received when he was in Herod's pithole prison—a moving site up near Sychar and Nablus—"Are you *beneyedee* and *agapetos*? Are you Messiah, Jessie's branch, David's king . . . are you He who is to come, or shall we look for another? And Jesus' retort, "What do you see? What's happening?" The blind see, the lame walk—even Tiny Tim and Amahl discard their crutches—and the poor hear the gospel of God. Dr. King put it this way toward the end of his own cruciform life: "We celebrate the Advent and Second Advent every time we open our heart to Jesus, every time we turn our backs on the lower road and accept the high road, every time we say no to self and yes to Jesus Christ, every time we turn from ugliness to beauty and forgive our enemies, when we turn our lives toward the highest and best, Christ is there."

Friends of God in Christ, we now break bread together as we take our leave for holy days at home and parish. In liturgy and song, in vestments and text, on advent wreath and candle "even in malls and on city sidewalks," the light of God transmutes like Monet's series on Rouen Cathedral, from purple to rose and Sarum blue. Anguish and brutality subside for a *Parousia* moment into the silence of joy and peace, for the Lord is come and Earth receives her king.

In the name of the Father, the Son and the Holy Spirit, One God, world without end. Amen.

PART FIVE

The Search for Legacy

Family

THIS AUTOBIOGRAPHY IS NOT complete without a word of tribute to those closest to me—my family. If father and husband sought to inculcate wife and children with truth and justice, much more would they educate him in those virtues.

SARA

In 2003, Sara and I celebrated our 40th wedding anniversary. It was Bastille Day at Jilly's or some other exotic French restaurant. In recent years, we have often repaired to *la belle France* (Strasbourg or Paris), where she will view two or three films per day, while I sit and write away on this or that metaphysical history of the world and everything therein. Every book bearing the Vaux name is collaboration in some way. All ideas and outlines take early form across the kitchen table with baguette, gruyere, and Côte du Rhône as encouragement. She has achieved the near impossible task of bringing five children into the world, raising four, and still managing a quite remarkable administrative, academic, and advising career. I have tried in recent years to back her up and support her profession, as she did mine those many years. As with most gifted women of her generation, there is some mourning for what could have been, sweetened by good memories of raising well her children, pretty much *sans père*.

In summer 2007, she began her *pièce de résistance* of family ministry with the birthing and initial raising of our granddaughter, Aislyn Moira, the first child of Catherine and Sean. Books and teaching on theology and film continue to absorb her attention, as she prepares an exciting study of Clint Eastwood under contract with Eerdmans Press.

Sara has been the cohesive force in the family, a community builder wherever we have lived, a friend, and consultant to students, but most of all—as I reflect across the years—a serious reader, thinker, and scholar. Like her dad, Dr. Bert Anson, she learns more for the sheer joy of it, although she does produce writings with frequency. A good friend, fun to be with, intellectual adversary, coverer of her husband's sins, homemaker-*par-excellence*, companion in the storm.

She also has led the way in the theological/ethical formation of our family. Brutally honest and unequivocal in her truth and justice, we all have followed her lead in commitments to "the least of these," to the poor, to peacemaking, racial justice, international and interreligious commitment, and hospitality. She sets and provides a family table that is Teilhard de Chardin's "mass upon the Earth," where all are welcome. We feast with her there.

CAT

Speaking of humanitarian service and care for the least of these, we knew Catherine was an extraordinary girl long before she first worked as a counselor at The Fowler Center in Michigan, the camp that she directed before taking over Latin School's urban-camp program. She attended several totally incapacitated persons with disabilities, being there through the night to swat a fly, to fetch a cup of water. Now in her 30s with her own child, she not only served tender care but trained staff, administered a complex organization, oversaw development and all the remaining tasks of directing one of the leading camps for persons with disabilities and one of the best urban summer camps in the country. She has extraordinary patience, combined with the tough-skin needed to raise money—a rare combination.

I love most to hear her play the violin. A graduate of the Suzuki method, taught by Brenda Wurman in Oak Park and other great teachers, Cat has played in the Chicago Youth Orchestra in Japan and the University of Chicago Orchestra. I often had her play for my sacred services. I remember her offering of Bach's double violin concerto with a talented classmate on Christmas Eve at Second Presbyterian in Chicago.

She has found her man. Although the Vaux clan couldn't travel so close to September 11th, her wedding to Sean was a beautiful event at the seminary. It seems that he had been hanging in the wings since she entered University of Chicago. This boyfriend, then that. He waited for his chance, until finally, like her mother, she reluctantly gave in to persistence. He is a chiropractic physician, while she continues her work in camping. They have moved close at hand, providing comfort to her aging folks and finding ready and willing babysitters.

KEITH

I've often spoken to his medical colleagues. Once, at University of Chicago, while he was in medical school, I spoke on "informed consent." Then, in summer of 2000, when he was a young "attending" in Pediatrics at San Diego Hospital, I presented department "rounds" on the "Human Genome" project. To bring him down to Earth, I brought his baby picture and jested that he was the model of the "Bob"/"Shaq" television commercial, where baby "Bob" betrays that "Shaq and I both like powder on the bottom when our diapers are changed." He has lived in San Diego with Cathy, the mother of his children. His splendidly raised family now makes four, with Margo, his excellent new wife, as he musters out of the Navy into civilian health ministry. He now leads the Pediatric Genetics unit at Children's Hospital.

Keith has always had a brilliant technical mind. I remember in the Pennsylvania forest one summer purchasing two broken-down Evinrude boat motors: five dollars for the pair. We unloaded the pieces in the garage, and I went back to the books. In a few hours, we heard a roar from the back drive. He had assembled and gotten one motor running.

Keith learned this technical virtuosity from his Grandpa Vaux and at our Riverside home. This Victorian monstrosity had to be rebuilt, rewired, replumbed, and the rest—and Keith did it all. With us from the beginning of our first crisis in ministry at Pittsburgh, and through the loss of Kerry in Illinois, he has always been the stalwart leader of our family and an exemplary fellow.

He also loves to read. I think it was in Oxford at the end of his high-school years at Magdalene College School, then beginning University studies at Mansfield College, that first turned him onto things of the mind.

I've gained enormous respect for Keith, as I have for my own dad, who in his waning years cared tenderly for my Alzheimer's-debilitated mom. Keith is a great dad, reading, spending time enjoying the kids (Samantha and David), just as his mother did. It seems he prefers to be with them, unlike his dad, who resented the distraction from his monumental, Earth-saving work. This he manages on top of a burgeoning career as a pediatric-geneticist in San Diego.

His commitments to truth and justice are perhaps even more strenuous than his mom's. He soundly critiques American war and foreign policy and, in good University-of-Chicago loyalty, he lives out a "great books, great ideas" humanism.

BERT

"Bo," as he was nicknamed by his nine-year-old brother, Keith, was the budding genius of the family. We had to decide before he was 10 how to channel the enormous intellectual curiosity, and together we chose languages. But, languages seemed to be a subject involving science and humanities, and in grad school he was one of the rare fellows to hold both National Science Foundation and Mellon fellowships.

He did his music, sports, math, and sciences while we started him in Spanish, French, and Latin early, so that by high school he was studying Greek, then Sanskrit, and Armenian in college. He can now play around with 30 or so languages. Guided through the maze of practical living by the cleverness of his younger sisters, he emerged out of a bachelor's at University of Chicago and a Ph.D. from Harvard to a beginning teaching post on the Square. He has subsequently taught at University of Wisconsin-Milwaukee and Cambridge.

Even in a young teaching career, he was awarded "Best Teacher" award by the graduating class. Only at Hasty-puddingdom could one find in the yearbook his full-page photo, there with Robert Coles and Cornel West in their bow-tie best, he in his Chicago Bulls sweatshirt.

In a *tour de force* of sheer *bonne chance*, his social awkwardness met the lovely Cristina Maranci at a lecture he was giving to an American gathering. An art history Ph.D. from Princeton, their professional ambition synchronized beautifully. His wedding to Cristina was a masterpiece of the ancient liturgy, composed and translated with moving explanations by *la belle couple*. But the marriage was short-lived. His new wife, Sahar Nateghi, is also an enchanting beauty and skilled businesswoman.

We witnessed his virtuosity on occasion. In Paris, he gave a paper on Black Sea Armenian dialects, which wowed even the scholars from Armenia and Russia.

In commitments to truth and justice, he has paid the price of *Akedic* witness more than the rest of us. In my theology of Jew, Christian, Muslim, I argue that wisdom (truth and right) strive into realization in the world through witnesses (martyrs) who live into messianic *Sophia* against the repudiation of the world (*peccata mundi*). They suffer. They prevail. Those who bear witness to righteousness change the world along the long arc of goodness (J.R. Lowell)

Bert's Abrahamic trial was taking a firm, but immensely unpopular stand, supporting the Palestinian people against the injustices and violence of the state of Israel's occupation. He condemned the attack, occupation, and deportation of the Palestinians and joined a handful of Harvard and MIT professors in making that witness shortly after the events of September 11th. Even President Larry Summers invoiced the frightful charge of anti-Semitism—a devastating indictment especially at one whose every fibre of being was deep solidarity with the Jewish people and abhorrence of the Holocaust. As Judith Butler of Berkeley has shown,[1] those who condemned genocide and *Shoah*, must (in defiance of AIPAC and "campus watch") condemn the "cleansing" (attack and dispersal) of the Palestinian peoples. This greatest ethical calamity of the post-*Shoah* world history (4 million forced to be refugees), to my mind, is the major cause of Huntington's "clash of civilizations" (if such really exists), the events of September 11th, and the war on terrorism.

In a celebrated fiasco, Bert was denied the due tenure process promised him, and he was forced to leave Harvard, despite being voted multiple times by the graduates an outstanding professor. His witness has helped me formulate more carefully my own views that ethical integrity for any human being after the late 20th century demands full acknowledgment and accountability for the *Shoah*, a resolve to never allow it to happen again anywhere and to anyone. That implies a forceful solidarity with the sequel instance of similar inhumanity—the victim (vicar, lamb of God) people of Palestine, and all others (*e.g.*, Darfur).

1. See Butler, *Precarious Life*.

Bert's family is deeply proud and honored by his stance, though it has cost him dearly.

JUNIOR (SARAH)

We saved the best (and the toughest) for last. No University of Chicago for her. She was her own person. No scholar her, no way! No professional geek, but a survivor, and in many ways, she is the family leader. She was about 13 when we first sent her to France for the year. She schlepped her bags across Luxembourg and down to Strasbourg. A bit too much, too soon. In two weeks, she was back home. So we were, of course, elated when she completed (with flying colors) her junior year abroad in Paris at the Sorbonne. And you guessed it, soon, there she was with her sister, Cat, running the waterfront at The Fowler Center.

Sarah returned for her senior year at Scripps College with interest budding in French, school teaching, Francophone Africa, the Peace Corps, and the like. She caught hold beautifully—reading, engaging great ideas, and still—her own woman! She became Program Assistant at PAS (Program in African Studies), Northwestern University, and eventually met her man, Kris de Roeck, from Antwerp, Belgium. She now lives there, with Kris and baby Fiona, shifting the epicenter of our family to Europe, and works in Brussels on an international platform in rehabilitation. Kris is my major data bank on Chicago sports statistics: Bulls, Bears, White Sox, and da Cubs—and Sarah has been known to cheer for KG (Kevin Garnett) in the 2008 NBA Championship.

CONCLUSION

I've written much about war these last years and less about medicine, although a sabbatical project dealing with Avicenna, Maimonides, Schweitzer, and Leon Kass culminated in the 2007 publication of *An Abrahamic Theology for Science*. My agenda remains to relate theology to cultural issues. I am concerned more than I was 20 years ago, when I began this work, that theology must get its act together and its messages right. The crisis of recent years among the Abrahamic faiths makes clear how muddled are our self-understandings. They, therefore, render ineffective our witness in the world. Laypersons in the three faiths seem totally adrift when it comes to applying faith to concrete issues in the world.

Now a fellow at the Centre for Advanced Religious and Theological Studies at Cambridge (a convenient place to stay with Sahar and Bert), I continue to write foundational theological essays (*e.g.*, Scriptural Reasoning pamphlets) and occasional practical papers—especially on war and health issues and on inter-Abrahamic themes. Garrett has gratefully allowed me to teach beyond customary retirement, providing ongoing stimulus from students, faculty, and Northwestern colleagues on these complex and compelling issues.

The life and work you have troubled yourself to read is obviously pedestrian—closer to a family history than an autobiography—with, I hope, some universal caches. I had to write it for my family first and my students and friends—and myself—seeking now as ever to synthesize faith and worldly reality and synchronize *Heilsgeschichte* with our space and time—here-and-now world. You, good reader, have accompanied and instructed me in this pilgrimage. I remain your servant and friend.

Ken Vaux, January 2010

Appendix

CURRICULUM VITAE

Kenneth L. Vaux
Professor of Theological Ethics
Garrett-Evangelical Theological Seminary
2121 Sheridan Road
Evanston, Illinois 60201
847.866.3887 • ken.vaux@garrett.edu

Education

Th.D.	University of Hamburg, Hamburg, Germany, 1968
M.Div.	Princeton Seminary, Princeton, New Jersey, 1963
B.A.	Muskingum College, New Concord, Ohio, 1960
Additional Study	University of Pittsburgh, Pittsburgh, Pennsylvania
	University of Edinburgh, Edinburgh, Scotland, U.K.
	University of Illinois, Champaign, Illinois

Previous Professional Experience

1993–2001	Founder and Director of the Ethics Center, Garrett-Evangelical Theological Seminary, Evanston, Illinois
1979–1993	Professor of Ethics in Medicine, The University of Illinois Medical Center, Chicago, Illinois
1967–1978	Professor and Director, Institute of Religion, Texas Medical Center, Houston, Texas
1971–1973	Adjunct Associate Professor of Law, University of Houston Law School, Houston, Texas

Pastoral Experience

1961–1964	One-year pastoral assignments in Scotland, New Jersey, and Pittsburgh
1964–1967	Minister, United Presbyterian Church, Watseka, Illinois
1967–1974	University Pastor, Rice University, Houston, Texas
1987–1993	Parish Associate, Riverside Presbyterian Church, Riverside, Illinois
1991–1992	Interim Minister, Second Presbyterian Church, Chicago, Illinois
1993	Interim Minister, Church of Christ Presbyterian (Asian), Park Ridge, Illinois
1993	Parish Associate, First Presbyterian Church, Evanston, Illinois

Clinical Experience

One year of CPE at Cambridge State Mental Hospital, Cambridge, Ohio

Two years extended clinical supervision at Princeton Seminary, Princeton, New Jersey

Books Published

America in God's World (Eugene, Ore.: Wipf and Stock, 2009).

An Abrahamic Theology for Science (Eugene, Ore.: Wipf and Stock, 2007).

Jew, Christian, Muslim (Eugene, Ore.: Wipf and Stock, 2003).

Ethics and the War on Terrorism (Eugene, Ore.: Wipf and Stock, 2002).

Being Well (Nashville: Abingdon Press, 1997).

Dying Well (Nashville: Abingdon Press, 1996).

Death Ethics: Religious and Cultural Values in Prolonging and Ending Life (Philadelphia: Trinity-SCM, 1992).

Ethics and the Gulf War: Religion, Rhetoric, and Righteousness (Boulder: Westview, 1992).

Birth Ethics: Religious and Cultural Values in the Genesis of Life (New York: The Crossroad Publishing Company, 1984).

Health and Medicine in the Reformed Tradition: Promise, Providence, and Care *(New York: Crossroad, 1989)*.

Will to Live/Will to Die: Ethics and the Search for a Good Death *(Minneapolis: Augsburg Fortress, 1978)*.

This Mortal Coil: The Meaning of Health and Disease *(New York: Harper and Row, 1978)*.

Biomedical Ethics: Morality for the New Medicine *(New York: Harper and Row, 1974)*.

Subduing the Cosmos: Cybernetics and Man's Future *(Atlanta: Knox, 1970)*.

Editorial Projects

Covenants of Life: Contemporary Medical Ethics in Light of the Thought of Paul Ramsey, with Sara Vaux and Mark Stenberg *(Dordrect, The Netherlands: Kluwer, 2002)*.

Memoir of an Ex-radical: The Story of Joseph Fletcher *(Louisville: Westminster-John Knox Press, 1992)*.

Powers that Make Us Human *(Urbana: University of Illinois Press, 1985)*.

Health and Medicine in the Faith Traditions *(New York: The Crossroad Publishing Company)*, multi-volume series with Martin E. Marty, beginning in 1983.

Health, Medicine and the Faith Traditions: An Inquiry into Religion and Medicine, with co-editor, Martin E. Marty *(Philadelphia: Fortress, 1982)*.

To Create a Different Future *(New York: Friendship, 1972)*.

Who Shall Live: Medicine, Technology, Ethics *(Philadelphia: Fortress Press, 1970)*.

Books, Chapters, and Articles

Two-hundred articles, newspapers essays, reports, book reviews, juried papers, etc.

Bibliography

American Medical Association Council of Ethical and Judicial Affairs, "Withholding or Withdrawing Life-prolonging Medical Treatment," March 15, 1986.

Anonymous, "It's Over, Debbie," *Journal of the American Medical Association* 259 (1988).

Aries, Philippe. *Centuries of Childhood: A Social History of Family Life.* New York: Random House, Inc., 1962.

Barnard, Christiaan N. "Face the Nation" interview, December 24, 1967.

Barth, Karl. *Church Dogmatics.* Edinburgh: T & T Clark, 1958.

Beker, Johan Christiaan. *Paul, the Apostle: The Triumph of God in Life and Thought.* Minneapolis: Fortress, 1980.

Bernardin, Cardinal Joseph. *The Gift of Peace: Personal Reflections.* Chicago: Loyola Press, 1997.

Bloom, Harold. *Jesus and Yahweh: The Names Divine.* New York: Riverhead, 2005.

Bonhoeffer, Dietrich. *No Rusty Swords: Letters, Lectures, and Notes, 1928–1936, from the Collected Works of Deitrich Bonhoeffer, Volume* 1, Edwin H. Robertson, ed. London: Collins, 1965.

Bonhoeffer, Dietrich. *Letters and Papers from Prison.* New York: Touchstone/Simon & Schuster, 1997.

Bonhoeffer, Dietrich, Green, Clifford J., Krauss, Reinhard, West, Charles C., and Stott, Douglas W. *Ethics: Dietrich Bonhoeffer Works, Vol.* 6. Minneapolis: Fortress, 2005.

Boyarin, Daniel. *Border Lines: The Partition of Judaeo-Christianity.* Philadelphia: University of Pennsylvania Press, 2004.

"Bring Him Home," *Les Misérables* soundtrack, www.stlyrics.com/lyrics/lesmiserables/bringhimhome.htm.

Butler, Judith. *Precarious Life: The Power of Mourning and Violence.* New York: Verso, 2004.

Crossan, John Dominic. *Jesus: A Revolutionary Biography.* New York: HarperCollins, 1994.

Domenach, Jean-Marie. "Malraux and Death," in *New York Times Book Review,* December 8, 1977, 37–38 (review of André Malraux, *Lazarus.* New York: Holt, Rinehart and Winston, 1977).

Eliot, T.S. "Choruses from 'The Rock,'" in *Collected Poems,* 1909–1962. New York: Harcourt Brace & World, 1963/1964.

Elkington, John R. "Moral Problems in the Use of Borrowed Organs, Artificial and Transplanted," in *Annals of Internal Medicine,* February 1, 1964 60: 309–313.

Erikson, Erik H. *Young Man Luther: A Study in Psychoanalysis and History*. New York: Norton, 1958.

Fish, Stanley. "Religion Without Truth," the *New York Times*, March 31, 2007.

Fletcher, Joseph. *Joseph Fletcher: Memoir of an Ex-Radical—Reminiscence and Reappraisal*, Kenneth L. Vaux, ed. Philadelphia: Westminster John Knox, 1993.

Ford, David F. "An Interfaith Wisdom: Scriptural Reasoning Between Jews, Christians, and Muslims," in *The Promise of Scriptural Reasoning*, David Ford and C.C. Pecknold, eds. Hoboken, NJ: Wiley-Blackwell, 2007.

Fox Renee C. and Swazey, Judith P. *The Courage to Fail: A Social View of Organ Transplants and Dialysis*. Chicago: University of Chicago Press, 1978.

Hellholm, David, ed. *Apocalypticism in the Mediterranean World and the Near East*. Tübingen: J.C. B. Mohr/Paul Siebeck, 1979.

Holden, John. "Some Ethical Considerations in the Transplantation of Organs," in *Existential Psychiatry*, 1966.

"I Know Not Why God's Wondrous Grace," Psalter Hymnal #495, www.hymnary.org/hymn/PsH/495.

Illich, Ivan. *In the Vineyard of the Text*. Chicago: University of Chicago Press, 1993.

Jewett, Robert. *A Chronology of Paul's Life*. Minneapolis: Fortress, 1979.

Jewett, Robert, et al. *Romans: A Commentary (Hermeneia: A Critical and Historical Commentary on the Bible)*. Minneapolis: Fortress, 2006.

Jonas, Hans. "The Burden and Blessing of Mortality," *The Hastings Center Report* 22 (1992).

Jonsen, Albert R. *The Birth of Bioethics*. New York: Oxford University Press, 1998.

Juul, Donald. *Messianic Exegesis: Christological Interpretation of the Old Testament in Early Christianity*. Minneapolis: Fortress, 1992.

Kazantzakis, Nikos. *Zorba the Greek*. New York: Simon & Schuster, Inc., 1952.

Kevles, Daniel J. *In the Name of Eugenics: Genetics and the Uses of Human Heredity*. New York: Knopf, 1985.

"La Mamma Morta," www.allthelyrics.com/lyrics/philadelphia_soundtrack/.

Leach, Edmund. "Doctors' Powers 'Unbelievable'" in the *London Times*, December 4, 1967, 2.

Levenson, Jon. *The Death and Resurrection of the Beloved Son*. New Haven: Yale University Press, 1995.

Lewis, C.S. *Mere Christianity*. New York: HarperCollins, 2001.

———. *Out of the Silent Planet: Space Trilogy, Book One*. New York: Scribner, 1996.

Liturgy for Yom Kippur, www.jewfaq.org/holiday4.htm.

Mailer, Norman. *Of a Fire on the Moon*. New York: Grove, 1985.

Marty, Martin E. and Vaux, Kenneth L. *Health/Medicine and the Faith Traditions: An Inquiry Into Religion and Medicine*. Philadelphia: Fortress, 1982.

Outler, Albert C. *Evangelism and Theology in the Wesleyan Spirit*. Nashville: Discipleship Resources, 1996.

Pelikan, Jaroslav. *Mary Through the Centuries: Her Place in the History of Culture*. New Haven: Yale University Press, 1998.

Polkinghorne John and Welker, Michael. *The End of the World and the Ends of God: Science and Theology on Eschatology*. Harrisburg, PA: Trinity Press International, 2000.

Rae, Scott B. and Cox Paul M. *Bioethics: A Christian Approach in a Pluralistic Age*. Grand Rapids: Eerdmans, 1999.

Ramachandra, Vinoth. "What is Integral Mission?" (unpublished paper).

Raven, Charles E. *St. Paul and the Gospel of Jesus: A Study of the Basis of Christian Ethics.* London: SCM, 1961.

————. *Teilhard de Chardin: Scientist and Seer.* London: Collins, 1962.

Sandburg, Carl. *Always the Young Strangers.* New York: Harcourt Brace, 1953.

Sandel, Michael J. *The Case Against Perfection: Ethics in the Age of Genetic Engineering.* Cambridge: Harvard University Press, 2007.

Sanders, E.P. *Jesus and Judaism.* Minneapolis: Fortress, 1985.

————. *Paul: A Very Short Introduction.* Oxford, UK: Oxford University Press, 1991.

Smith, Jonathan Z. *Relating Religion: Essays in the Study of Religion.* Chicago: University of Chicago Press, 2004.

Spiegel, Shalom. *The Last Trial: On the Legends and Lore of the Command to Abraham to Offer Isaac as a Sacrifice, The Akedah* 1899-1984. Woodstock, VT: Jewish Lights, 1993.

Spinetta, John and Patricia, eds. *Living With Childhood Cancer.* St. Louis: Mosby, 1981.

Stolberg, Sheryl Gay. "Ought We Do What We Can Do?" *The New York Times,* August 12, 2001.

"Surgery: The Ultimate Operation," *Time* magazine, December 15, 1967.

Teilhard de Chardin, Pierre. *On Suffering.* New York: Harper & Row, 1974.

Toynbee, Arnold J. *A Study of History.* New York: Oxford University Press, Inc. 1947, vol. 12.

"Transplant Surgery," *Newsweek,* December 18, 1967.

Trimingham, J. Spencer. *Islam in Ethiopia.* Oxford, UK: Oxford University Press, 1952.

Van Eys, Jan. *The Truly Cured Child: The New Challenge in Pediatric Cancer Care.* Baltimore: University Park Press, 1977.

Van Buren, Paul Matthews. *According to the Scriptures: The Origins of the Gospels and of the Church's Old Testament.* Grand Rapids: Eerdmans, 1998.

Van Leeuwen, Arend Theodoor. *Christianity in World History: The Meeting of the Faiths of East and West.* New York: Scribner, 1966.

Vaux, Kenneth L. *An Abrahamic Theology for Science.* Eugene, OR: Wipf & Stock, 2007.

————. *Being Well.* Nashville: Abingdon, 1997.

————. *Birth Ethics: Religious and Cultural Values in the Genesis of Life.* New York: Crossroads, 1989.

————. *Death Ethics: Religious and Cultural Values in Prolonging and Ending Life.* New York: Continuum, 1996.

————. *Ethics and the War on Terrorism.* Eugene, OR: Wipf & Stock, 2002.

————. *Jew, Christian, Muslim: Faithful Unification or Fateful Trifurcation? Word, Way, Worship, and War in the Abrahamic Faiths.* Eugene, OR: Wipf & Stock, 2003.

————. *Subduing the Cosmos: Cybernetics and Man's Future.* Louisville: Westminster John Knox, 1970.

————, ed. *To Create a Different Future: Religious Hope and Technological Planning.* New York: Friendship, 1972.

————, ed. *Who Shall Live: Medicine, Technology, Ethics.* Philadelphia: Fortress, 1970.

Vaux, Kenneth L., Vaux, Sara and Stenberg, Mark, eds. *Covenants of Life: Contemporary Medical Ethics in Light of the Thought of Paul Ramsey.* Amsterdam: Kluwer, 2002.

Vermès, Géza. *The Religion of Jesus the Jew.* Minneapolis: Fortress, 1993.

"What Wondrous Love Is This," www.hymnary.org/text/what_wondrous_love.

Wink, Walter. *The Human Being: Jesus and the Enigma of the Son of Man.* Minneapolis: Augsburg Fortress, 2002.

Yancey, Philip. *The Bible Jesus Read.* Grand Rapids: Zondervan, 1999.